LEARNING
ECONOMICS

Learning Economics

Arnold Kling, Ph.D

Copyright © 2004 by Arnold Kling.

Library of Congress Number: 2004094344
ISBN : Hardcover 1-4134-6027-5
Softcover 1-4134-6026-7

All rights reserved. No portion of this book may be reproduced, stored in a retrieval system, or transmitted in any form or by any means—electronic, mechanical, photocopy, recording, or any other—except for brief quotation in printed reviews, without the prior permission of the publisher.

This book was printed in the United States of America.

To order additional copies of this book, contact:
Xlibris Corporation
1-888-795-4274
www.Xlibris.com
Orders@Xlibris.com
25220

Contents

Acknowledgments 9
Author's Introduction 11

PART I: WHAT'S DIFFERENT ABOUT ECONOMICS?

Introduction 19
Chapter 1: Sweetwater vs. Saltwater 25
Chapter 2: The Omniscient Voyeur 32
Chapter 3: Can Money Buy Happiness? 36
Chapter 4: Type C and Type M Arguments 41
Chapter 5: There Is No Labor Shortage 47
Chapter 6: Quack Economic Prescription 52
Chapter 7: Economics vs. Populism 57
Chapter 8: Economic Attribution Errors 63

PART 2: GROWTH, TECHNOLOGICAL PROGRESS, AND DECENTRALIZED INNOVATION

Introduction 71
Chapter 9: Growth Across Time 75
Chapter 10: Progress and Displacement 82
Chapter 11: Rational Exuberance 87
Chapter 12: The Elastic Economy 91
Chapter 13: What Causes Prosperity? 96
Chapter 14: The Statism Trap 103
Chapter 15: Substitution, Technological Change, and the Environment 108
Chapter 16: Nonlinear Thinking 113
Chapter 17: Hayek, Stiglitz, and Michael Powell 120

PART 3: MOORE'S LAW, PROGRESS, AND DISPLACEMENT

Introduction 127
Chapter 18: Listen to the Technology 131

Chapter 19: The Death of Newspapers 135
Chapter 20: The Internet Packet Express 140
Chapter 21: The Wireless Last Mile 144
Chapter 22: Asymptotically Free Goods 148
Chapter 23: Legamorons in a Trackable Society 154
Chapter 24: Metaphors for Intellectual Property 159
Chapter 25: The Club vs. the Silo 164
Chapter 26: Equilibrium in the Market
    for Rock 'n' Roll 168
Chapter 27: Moore vs. Plato 172

PART 4: FREE TRADE

Introduction 179
Chapter 28: Roll Over, Ricardo 183
Chapter 29: Don't Smoot the Weasels 192
Chapter 30: Please Outsource to My Daughter 195
Chapter 31: Manufacturing a Crisis 199
Chapter 32: The Language Barrier 204
Chapter 33: Oil Econ 101 208
Chapter 34: The Balance of Saving 212

PART 5: MACROECONOMICS AND BUBBLES

Introduction 219
Chapter 35: Arithmetic in a Bubble 223
Chapter 36: Briefing the President 226
Chapter 37: Some Keynes for Bush 232
Chapter 38: Labor Force Capacity Utilization 237
Chapter 39: The President's Macroeconomic
    Report Card 241
Chapter 40: The Great Displacement 246
Chapter 41: Can Greenspan Steer? 251
Chapter 42: The Bitterness of Supply-Siders 256
Chapter 43: Would Keynes Change His Mind? 260
Chapter 44: What's Your Margin of Safety? 265
Chapter 45: The Dollar Bubble and the Bond Bubble 270

PART 6: SOCIAL SECURITY, HEALTH CARE, AND EDUCATION

Introduction 277
Chapter 46: Bleeding-heart Libertarianism 279
Chapter 47: A Social Security Policy Primer 285
Chapter 48: America Is Mentally Ill 293
Chapter 49: Health Insurance Do-Nots 298
Chapter 50: Phase Out Medicare 302
Chapter 51: The Great Race 306
Chapter 52: The World's Nicest Holding Pen 312
Chapter 53: Efficiency, Entrepreneurship,
    and Education 318
Chapter 54: Equity, Entrepreneurship,
    and Education 323
Chapter 55: Mandatory Libertarianism 327
Chapter 56: True or False: Does Standardized
    Testing Promote School Reform? 332
Chapter 57: Government: The High-Cost Producer 337

A Final Note 343
Endnotes 345

ACKNOWLEDGMENTS

I would like to thank several economists who imparted to me their enthusiasm for the subject when I was younger. Bernie Saffran's seminar on economic theory at Swarthmore College was particularly influential. Alan Blinder, for whom I worked one summer at the Congressional Budget Office, and Robert Solow, who supervised my doctoral dissertation, were also stimulating early role models.

Nick Schultz, the editor of TechCentralStation.com, "discovered" me as an essayist. I appreciate his enthusiastic support, encouragement, and suggestions for topics. Most of the chapters in this book originally appeared as essays on TCS.

The introductory chapters and the chapter "Growth Across Time" were written for this volume. The chapter "Hayek, Stiglitz, and Michael Powell," was published in abbreviated form in the *Washington Times*. Other chapters, which were written for my web site (arnoldkling.com) but have not appeared elsewhere, are: "There is No Labor Shortage," "Asymptotically Free Goods," "The Club Vs. the Silo," "Equilibrium in the Market for Rock 'n' Roll," "Arithmetic in a Bubble," "Briefing the President," "Some Keynes for President Bush," "Efficiency, Entrepreneurship, and Education," and "Equity, Entrepreneurship, and Education."

Teri Wilhelms of Content Resources, Inc., served as editor of this book. She provided valuable assistance and advice.

About the Cover

The cover shows a position in Othello(TM), marketed by

Pressman Toys, from a game that I played at the U.S. Natonal Championships in 1986, against the eventual winner, David Shaman. Playing White, I made an unusual move, to the square in the second column, fourth row (b4). At the International championship that year, Shaman showed my b4 move to a top British player, who used it against the French champion. The Japanese champion, who won the world title, later used b4 in a prestigious tournament back home, and the Japanese Othello journal still credited me with the idea. However, when the Japanese report was translated into Italian, the printer read "Kling" as "Kung," and thus it became known as the Kung Opening. It is now considered the wrong move to make in this position.

The story of the Kung Opening illustrates the process of information diffusion, trial and error, accident, and sifting out of unsuccessful ideas that I see as the learning mechanism of the market economy. In that way, it symbolizes "learning economics."

—Arnold Kling

Author's Introduction

Each year, thousands of people study economics, but not many learn it. Most of them leave their economics courses ignorant of important basic facts, such as the differences in the standard of living over time and across countries, as well as basic economic principles, such as the way that a global oil market renders meaningless the notion of "energy independence."

Of course, there are many educational deficits to complain about in the United States—science, geography, mathematics, and so on. What is frustrating about the deficit in economic education is that it afflicts journalists, policy analysts, and other professionals whose work requires basic competence in economic analysis. Their failure to learn economics is equivalent to the failure of a physician to learn basic human anatomy.

I believe that some of the fault lies with the top graduate schools in economics, such as the Massachussets Institute of Technology, where I obtained my Ph.D. The focus on mathematical training in these programs is so intense that they tend to produce a sort of *idiot-savant*, competent only to publish in academic journals. It pains me to see economists for whom expounding economic principles and speaking in plain English are mutually exclusive activities.

Ours seems to be the age of the Partisan Hack. Looking over the list of best-selling books or the roster of columnists at top-drawer newspapers, success appears to correlate with mean-spirited attacks and heavy-handed rhetoric. Whatever happened to logical analysis of economic policy designed to illuminate as opposed to rabble-rouse?

When I was young, economists Milton Friedman and Paul

Samuelson wrote regularly for a major news magazine. They wrote to educate and to persuade. If their columns were to appear among today's journalistic mudball fights, they would seem as quaint and unfamiliar as opera would be to a pop-music audience.

This book attempts to express what I call passionate reasonableness. By reasonable, I do not mean centrist, indecisive, or compromising to settle differences. I mean taking positions on public affairs based on facts, knowledge, and intelligent analysis of the consequences of policy proposals. I mean trying to persuade rather than mock those who take a different point of view. I mean trying to appeal to rather than insult the intelligence of the average reader.

In addition to an absence of reasonableness, today's economic journalism lacks perspective on technological dynamism. When I gaze into the future, I see rapid economic and technological change. While the economy as a whole will grow rapidly, the majority of today's companies may disappear in the next twenty years! Entire industries will be born, thrive, and die within a decade. Children born in the early part of this century will grow up with totally different concepts of privacy, mental and physical well-being, and the relationship between humans and technology than what we are used to.

Unfortunately, few people today are in a position to see what is happening. Those who are not familiar with either leading-edge technology or economics—including the overwhelming majority of high school teachers and probably the vast majority of college professors—have almost no sense of the pace of change. People who are involved with information technology, nanotechnology or biotechnology can see the excitement within their own fields, but they may fail to apply the logic of exponential growth to the whole picture. Most economists, who can calculate exponential growth and appreciate its impact, seem to ignore or deny what is happening in the key technology sectors.

William Gibson, the science fiction author who coined

the term "cyberspace," has been quoted as saying "The future is here. It just hasn't been distributed yet." Today, it feels to me as if the future has been distributed to only a select cadre of science fiction writers, technology executives, and a handful of economists.

This book can help you think about public policy and rapid technological change. For those who do not have time to take a formal economics course, it can provide some insight into the economist's thought process. For those who are studying introductory economics, this book can provide additional food for thought, the way that Robert Heilbroner's *The Worldly Philosophers* and Alan Blinder's *Hard Heads, Soft Hearts* helped to illuminate economics courses in past years.

The title *Learning Economics* has a double meaning. It suggests a book that is intended to have educational value. However, it also refers to the economy itself as a system for learning. Traditional textbooks define the economic problem as "allocating scarce resources among competing ends." This completely misses what is arguably the most important economic phenomenon of all—the rise in the standard of living that represents what economists call growth. Economic growth is due primarily to the accumulation and successful application of knowledge.

This concept of economic growth as a learning process, which might receive offhand mention in mainstream textbooks, is central to the thinking here. Thus, even professional economists may find the perspective here to be somewhat novel.

The Plan of the Book

Each chapter in the book is a self-contained essay. The essays are grouped into main topic areas, each with its own themes.

The first topic area is called "What's Different About Economics?" The chapters emphasize the contrast between the way non-economists think about markets and behavior with the analysis that economists have developed. An important theme is that market-mediated trading among strangers is a distinctive form of human interaction. Many stubborn economic fallacies consist of people confusing trading with sharing. Another common misconception is failing to appreciate the difference between voluntary economic exchange and the exercise of coercive political power.

Economists are known for cynical realism, as embodied in the saying "There is no such thing as a free lunch." Nonetheless, the economics of learning is optimistic in an important sense. Many forms of human interaction are zero-sum games, meaning that one person's gain is another person's loss. In contrast, the economic processes discussed in the first half of this book are all positive-sum games, meaning that on average they produce benefits. Economic growth raises the standard of living for the entire society. The discoveries taking place in the field of computer science, which follow something called Moore's Law, are supporting economic growth at an accelerated pace. The phenomenon of international trade, which economists have understood for over 200 years to be a positive-sum game, is potentially enhanced by new information and communication technology.

The second topic area is called "Growth, Technological Progress, and Decentralized Innovation." The chapters emphasize the causes, consequences, and challenges of a learning economy, in which new production techniques are discovered and older techniques are discarded. An important theme is that the widespread improvement in our standard of living is a relatively recent phenomenon. Economic existence was stagnant and squalid throughout much of history, and even today prosperity is elusive in many parts of the world.

The third topic area is called "Moore's Law, Progress, and Displacement." The chapters draw out the benefits and dislocations brought about by rapid ongoing innovation in the design of microprocessors for computers. An important theme is the disruptive impact on mass media industries, such as news and music publishing.

The fourth topic area is called "Free Trade." The chapters renew the classic economic arguments for free trade by applying them to current issues, such as the rise of China in manufacturing, the outsourcing of white-collar work to India, and our "dependence" on foreign oil. An important theme is that punishing another country by reducing imports is a policy idea that does not hold up under close examination.

The fifth topic area is called "Macroeconomics and Bubbles." The chapters focus on the episode of the Internet Bubble in the stock market, with the subsequent crash and its consequences for the economy. A main theme is that economic policy in the post-bubble recession, while not perfect, was surprisingly constructive, and certainly did a better job of cushioning the economy than the policies that followed the stock market crash of 1929.

The sixth topic is called "Social Security, Health Care, and Education." These chapters offer alternatives to our current way of thinking about government involvement in those important areas. One theme is that in order to keep Social Security and Medicare from taking an ever-growing share of national income, we probably need to adjust the retirement age upward as the quality and longevity of life continues to increase. On education and health care, I make the case for radically less government service provision. Instead, I argue for a "bleeding-heart libertarian" approach to government that I suppose more than three-fourths of all economists would view as too libertarian, with a smaller proportion finding my approach congenial and an even tinier proportion finding it too paternalistic.

If you have browsed this far, then I challenge you to read the rest of the book. I expect that you will find many ideas to mull over—more than what can be absorbed on one plane ride or a day at the beach. I hope that you find it rewarding, and that you may even find yourself referring back to and re-reading some of the chapters. I appreciate your sharing your time with me.

—Arnold Kling

PART I

What's Different About Economics?

INTRODUCTION

"*Excuse me while I have a brief Hayekian moment. Clementines. From Australia. Big juicy sweet—amazingly sweet—Australian clementines...*

Isn't the world market marvelous! Nobody human knows—no machine has in its memory banks—the knowledge that an extra clementine tree should be planted in Australia in order to provide J. Bradford DeLong, a U.C. Berkeley professor, with big, sweet, juicy clementines in the northern-hemisphere summer. But the world market—our system of economic interrelationships considered as a social mechanism for guiding the production, transport, distribution, and allocation of goods and services—knows this. How wise it is! How fortunate the catallaxy! How big, juicy, and sweet the Australian clementines are! Clementines!"—Brad DeLong[1]

(DeLong refers to Friedrich Hayek, a Nobel prize-winning economist whose work I will discuss in the chapter "Hayek, Stiglitz, and Michael Powell.")

Let's start with something simple. Consider the cup of coffee that you drink in the morning (if you don't drink coffee, then just play along). Do you know anyone involved in the process of getting you that cup of coffee?

Do you know on whose land the coffee plants grow? Do you know who planted them? Do you know who harvested the beans? Do you know who shipped the beans to a processing plant? Do you know who made any of the containers and equipment used in shipping? Do you know who worked in the processing plant? Do you know who ran the machinery that packaged the coffee? Do you know who delivered the coffee to a retail outlet? Do you remember the person who sold you the coffee—do you know that person's last name?

We live in an impersonal world. If you lived in prehistoric times, in a tribe of hunter-gatherers or a small farming village, you would know everyone involved in your life. You would not be eating things or using things touched by strangers.

Look at the clothes that you are wearing. Do you have any idea who made them? Look at the objects around the room or office or airline terminal where you might be reading this. How many strangers did it take to create those surroundings?

Some services are still personal. You know your doctor's first and last names. Of course, the specimen that you leave in the doctor's office will be analyzed by someone you do not know at all, perhaps in a lab located in a different state. And the insurance forms you fill out are going to be processed by strangers. And the medications that the doctor prescribes for you were researched, tested, manufactured, distributed, and sold in a complex process involving thousands of people unknown to you.

Economics is about the transactions that take place in this complex, impersonal world. However, we do not look at it transaction by transaction. Instead, what we focus on is the overall outcome of the system of transactions. What can one say about the likely results from such a process? What are the benefits and harms of government intervention in that process?

The market system for interaction among strangers is mysteriously decentralized. What force keeps this system together? What is it that binds all of the separate activities into a coherent process that delivers coffee or clothing or medicine to people who do not know one another?

When I ask this question to people who have never taken a course in economics, often their first answer is "money." That is not a bad answer. Money certainly plays a major role in making impersonal transactions more efficient. But it is not the answer that I am looking for—not the answer that an economist would give.

For economists, the binding force is the price system. Prices are the terms of exchange between different goods and services. You do not know who sold you the coffee, but you know the price that you paid. The retailer knows the price paid to the wholesaler, who knows the price paid to the shipper and the price paid to the processor. The processor knows the price paid to the plantation operator, who knows the price paid to the harvesters and the landowners.

But who is it that sets these prices? If prices are the binding force in our impersonal web of transactions, then the person or persons who set prices must be awfully important. Who are they?

Here, the economist answers enigmatically. We say that no one sets prices. The market sets prices.

The wholesaler with bags of coffee for sale gives a price list to the retailer. But an economist would deny that the wholesaler *sets* the price. The wholesaler is constrained by market forces. If the wholesaler sets a price that is too high, retailers will switch to a different wholesaler. If the wholesaler sets the price too low, she will not recoup her costs of purchasing and shipping the coffee, and she will have to go out of business. Thus, although she is technically free to post any price she wants, in practice the range of prices that she can charge for her coffee in the context of the market is quite limited. Like the transactions that they serve to facilitate, prices are impersonal.

Nonmarket Transactions

One way to appreciate the distinctiveness of market-mediated trade among strangers is to contrast it with other ways in which people transact with one another. Anthropologist Alan

Fiske[2] suggests that all interpersonal transactions can be sorted into four relational models:

In a *Communal Sharing* transaction, such as a family dinner, every member of the relationship is entitled to share in what is available.

In an *Authority Ranking* transaction, such as a decision made in a traditional military unit or within a corporation, there is a clear hierarchy, with people lower in the hierarchy deferring to those who are higher up.

In an *Equality Matching* transaction, such as taking turns going through a four-way stop, people operate according to an intuitive sense of balance and fairness.

In a *Market Pricing* transaction, such as buying a used car, people make decisions on the basis of calculating costs and benefits.

Cognitive psychologist Steven Pinker, author of *The Blank Slate*, argues that of these four modes of transactions, Market Pricing is a relatively new phenomenon in the development of the human species.

Market Pricing is absent in hunter-gatherer societies, and we know it played no role in our evolutionary history because it relies on technologies like writing, money, and formal mathematics, which appeared only recently.[3]

Another aspect of hunter-gatherer societies is that people belonged to tribes or bands of fewer than 150 people. Everyone knew everyone else, and people expected to interact with one another repeatedly. Small groups with repeated interactions are conducive to establishing trust and confidence in reciprocity, which are requirements for Communal Sharing and Equality Matching. When societies become larger and people must interact with strangers, something must replace trust and confidence. Only Authority Ranking or Market Pricing can "scale up" to large groups.

What I have noticed is that many anti-economist fallacies

treat Market Pricing as if it were one of the other modes of transactions. It is as if our instinct is to see the world from a hunter-gatherer's perspective, which omits Market Pricing. For example, it is common to believe that trade with a poor country reduces income for the workers in a rich country. This would certainly be true if the transactions consisted of Communal Sharing. However, when the mode of interaction is trade at market prices, workers benefit in both countries. This will be discussed further in part four of this book.

Another example is the doctrine of Karl Marx. Marx did not portray our economy as an impersonal system of Market Pricing. Instead, he described capitalism as if it were Authority Ranking, in which the capitalist class exploits the working class. The alternative, naturally, was Communal Sharing: from each according to his abilities, to each according to his needs.

Although few people today believe in Marxist Communism (because in practice it turned out to be a corrupt and dysfunctional system based on Authority Ranking), many people instinctively view the economy through Marxist eyes. That is, they believe that capitalism is an exploitative Authority Ranking system, and it would be more "progressive" or "just" to have Communal Sharing. For example, the phrase "tax cuts for the rich" is used to arouse a feeling that the income earned by the well-off really should be Communally Shared, and only because of Authority Ranking are they allowed to keep it.

The last decade witnessed a political and legal assault on "Big Tobacco." The lawsuits against the tobacco companies were treated by most people as a victory for Communal Sharing and a defeat for Authority Ranking. However, from a Market Pricing perspective, this is not so clear. An alternative point of view is that smokers are people who bought products at market prices rather than as passive victims of tobacco companies; and the winners of the lawsuits were the individual attorneys who collected huge fees, not the community as a whole.

In a Market Pricing system, the protection that we enjoy against exploitation is the availability of choice. If the wage that you offer me is too low, I can work for a different employer. If the price that you charge is too high, I can try to find a seller with a lower price, or I can do without the product and substitute something else. Only the government has the Authority-Ranking power to force me to buy a particular product or work at a particular job.

Critics of our economy discredit themselves when they confuse Market Pricing with Authority Ranking, or when they measure it against an ideal of Communal Sharing that is unworkable in any society that has moved beyond the simplicity and small scale of a hunter-gatherer tribe. The elegance of Market Pricing can be overstated, and there are valid criticisms of our economic system. But in order to become an informed critic, one first must learn how a market system works, rather than rely on intuition derived from Communal Sharing or Authority Ranking.

The chapters in this section explore the framework that economists use to analyze the Market Pricing system. The "Sweetwater vs. Saltwater" chapter looks at doctrinal differences among a number of Nobel Prize-winners in the economics profession. The other chapters look at issues where economists tend to be on one side and non-economists on the other. Overall, these chapters provide a philosophical and scientific foundation for economics.

CHAPTER 1

SWEETWATER VS. SALTWATER

Economists agree on many things. We are all for free trade. On environmental issues, we are more persuaded by Bjorn Lomborg[4] than by Edward O. Wilson (see chapter on "Substitution, Technological Change, and the Environment"). We believe that government support for scientific research helps the economy. We supported Lawrence Lessig[5] in his attempt to overturn copyright extension (the Sonny Bono Act).

However, the economics profession divides on a number of issues. The 2002 Nobel Prize in economics, awarded to Vernon Smith and Daniel Kahneman,[6] may prove to be the most controversial in its 34-year history. In general, I would expect that Saltwater economists (from Berkeley, MIT, and Harvard, near the oceans) would approve, while Sweetwater economists (from Chicago, Minnesota, and Rochester, near the Great Lakes) would not.

The year 2002 Nobel laureates are known for evaluating the validity of two sacred assumptions in economics: the assumption that individuals optimize and the assumption that real-world markets lead to competitive outcomes. Kahneman has found systematic exceptions to the assumption that individuals optimize. Smith uses human experimental subjects to simulate market behavior, and on occasion his simulations have found that different market structures lead to different outcomes.

Can We Live Without our Assumptions?

The Sweetwater and Saltwater schools differ on the significance of the underlying postulates. Here are two representative points of view.

"Economics is that way of understanding behavior that starts from the assumption that individuals have objectives and tend to choose the correct way to achieve them."—David Friedman [7]

"The only sane answer to the questions 'do markets work well?' and 'do people act in their own interest?' is 'sometimes.' Smith and Kahneman have done a huge amount of productive work in helping us to understand that 'sometimes.'"—Brad DeLong [8]

David Friedman, the son of Milton Friedman (Nobel 1976), represents the Sweetwater school. The standard definition of economics is "the study of the allocation of scarce resources for competing ends," which does not rule out irrational behavior. However, for Chicago-trained professors, economics *is* the study of rational behavior. In their view, work such as Kahneman's, which looks at irrational behavior, is outside of economics *by definition*. Although Milton Friedman is the most well-known exponent of the Sweetwater school, within the profession Gary Becker[9] (Nobel, 1992) is considered the economist most closely identified with the doctrine that economics is the study of rational behavior.

Milton Friedman's defense of the rationality assumption is pragmatic. He does not ask us to believe that people *do* behave rationally. Instead, he asks us to evaluate the predictions that he makes when he treats people *as if* they behave rationally. In Friedman's famous metaphor, he says that we know that billiard players do not use the laws of physics to line up their shots. However, we can best predict how they will line up their shots by treating them as if they were using those laws.

Brad DeLong, who is also the son of an economist (James V. DeLong), represents the Saltwater school. Saltwater economists believe that examples of irrational behavior and imperfect markets are interesting and important. In principle, a Sweetwater economist might agree with DeLong that people are rational only sometimes and that markets are perfectly competitive only sometimes. However, the Sweetwater economists do not view this as a reason to pursue economics differently.

The Sweetwater school views the economist as a prediction-making machine. As long as the economist's predictions are nontrivial and accurate, the underlying assumptions themselves do not need to be examined. By the same token, Sweetwater economists would argue that in order to show that irrational behavior and imperfect markets matter, you must use your theories to make nontrivial and accurate predictions. It is not sufficient to demonstrate in a psychological experiment that people miscalculate. It is not sufficient to demonstrate in a simulated market that strange outcomes occur. The relevance of such findings depends on one's ability to use them to make valuable predictions about the behavior of prices and trade patterns in the real world.

By these standards, I believe that the 2002 Nobel laureates fall short. The "experimental economics" that follows Vernon Smith has generated very few predictions about real-world markets that differ from the predictions of standard mathematical models. To the extent that there have been unique predictions, to my knowledge they have not been demonstrated to be valid in any real-world setting.

Similarly, the "behavioral economics" that follows Daniel Kahneman has not developed much empirical traction. There are some hints of interesting results, particularly concerning how much income individuals choose to save[10] and how they manage their portfolios,[11] but giving a Nobel Prize to behavioral economics at this stage is like putting a promising rookie in the Hall of Fame.

Macroeconomics

In the 1970's, the great divide between Sweetwater and Saltwater economists concerned macroeconomics. Saltwater economists, such as James Tobin (Nobel, 1981) battled Sweetwater economists, including Milton Friedman and Robert E. Lucas, Jr. (Nobel, 1995).

The conflict began over the importance of monetary policy. Saltwater economist Robert Solow (Nobel, 1987) once quipped that "Everything reminds Milton Friedman of the money supply. Everything reminds me of sex, but at least I keep it out of my papers."

Eventually, however, the war spread to the very issue of whether unemployment in recessions is involuntary. In the latter part of the 1970's, Sweetwater economists began to respond to the natural gravitational pull of the assumptions of optimization and well-functioning markets, which tend to rule out the possibility of involuntary unemployment. Saltwater economists were outraged—Franco Modigliani (Nobel, 1985) once protested "Was the Great Depression nothing but an outbreak of laziness?" Sweetwater economists, notably Edward Prescott,[12] believe that unemployment indeed can be explained by changes in the incentive to work, rather than the Keynesian mechanism of effective demand failure.

In my view, if we use the "prediction machine" concept of economics, then Keynesian Saltwater economics works better (see part five of this book, "Macroeconomics and Bubbles").

The "prediction machines" of Keynesian macroeconomists have been far from perfect. However, Herbert Stein once wrote that although economists do not know very much, noneconomists know even less. Similarly, I would say that Saltwater economists do not know very much about macroeconomics. However, Sweetwater economists, who deny that there is such a thing as involuntary unemployment, know even less. For more on the Saltwater point of view, see this interview with Solow.[13]

Policy Differences

Sweetwater and Saltwater economists tend to differ on policy issues. Saltwater economists see opportunities for government to fix private-sector outcomes. Sweetwater economists are less likely to view private sector outcomes as broken. Rather than assume that government seeks to improve social welfare, Sweetwater economists are more likely to adopt the cynical view of the Public Choice[14] school, associated with James Buchanan (Nobel, 1986). The Public Choice school views government policy as the outcome of interest-group politics, with government employees ultimately acting in their own interests.

Here are a few examples of policy differences:

1. The Distribution of Income

Sweetwater economists tend to favor ensuring that each family enjoys a minimum level of income. However, they would take no further steps to reduce income inequality.

In contrast, Saltwater economists believe that government must pay more attention to the distribution of income, and in particular the government should try to reduce the discrepancies between the very wealthy and the middle class.

What the money supply is to Milton Friedman and sex is to Robert Solow, the distribution of income is to Paul Krugman[15] and other Saltwater disciples.

2. Monopoly

When it comes to monopoly, Saltwater economists tend to see government as the solution, while Sweetwater economists tend to see government as the problem.

Historically, governments granted monopolies as a revenue source. For example, a private firm might operate a canal, while giving the government a fraction of all tolls collected. Most Sweetwater economists believe that no monopoly can persist without government protection. Indeed, residues of the symbiotic relationship between monopoly and government revenue can still be seen today, for example, in the high tax rates on regulated telephone service.

In the Microsoft case, there are Saltwater economists who take the view that Microsoft is a monopoly and that government should take strenuous action. Sweetwater economists tend to believe that the market is capable of providing checks and balances against Microsoft. I myself cited Thomas Sowell, a disciple of Milton Friedman, in my skeptical survey[16] of the case for government intervention in the market for operating systems.

3. Growth Policy

Saltwater economists tend to think in terms of opportunities for government to make positive contributions to economic growth. These might include spending on health and education, helping to retrain workers displaced by economic progress for new jobs, increasing taxes to reduce government deficits and interest rates, and intervening in situations where markets produce flawed outcomes.

Sweetwater economists tend to think that government's best contribution to growth would be to get out of the way. They favor deregulation, lower tax rates to reduce the deadweight loss from taxes, and letting the private sector sort out economic choices.

Chapter 2

The Omniscient Voyeur

When I teach high school statistics, I try to warn my students to be skeptical of survey results. The example that I use to illustrate a biased statistic is what I call the omniscient voyeur.

Newspapers and magazines love to report sex surveys. With a straight face, a publication will report a finding like "The average male has five times the number of sex partners as the average female."

I ask students to imagine that there is an omniscient voyeur, who observes every heterosexual relationship that takes place. The voyeur counts the total number of relationships, which he calls N. Suppose that the number of males in the population is M, and the number of females in the population is F. Then the average number of heterosexual relationships per male is N/M, and the average number of heterosexual relationships per female is N/F. Assuming that the average number of males is close to the average number of females, then N/F has to be close to N/M, so that it is impossible for the average male to have five times as many heterosexual partners as the average female. The omniscient voyeur knows that the survey obtained biased results.

Revealed Preference

Iain Murray criticized[17] the methods used in a survey of attitudes on America. The findings were broadly anti-

American, and Murray pointed out a number of ways in which the design and execution of the survey influenced those results.

Another way to see the flaws in the survey is from the perspective of the omniscient voyeur. To assess people's real attitudes about America, we can look at immigration and emigration statistics. Unfortunately, the data available on the Internet from the U.S. Immigration and Naturalization Service are not fully up-to-date (why am I not surprised?).

For the latest period available, the 1980's, the Immigration and Naturalization Service reports that there were 7.3 million immigrants and only 1.6 million emigrants.[18] Somewhere between four and five times as many people chose to come into the United States as chose to leave. I would venture to guess that this ratio has held up in recent years.

The demand for immigration to the United States is even greater than the official statistics suggest. In the 1990's, the *un*authorized immigrant population is estimated to have doubled,[19] from 3.5 million to 7.0 million. In spite of these large figures, one can presume that immigration laws kept out some would-be immigrants, so that the true demand to live in the United States is even higher.

Inferring people's attitudes from the choices that they make rather than from their responses to a survey is a well-established doctrine in economics, known as revealed preference.[20] Observing market behavior is the economist's equivalent of acting as an omniscient voyeur.

Another illustration of revealed preference is the behavior of teachers in public schools. As the Friedman Foundation reports,[21] "50 percent of Milwaukee's and 40 percent of Cleveland's public school teachers send their own children to a private school."

Income and Happiness

Yet another example of questionable survey research is a study that purports to show that people obtain little incremental happiness beyond a certain level of income. As reported in the *Atlantic Monthly* by Don Peck and Ross Douthat,[22] the results suggest that "Above about $20,000 per capita, increases in wealth [sic] yield at best minimal increases in happiness." (Presumably, the $20,000 per capita figure refers to annual income, not cumulative wealth.)

From the standpoint of revealed preference, the statement that income over $20,000 does not raise happiness simply falls apart. Observing the fact that even people with very high incomes choose to work, an economist would infer that for most people the point at which income brings sharply diminishing returns to happiness must be much higher than $20,000. If $20,000 were the point of diminishing returns, then people who earn more than that would reduce their work effort and consume more leisure.

If anything, market behavior under-estimates the relationship between income and happiness. That is because taxes drive a wedge between market earnings and consumer well-being. An individual who faces income taxes, payroll taxes, and sales taxes has an incentive to sit around and consume leisure rather than go into the market and earn taxable income in order to obtain taxable consumer goods and services.

Tax disincentives toward earning market income are even higher in other countries. For example, Edward Prescott argues[23] that a significant portion of the difference in economic performance between France and the United States is caused by the higher tax rates faced by French workers. Because of this tax factor, Prescott says, "market time is about 30 percent lower in France than it is in the United States." In other words, if French tax rates were reduced to U.S. levels, French workers would increase their market labor significantly, because earning more income would increase their happiness.

The lesson here is that consumers' market behavior represents an important indicator of their preferences. When a survey produces reported attitudes that are inconsistent with behavior, skepticism is in order. Remember that the omniscient voyeur might be able to easily discredit the survey.

Chapter 3

Can Money Buy Happiness?

Many years ago, some friends of mine who were taking a class from popular Swarthmore economics professor Bernard Saffran thought that it would be amusing to ask him if money could buy happiness. Bernie's answer was, "Yes, to a first approximation."

This is not a frivolous issue. Many people instinctively distrust or dislike economics. However, once you concede that people with higher incomes are better off than people with lower incomes, you have conceded home field advantage to the economists. To the socialists, we can demonstrate that free markets, capital accumulation, strong property rights, and governments that serve the people rather than oppress them are factors that lead to higher incomes (see chapter on "What Causes Prosperity?"). To the environmentalists, we can show that the keys to environmental sustainability are substitution and technological change (see chapter on "Substitution, Technological Change, and the Environment"), not anti-capitalist primitivism.

A Basic Challenge

British economist Richard Layard spelled out a fundamental challenge[24] to mainstream economics. He argues that higher incomes do not lead to greater happiness. This in turn threatens much of the conventional wisdom among economists concerning policy issues.

To an economist, it is literally axiomatic that if people pursue higher incomes, then higher incomes make them happier. We do not believe that people do things that are contrary to their interests.

Layard argues instead that people pursue higher incomes even though collectively it is not in their interest to do so. He says that people are deluded into pursuing higher incomes by distortions in perception.

"First, I compare what I have with what I have become used to (through a process of habituation). As I ratchet up my standards, this reduces the enjoyment I get from any given standard of living. Second, I compare what I have with what other people have (through a process of rivalry). If others get better off, I need more in order to feel as good as before. So, we have two mechanisms which help to explain why all our efforts to become richer are so largely self-defeating in terms of the overall happiness of society."

According to Layard, we are on a happiness treadmill. Once we get used to air conditioning, having air conditioning no longer makes us happy. Once we get used to surfing the Internet, surfing the Internet no longer makes us happy. Once we get used to living longer because of modern medicine, our greater lifespan no longer makes us happy.

Furthermore, according to Layard, being aware of other people with higher incomes makes us unhappy. Lowering other people's incomes would make us just as happy as raising our own. He concludes that "in an efficient economy, there will be substantial levels of corrective taxation."

The Evidence

Layard's analytical edifice rests on an empirical foundation of survey evidence known as "happiness research." Psychologists will ask people questions such as "would you rather earn $50,000 in a world where others earn half that or earn $100,000 in a world where others earn double that?" The responses are used as indicators of whether people value relative or absolute income. Layard reports that these surveys indicate that most people would prefer higher relative income to higher absolute income.

Economists tend to distrust survey research. We believe that people indicate their desires by how they behave—we call this "revealed preference." For example, we rarely see affluent people move into poor neighborhoods in order to enjoy higher relative incomes. We often see immigrants come to the United States knowing that they will be relatively poor. Thus, their behavior appears to suggest that people value absolute income rather than relative income. Given a conflict between surveys and behavior, economists tend to view the survey results as unreliable.

Layard defends survey research on happiness, arguing that people have shown an ability to self-report happiness accurately. He reports on results showing that people's answers to questions about whether they are feeling happy are correlated with increased activity in certain parts of the brain. Therefore, something "real" is going on when people say that they are happy.

However, the fact that people can report their own happiness correctly does not mean that they can correctly articulate what makes them happy. Going from the fact that brain activity changes when people say that they are happy to the conclusion that surveys can correctly identify the causes of happiness is not a valid logical leap.

More important, the fact that subjective happiness and measurable brain activity are correlated does not imply that we can make a meaningful comparison between the happiness reported by one person and the happiness reported by another person. In particular, if I do a survey and find that two people with incomes of $20,000 and $40,000 report happiness of X and Y, I cannot draw any conclusion based on the relative values of X and Y. Even if we are talking about one person, and X and Y represent their reports at two different points in their lives, it is not clear that we can make a meaningful comparison between X and Y. Thus, it is unlikely that survey research can shed light on how happiness is affected by a change in income from $20,000 to $40,000.

What Is Socially Constructed?

Layard writes that "My main message will be that happiness depends on a lot more than your purchasing power. It depends on your tastes, which you acquire from your environment—and on the whole social context in which you live." He is saying that you cannot trust people's behavior as an indicator of their preferences, because their tastes may be socially constructed.

However, if tastes are socially constructed, then it seems to me that social context is at least as likely to affect survey research as it is to affect behavior. For example, Layard reports that marriage increases happiness, based on survey research. Even if we overlook the issue that interpersonal and intertemporal comparisons of subjective happiness have not been demonstrated to be meaningful, it could easily be that the difference in reported happiness reflects respondents' views of how they are *expected to feel* about being single or married.

As an economist, I do not worry about whether tastes are innate or acquired. I am pretty sure that I was not born with an innate taste for reading. However, reading presumably satisfies an innate desire, so that I have acquired a taste for reading. Does it matter how I acquired that taste? The fact is, I buy books and I spend time reading them. Often, I read books that make me unhappy. Yet I find them worth reading.

Overall, the more one compares Layard's survey-centric "happiness research" to the traditional approach of revealed preference, the more one appreciates the latter. One can make better predictions and arrive at more robust policy conclusions by watching what people do, not what they say.

Chapter 4

Type C and Type M Arguments

(An open letter to Paul Krugman, a columnist for the New York Times who was a contemporary of mine in graduate school.)

Dear Paul,

You might remember me from graduate school at MIT. I would like to ask you a question about what constitutes a reasonable argument.

For example, suppose I were to say, "We should abolish the minimum wage. That would increase employment and enable more people to climb out of poverty."

There are two types of arguments you might make in response. I call these Type C and Type M.

A hypothetical example of a Type C argument would be, "Well, Arnold, studies actually show that the minimum wage does not cost jobs. If you read the work of Krueger and Card, you would see that the minimum wage probably reduces poverty."

A hypothetical example of a Type M argument would be, "People who want to get rid of the minimum wage are just trying to help the corporate plutocrats."

Paul, my question for you is this:

Do you see any differences between those two types of arguments?

I see differences, and to me they are important. Type C arguments are about the *consequences* of policies. Type M arguments are about the alleged *motives* of individuals who advocate policies.

In this example, the type C argument says that the consequences of eliminating the minimum wage would not be those that I expect and desire. We can have a constructive discussion of the Type C argument—I can cite theory and evidence that contradicts Krueger and Card—and eventually one of us could change his mind, based on the facts.

Type M arguments deny the legitimacy of one's opponents to even state their case. Type M arguments do not give rise to constructive discussion. They are almost impossible to test empirically.

Here are some more examples of issues where liberals could choose to use either type C or type M arguments:

Tax Cuts

Suppose that someone were to say, "The Bush tax cuts will increase long-term growth." You might raise various objections.

One possible type C argument would be that even if the tax cuts increase long-term growth, they will increase inequality. Thus, the consequences are not good. We could have a constructive discussion of that issue, although we may not come to agreement.

Another possible type C argument would be that the tax cuts will reduce national saving, thereby lowering the capital stock, thereby reducing economic growth. They will have the exact opposite of the consequence that is claimed for them. I think that this is an important argument. I have the discomfiting impression that many in the Bush Administration and its supply-side supporters fail to understand this argument.

A type M argument would be, "So what were the Bush tax cuts really about? The best answer seems to be that they were about securing a key part of the Republican base. Wealthy campaign contributors have a lot to gain from lower taxes, and since they aren't very likely to depend on Medicare, Social Security or Medicaid, they won't suffer if the beast gets starved." In fact, this is what you wrote in "The Great Tax Cut Con."[25]

To me, this is not a helpful argument. Imagine that we could somehow prove that the motives of the supply-siders were pure, and that they really did want to improve economic growth. Would that purity of motive outweigh the argument that the higher deficits will actually have the consequence of reducing growth? I would hope not. Conversely, if the motives are wrong but the consequences are good, to me that would argue in favor of the tax cuts, not against them.

School Vouchers

Suppose that I were to say, "I believe that school vouchers would increase the quality of education and reduce the gap between the quality of schools attended by the poor and that of those attended by the rich."

A type C argument would be that there are other values that are more important, so that public education, whatever its flaws, should be maintained as it is. If you took such a position, we could have a constructive discussion, but we might end up having to disagree.

Another type C argument, which you raised in an essay in *Mother Jones*, would be, "Upper-income families would realize that a reduction in the voucher is to their benefit: They will save more in lowered taxes than they will lose in a decreased education subsidy. So they will press to reduce public spending on education, leading to ever-deteriorating quality for those who cannot afford to spend extra. In the end, the quintessential American tradition of public education for all could collapse." This is an argument about consequences. I believe that it is wrong, because I think that upper-income families would be happy to pay higher taxes to support an education system that works rather than one that fails. But at least we are talking about an empirical question.

A type M argument would be the one you made in the next paragraph of your essay. "The leaders of the radical right want privatization of schools, of public sanitation—of anything else they can think of—because they know such privatization undermines what remaining opposition exists to their program." This argument shuts off any constructive debate. It dehumanizes me to the point where I am not even given credit for knowing what my own motives are.

The War in Iraq

Suppose that someone says, "The war in Iraq has made us safer from terrorism." You would disagree.

A type C argument would be to suggest that in fact the war in Iraq has made us less safe from terrorism. One view might be that if we had backed down, we would have had broader support in the world and more resources to deal with terrorism elsewhere. It is a difficult question to settle empirically, but we can have a reasonable argument.

A type M argument would be to write, as you did on September 9, that, "It's now clear that the Iraq war was the mother of all bait-and-switch operations. Mr. Bush and his officials portrayed the invasion of Iraq as an urgent response to an imminent threat, and used war fever to win the midterm election." This is not a constructive argument. My opinion is that it requires an implausible degree of complicity among highly dedicated civil servants. Would Colin Powell *not* have resigned if the purpose of the war were to win an election? Furthermore, I still care far more about consequences than about motives. If the consequences of the Iraq war are that it leads to increased terrorism and conflict, then even the purest motives would not make it a good war, and vice-versa.

The Economic Consequences of Mr. Krugman

Paul, your columns consist primarily of type M arguments. Either you do not see the difference between type C arguments and type M arguments, or you do not care.

I am not going to try to guess your motives for relying on type M arguments. However, I can tell you some of the consequences.

One consequence is to lower the level of political discourse in general. You have a lot of influence with those who sympathize with your views. When they see you adopt type M arguments, they do the same.

Conversely, many of your opponents are stooping to your level. I see type M arguments raised by many of your enemies on the Right. As horse manure draws flies, your columns generate opposition that is vindictive and uninformed.

Another consequence is to lower the prestige and impact of economists. We are trained to make type C arguments. Instead, you are teaching by example that making speculative assessments of one's opponent's motives is more important than thinking through the consequences of policy options. If everyone were to use such speculative assessments as the basis for forming their opinions, then there would be no room for economics in public policy discussions.

You could express your point of view using type C arguments and still take strong stands for what you believe is right. In fact, you might find that doing so would make you more effective. Even if that is not the case, even if there is a sort of media version of Gresham's Law in which specious reasoning drives out careful analysis, then that is a challenge for all of us who are trained as economists. I believe that we have a professional duty to try to be part of the solution, not part of the problem.

CHAPTER 5

THERE IS NO LABOR SHORTAGE

"Two main lessons derived from [my experience as an economist] are:

1. *Economists do not know very much*
2. *Other people, including the politicians who make economic policy, know even less about economics than economists do."* —Herbert Stein[26]

Late in the fall of 1997, I attended an annual meeting of Management Recruiters International, a headhunting firm that focuses on mid-level technical, management, and sales positions. They were a sponsor of a web site that I had launched a few years earlier, which offered relocation information.

A keynote speaker addressed the conference on the outlook for the executive recruiting industry. He forecast a 20-year shortage of workers, which meant that the staffing industry would not have to worry about finding positions for individuals—it would only have to worry about finding candidates to fill an abundance of positions.

The speaker made his presentation using fancy charts and graphs. He obviously had studied the data extensively, and he cited a recent report by the United States Department of Commerce that also forecast a long-term labor shortage.

I had never considered the issue before. I had been putting all of my thought and energy into my own business, as any entrepreneur can appreciate. I was not familiar with the data or the previous studies that the speaker referenced. Everything about the presentation, in an auditorium packed with hundreds of rapt listeners, suggested that he was an expert on the subject. *And I was absolutely certain that he was wrong.*

I knew he was wrong because the notion of a long-term shortage is a violation of elementary economics. Economics professors reveal most of our knowledge to first-year students. Not much is held back for later courses. Certainly, no one has to wait for an advanced course to be exposed to the proposition that supply and demand curves intersect—that the price system adjusts so that neither demand nor supply is in excess. Nonetheless, in the media and government, non-intersecting supply and demand curves are drawn with disturbing frequency.

For example, in the 1970's the public was told to expect a chronic shortage of oil. Graphs depicted "demand" for oil increasing indefinitely, getting further and further away from "supply," which was shown increasing less rapidly, or perhaps falling. Thus, an "energy crisis" was proclaimed. Billions of dollars of taxpayer money were wasted on research into synthetic fuels and pouring oil down a hole in Louisiana called the "strategic petroleum reserve."

In contrast, the proposition that supply and demand curves intersect implied that there was a price that would eliminate the oil shortage. When the market mechanism was tested by the Reagan Administration, it proved to work.

Late in 1997, the economy was booming, which led to talk of a "labor shortage," or a "skilled labor shortage." At the MRI conference, the keynoter showed graphs of "demand" for workers growing faster than "supply."

The causal factor in his analysis is the proposition that demographic trends imply slow labor force growth in the U.S.

relative to overall population growth. The baby boomers will reach retirement age, while a smaller cohort enters the working age. A smaller cohort of working-age Americans implied a labor shortage.

Pose the question to any first-year economics student: what happens to the new equilibrium in the labor market if there is a decline in the working-age population? The answer will be that employment is reduced and the wage rate increased. The increase in the wage rate is what chokes off the incipient shortage. At higher wages, more people are willing to work. As the late-1990's boom continued, elderly people came out of retirement and young people dropped out of college to take advantage of the available opportunities. Also, at higher wages, businesses try to get by without hiring new workers. Greater efficiency and outsourcing (using overseas workers) were responses to the tight conditions of the labor market.

Fortunately, a foolish prediction of a 20-year labor shortage probably did not cause the staffing industry to make any mistakes over its relevant time horizon, which probably is closer to 20 days. More ominous were the rumblings from the Department of Commerce, which had published its study purportedly showing that the U.S. faces a future scarcity of skilled labor.

The prediction of a skilled labor shortage gave me the feeling that we were being softened up for some foolish policy initiatives: perhaps a crash program to develop "synthetic nerds," or maybe an underground facility to store network engineers as a "strategic reserve."

In 1997, one of the biggest shortages was for computer programmers with proficiency in a new language called Java, developed by Sun Microsystems. I posed this question:

> Suppose that we took a survey of all employers and asked, "At a salary of $30,000 per year, how many Java programmers would you hire?"

Adding up the answers, one might obtain a somewhat larger total than the number of people willing to supply Java programming skills at that salary. But I conjectured that a shortage of Java programmers would disappear if we surveyed employers and programmers assuming a salary of $300,000 a year. Somewhere between $30,000 and $300,000 is a salary that will balance demand and supply.

My prediction was that wages for computer programmers would rise too slowly in the "Dilbert" sector of the economy (government agencies, financial services companies, telecommunications companies, and other firms whose primary business is not software, but who currently maintain large software development organizations). Consequently, the best programmers would leave the Dilbert sector to join companies whose sole focus is software development. I viewed this as a healthy economic process, but it was widely interpreted as a shortage.

The natural economic tendency is for resources to move to where they are most productive. Market prices act as signals to bring about these shifts. The market price for computer programmers has soared in recent years. Small, specialized software companies are more effective than the Dilbert sector at using programmers. Thus, they can afford to pay programmers higher wages, while the Dilbert sector cannot. The more complaints that one hears from such firms of a shortage of technical workers, the more confident one can be that market forces are working to allocate technical workers to their most productive uses.

Late in 1997, I wrote that:

> Although most economists would share my confidence that the market can take care of a labor shortage, there is much that we do not know. We do not know how far away the current wage rate is from the one that is consistent with no excess demand for

labor. We do not know if the process of wage adjustment will be inflationary (nominal wages rising) or deflationary (prices falling relative to wages). We do not know how long the process may take.

Noneconomists, who forecast a chronic labor shortage as if there were no equilibrium wage rate, know even less than economists do.

As it transpired, it took a little over two years for the shortage in technical workers to evaporate. Once the Internet Bubble burst in March of 2000, the demand for programming began to slip. By 2002, the shortage was not in workers but in jobs. There were computer programmers complaining that they had been out of work for months, and they talked about sinister forces, including the outsourcing of work to India and elsewhere.

The shortage of computer programming jobs that emerged in 2002, like the shortage of workers that preceded it, had no permanent basis. One could be confident that wage rates will adjust downward, leading some workers to retire, return to school, or switch fields, and leading some firms to increase their hiring of software developers.

Herbert Stein was right. Economists may not know much, but we know more than non-economists. We know that wherever the price system is allowed to operate, shortages cannot last long.

Chapter 6

Quack Economic Prescription

In an opinion piece for the *Washington Post*,[27] physician Marc Siegel made a proposal for containing health care costs. The proposal was approximately as follows:

Physicians are ripping off the public with excess profits and overhead. The cost to the consumer of seeing a physician should be cut sharply, using at least one of two approaches. The first approach would be to enact price controls on all physician visits. The second approach would be to allow any patients who receive discounts (either because the physician chose to give the consumer a break or because the physician was required to give a discount by Medicare or another payer) to pass those discounts along to other patients. That is, if Fred gets a discount from Dr. X, then Fred can bring Ethel in to Dr. X for the same discount.

Physicians argue that they already are squeezed, and that the rates that they charge reflect the need to earn a return on the cost of going to medical school. Siegel's rejoinder is that physicians spend money on unnecessary overhead, such as nurses and assistants in the office. They could cut back on those expenses.

Just Kidding

As I said, this is *approximately* what Dr. Siegel wrote. Below is a comparison of this approximation to what he actually wrote.

Feature	Approximate Proposal	Actual Proposal
Price to be Reduced	Price of a physician visit	Prices of prescription drugs
Alternative to Price Controls	Allow patients with discounts to share discounts with other patients	Allow prescription drugs to be imported from countries with price controls
Fixed cost that prices would no longer recover	The cost of going to medical school	The cost of research and development of new drugs
Alleged excess overhead	nurses and assistants	drug company advertising
Economic impact not addressed	fewer people choosing to go to medical school	fewer new medications developed

I am sure that Dr. Siegel is well qualified to dispense medical advice. However, as far as economics is concerned, he is pushing harmful remedies.

Do the prices of prescription drugs exceed the marginal cost of manufacture? Definitely. But marginal cost pricing will not recover fixed costs. The marginal cost to a doctor of seeing a patient might be $10, but if that were the price hardly anyone would go to medical school. Similarly, the marginal cost of manufacturing a pill might be a few cents, but if that were the price then hardly any effort would be expended on research and testing of new drugs.

Do drug companies charge lower prices in other countries? Yes. Perhaps this is because the market will not bear higher prices in those countries. If so, then as long as overseas prices are greater than marginal cost the drug companies are recovering some overhead in other countries and this allows them to keep prices lower here than they otherwise would be.

There is, however, a less benign explanation for lower drug prices overseas. As 'Jane Galt'[28] pointed out, foreign governments have tremendous negotiating leverage with U.S. pharmaceutical companies. The foreign government has the option of telling local manufacturers that they do not have to honor U.S. drug patents. Because the chemical formulas of drugs are published, the drug companies are helpless unless they have legal protection for their intellectual property. Foreign governments could choose to take away this legal protection, and 'Jane Galt' believes that this potential threat is the reason that U.S. companies comply with foreign price controls. She believes that this allows foreign citizens to act as "free riders" on U.S. drug research—obtaining drugs at a cost below what is needed to support research and development and forcing American consumers to bear a disproportionate share of that cost.

Regardless of the reason for the success of foreign price controls, allowing importation of drugs for resale in the United States would drive prices down to the levels seen in other countries. While this indeed would serve as a short-term transfer from drug companies to consumers, it would have a chilling effect on pharmaceutical research and development.

Changing the Subject

When reminded of the issue of research and development, price-control advocates like Dr. Siegel respond by changing the subject. He writes,

"*When asked why pharmaceuticals cost so much, the drug companies often point to the high cost of that R&D. What they don't say is that they also spend an inordinate amount plying physicians with free lunches and over-packaged sample products. Or that they overspend on expensive advertising aimed at patients. (In fact, the industry's advertising costs exceed its R&D costs!)*"

Dr. Siegel's factual allegations are open to question. For example, I have seen references to data[29] that in 2001 the drug industry's direct advertising costs were $2.7 billion, compared with over $30 billion in research and development.

However, in terms of economics, those facts are not the issue. Economically, it would not matter if advertising were a hundred times research and development expenditures. What matters is whether or not the advertising is successful at increasing demand. If advertising is successful, then its economic effect is to increase the return on investment in new drugs. This either causes an increase in research and development spending, a reduction in drug prices (because with more demand firms can recover costs at lower prices), or both.

If drug company advertising is not successful at increasing the return on investment in drugs, then drug company advertising should be banned. It should be banned by drug company shareholders.

If drug prices were forced down, then drug companies might reduce advertising, because they would have less incentive to stimulate demand. However, in that case, the effect would be to *compound* the adverse impact on the rate of return on pharmaceutical research.

If physician payments were reduced sharply, many doctors would exit the business. If you told them to reduce the number of nurses and assistants, then the doctors' productivity would suffer, and they would have to exit the business even faster. Changing the subject to nurses and assistants does nothing about the physician's need to earn a return on investment for going to medical school.

Changing the subject to advertising does not solve the fundamental economic problem that the cost of up-front investment in drug research has to be recovered. Cutting spending elsewhere does not make money available for drug company research. Expected returns on investment are what make money available for research. That is basic, first-year economics.

Alternatives to the Status Quo

It is not my purpose to defend the status quo in the pharmaceutical industry. It is not my field of expertise, so I am reluctant to express more than a few hunches. However,

I am not convinced that pricing drugs above marginal cost is the best approach. There are viable economic alternatives that would allow drugs to be priced closer to marginal cost without destroying the incentive to innovate. For example, the patent system could be replaced by a cash prize system, in which the government or large charitable organizations provide rewards for successful drug research.

I am troubled by the degree of concentration in the pharmaceutical industry. My instinct is that decentralization is more conducive to innovation. I suspect that "big pharma" is protected by the complexity of the FDA regulatory structure, which I imagine requires a lot of overhead, making it difficult to be a sub-behemoth participant in the market.

But constructive reforms to improve the drug market should be guided by sound reasoning. It requires a combination of economic sophistication and industry expertise. It is disturbing that Dr. Siegel and others, who lack a basic understanding of the way markets work, can pass themselves off as authorities in economic policy. This is no field for quacks.

CHAPTER 7

ECONOMICS VS. POPULISM

"Each of the four schools that together represent the American foreign policy debate makes distinct contributions to national power, and each is well matched with the others—capable of complementing one another and of flexibly combining in many ways to meet changing circumstances."—Walter Russell Mead[30]

Historian Walter Russell Mead's *Special Providence: American Foreign Policy and How it Changed the World* is one of the most stimulating books that I have read in recent years. Although it is focused on American approaches to foreign policy, the off-hand insights that Mead offers about attitudes toward economic issues are also valuable.

Special Providence divides American foreign policy positions into four schools:

- **Hamiltonians.** They are the guardians of the international economic order. Think of Alan Greenspan or Robert Rubin.
- **Wilsonians.** They are the perfectionists who envision an international order governed by treaties and international institutions. I think of the Clinton Administration, which supported both NAFTA and Kyoto.
- **Jeffersonians.** They are idealists, the most emotional

57

of the four types, who believe in a moralistic approach to foreign policy. They believe that there are always better alternatives than war. The Jeffersonians are staunch opponents of the Iraq war, and many of them were none to keen on the war in Afghanistan.

- **Jacksonians.** They are the patriotic fighters for whom the worst sin is not going to war, it's losing one. Examples would be people who hung flags and attended pro-America rallies after 9/11. When Jeffersonians attack President Bush for acting unilaterally, they are probably helping his popularity with Jacksonians. For Jacksonians, unilateralism is a feature, not a bug.

I am also tempted to re-interpret Mead as providing a model with three elitist viewpoints and the Jacksonian populist viewpoint. The Hamiltonians are the banking elite, who believe that a good world is one where financial institutions are solvent and trade is brisk. The Wilsonians are the legal elite, who believe that a good world is one where democracy is widespread and the world's problems are addressed by international treaties. Finally, the Jeffersonians are the academic elite, who believe that a good world is one in which there is justice and equality, and the United States strives to lead by moral example rather than by force.

Where I Fit In

By temperament, I would be inclined to the view that an architecture of international institutions, as advocated by Wilsonians, is the ideal. You can see my reverence for elegant architecture in my fondness for the Internet and in my belief in the virtues of our Constitution. In fact, however, I am so enamored of our system of checks and balances, along with our Bill of Rights, that I distrust the Wilsonian project of bringing about international rule of law. I would be all for it if everyone were to adopt our system. However, compromising our elegant architecture for the sake of participating in a world architecture is repellent to me. Consequently, on foreign policy, and particularly after 9/11, I wind up a Jacksonian.

In the conclusion of *Special Providence*, Mead writes, "it seems to me that the voice of the Jeffersonian school is the one that currently most needs to be heard." This took me by surprise. Mead argues that the other elites—the Hamiltonians and the Wilsonians—are prone to overreaching. The Jeffersonians are needed, he says, in order to provide self-restraint on our hegemony.

On the other hand, Mead warns that "Jeffersonians can do as they did in the 1930's . . . rest in denial concerning the true extent of the nation's vital interests . . . confine themselves to sniping at the moral inconsistencies, blunders, and costs of American foreign policy . . ." In that case, he says, they will marginalize themselves and their potential contribution will be lost. It seems to me that the Jeffersonians have gone off-track in exactly the way that Mead feared.

I also believe that the Jeffersonians are off base on economic policy. The academic elite is eager to embrace any ideology, such as Marxism or radical environmentalism, that denigrates the market.

The Economic Consequences of the Populists

While I find Jacksonian populist foreign policy rather congenial, I part company with the populists on economics. The three most important quarrels I have with economic populism relate to free trade, Social Security, and thrift.

Mead points out that Jacksonians see ordinary working people as virtuous, justifying resentment of foreign competition. In this view, it is not fair for decent, hard-working Americans to lose jobs to alien workers.

In my view, international trade is only one aspect of the

overall phenomenon I call Progress and Displacement. Technological change is rapid and inevitable. It means that the employment base is constantly shifting, with some skills made obsolete while other skills become relevant. This wide river of technological change will not be dammed up by tossing in a few trade barriers. For example, it appears that the infamous steel tariffs of the Bush Administration probably cost more jobs in steel-using manufacturing firms than they saved in the steel industry itself.

Mead says that Jacksonians support Social Security because they respect the elderly. What I have tried to point out in numerous essays is that in a couple of decades Social Security (see chapter on "A Social Security Policy Primer") and Medicare (see chapter on "Phase Out Medicare") are going to pose an immense burden on the working population. I believe that the solution is for the population of people aged 50 and younger to be promised fewer benefits and instead be encouraged to save for their own needs later in life. It is urgent to resolve this matter soon, because it would be unfair to cut benefits at the last minute, when people already are close to or beyond retirement.

On the issue of thrift, Mead says that Jacksonians believe "that money, especially borrowed money, is less a sacred trust than a means for self-discovery and expression... The strict Jacksonian code of honor does not enjoin what others see as financial probity." In other words, thrift is not a Jacksonian virtue.

Our popular culture exalts the consumer. Most adherents of the elite schools are appalled by the spending mentality. Economists have shown that countries with high saving rates tend to have higher levels of income, because saving enables capital accumulation. Even modern followers of Keynes do not share his fear of excessive thrift. Instead, the belief is that with rare exceptions monetary policy can be used to maintain sufficient aggregate demand to support full employment.

On this topic, I confess to being in the same camp as the elites—I am in favor of more saving. In the wake of 9/11, when some Jacksonians talked about the need for consumers to keep spending as a patriotic duty, I was appalled. If we were truly at war, consumers would need to conserve resources, not spend them.

In my view, the populist exaltation of consumption is at odds with the Jacksonian emphasis on self-reliance. Without saving, people will find themselves unable to provide for their own retirement and unable to cushion their families from economic change and turbulence.

If Jacksonians strike me as overly casual about deficit spending at a personal level, they also strike me as overly casual about government deficits. I would like to see a tight lid kept on spending, so that deficits can be reduced. I would support deficits only in exceptional circumstances, notably a recession in which monetary policy is not sufficient to produce an adequate recovery.

The Bush Administration's supply-side economics strikes a populist chord. Combining tax cuts with spending increases, with little concern for deficits, is no problem for Jacksonians.

Jacksonians are happy with new government programs, such as a prescription drug benefit, that spend money on "deserving" middle-class families. Instead, what I see are the taxes that fund these programs. The tax bill falls on other middle-class families, creating new needs (such as more young people who cannot afford health insurance) for yet more government programs, in a vicious cycle.

As a Wilsonian architect, I like the elegant simplicity of my Bleeding-heart Libertarian (see chapter on "Bleeding-heart Libertarianism") tax-and-benefit formula, to replace the crazy quilt of government programs aimed at income redistribution. That tax formula also embodies my belief in encouraging saving rather than consumption. However, targeted government programs are what attract popular sentiment. Simple formulas have no emotional appeal to Jacksonians.

The Seeds of Education

If I were a demagogue, I would try to come up with emotional language that could be used to foist my economic policies on a reluctant Jacksonian populace. In fact, the game of manipulating the public is played by all members of the political elite, of both major parties.

Instead, I see myself as a teacher. The hope is to plant seeds so that the lawn of an educated viewpoint grows over the weeds of economic populism. In other words, my goal is that the Jacksonian middle class will come to support free trade, entitlement reform, and government that is small and efficient because people understand the arguments for these approaches.

CHAPTER 8

ECONOMIC ATTRIBUTION ERRORS

"Psychologists call this tendency the Fundamental Attribution Error (FAE), which is a fancy way of saying that when it comes to interpreting other people's behavior, human beings invariably make the mistake of overestimating the importance of fundamental character traits and underestimating the importance of the situation and context."—Malcolm Gladwell[31]

In the summer of 2003, a book club in which I participate met to discuss Gladwell's book. Ironically, one of the participants proceeded to commit what I think of as the Economic Attribution Error. That is when someone attributes the behavior of key macroeconomic indicators, such as the exchange rate, the Budget deficit, or the unemployment rate, to the fundamental character traits of government officials, such as the President or the Chairman of the Federal Reserve. In fact, the values of these variables depend mostly on the context provided by the private sector—the influence of fiscal and monetary policy tends to be vastly overstated.

What happened at the book club was that one participant complained that her forthcoming trip to Europe was going to be expensive, because of the recent decline in the value of the dollar. Another participant quickly assured her that this was due to the Bush Administration's irresponsible economic policies. Although I did not want to get into a heated argument (we were there to discuss Gladwell's book, not economic policy), I felt compelled to murmur something about Stein's Law.

I was hardly being original. Over three years previously, Paul Krugman warned,[32]

"Our current position, where we pay for many of our imports by attracting inflows of capital—in effect by selling the rest of the world claims on our future exports—cannot go on forever. And as the late economist Herbert Stein declared, 'If something cannot go on forever, it will stop.'

The most likely scenario is that the trade deficit will eventually be reined in by a decline in the foreign-exchange value of the dollar. The great dollar slide of 1985-87, precipitated by a trade deficit that was actually smaller compared with G.D.P. than the deficit today, reduced the value of a dollar by 40 percent in terms of German marks and Japanese yen. And there is no obvious reason why the same thing can't happen again.

... foreign investors, and therefore the value of the dollar, are arguably doing a Wile E. Coyote—one of these days they will look down, realize that they have already walked over the edge of the cliff, and plunge."

Similar warnings were made by Steve Roach in numerous settings (e.g., July, 2002)[33] and by Brad DeLong, who favorably passed this along[34] from *The Economist*, also July, 2002.

"There is also persistent concern among economists and, now, investors, about America's huge current-account deficit—now running at over 4% of GDP. In historical terms, that is a very high level for an economy just emerging from recession. Some research suggests that such high deficits tend to be unwound quickly, by a rapid downward adjustment in the currency."

Krugman's column about the dollar bubble appeared almost a year before President Clinton left office. Roach, DeLong, and *The Economist* gave their warnings without referring to any particular Administration's economic policies.

Instead, it is the public that appears inclined to believe that the President controls the economy.

The "Clinton" Surplus

Another case of the Economic Attribution Error concerns the Budget surplus. During the Clinton Administration, the projected Budget surplus improved by over one trillion dollars. However, most of this change came as a surprise to the Administration. A reasonably nonpartisan analysis by Douglas W. Elmendorf, Jeffrey B. Liebman, and David W. Wilcox[35] shows that less than 20 percent of the revision to the Budget outlook came from economic policy. (See figure 4 in their paper).

In fact, it appears from Table 2 of the paper that by the latter part of the Clinton Administration the policy contribution had turned adverse—in the absence of the policy changes made during those years, the surplus would have been higher. A cynic might say that throughout most of the 1990's fiscal restraint was adhered to only because policymakers underestimated the growth of the economy and tax revenues. Our representatives in Congress likely would have spent the surplus sooner had they known it was coming.

According to the economic attribution error, all of the movement toward surplus in the 1990's would be credited to the actions of President Clinton and Congress during that time. However, the best reading of the data would seem to indicate that at least 80 percent of the change reflected a context in which revenues grew faster than forecast.

Monetary Maestro?

Federal Reserve Chairmen are always revered. Even Arthur Burns, who unleashed a torrent of money during President Nixon's 1972 re-election year, thereby serving to aggravate the problem of inflation, was at the time viewed as wise and irreplaceable.

Today, Alan Greenspan is regarded, in Bob Woodward's term, as a maestro. Again the economic attribution error is at work. Journalists—and even some economists—will attribute every wiggle in macroeconomic performance to Federal Reserve policy. In fact, the Fed only affects one minor interest rate—the rate that banks charge one another for overnight loans—and for the most part the Fed is content to passively keep that rate in line with general market trends.

In his analysis of monetary policy in the 1990's, Greg Mankiw,[36] now President Bush's choice to be chairman of the Council of Economic Advisers, does not share the widespread view that Alan Greenspan's brilliance is what accounts for the strong economy.

"A large share of the impressive performance of the 1990s was due to good luck. The economy experienced no severe shocks to food or energy prices during this period. Accelerating productivity growth due to advances in information technology may also have helped lower unemployment and inflation."

Journalists see the economy as a puppet, with Greenspan pulling the strings. But the reality is quite different (see chapter on "Can Greenspan Steer"?).

Judging Policy

The economic attribution error means that people assign too much credit or blame for economic performance to the President and other officials. But shouldn't the President be held accountable, just as a corporate CEO is held accountable for corporate performance?

First, I believe that we commit attribution errors in our evaluation of corporate CEO's. The rise and fall of America Online had much more to do with the context in which it operated than with Steve Case's character traits. One of the

LEARNING ECONOMICS

reasons that I am not a fan of stock options as compensation is that their value tends to depend a lot on context rather than performance—options are worth more in a rising market than in a falling market.

In fact, the whole issue of CEO compensation is made murky by the economic attribution error. If CEO's really make enough of a difference to merit their centerfold spreads in business magazines, then they are badly underpaid. On the other hand, if context plays the dominant role in determining corporate profitability, then CEO pay is biased upward by the attribution error. I suspect the latter.

The President of the United States is not the CEO of our economy. The President operates under much tighter constraints—and we should be happy about that. Limitations on executive power are a good thing.

I do not think that the President should be held accountable for the decline in the dollar, the rise in unemployment, or the rise in the deficit so far. However, I want to make clear that while I am arguing against making the economic attribution error, I am not giving President Bush a "pass" on economic policy.

The Bush economic policy can be evaluated on its own merits. I would give the Administration a bad grade on trade, because of the steel tariffs. I would give the Administration a bad grade on fiscal policy, because it is making no attempt to identify and implement spending reductions, and because it has not pursued any sort of "exit strategy" for Medicare (see chapter on Phase Out Medicare"), which threatens to capture a huge share of GDP for the government. I would give the Administration a bad grade on energy policy, because the proposal to subsidize hydrogen fuel cells shows a failure to understand oil economics (see chapter on "Oil Econ 101"). I would give the Administration a bad grade on education policy, because it continues to undermine local control of schools (see chapter on "True or False").

These policy disappointments cannot be explained away by the economic attribution error. I can say only one thing in defense of the Republicans. On the issues that I just mentioned, their policies are only the second-worst of the two major parties.

PART 2

Growth, Technological Progress, and Decentralized Innovation

INTRODUCTION

"*The 7,500 calories in today's bag of flour would equal the diet of a four-person peasant family for a whole day; the difference is that it would take three days of medieval work to afford.*
... By the bags-of-flour standard, we are some 430 times wealthier than our typical rural ancestors of half a millennium ago."—Brad DeLong[37]

On December 11, 2002, Virginia Postrel, a Dallas-drawling libertarian who practices social science without a license (meaning that she lacks an advanced degree), noted for her weblog, or personal Internet journal, that she had just purchased a bag of flour for the low price of 69 cents.[38] "I find that amazing," she said. It was a typical observation for Postrel, who writes a monthly column on economics for the business section of *The New York Times* and is the author of *The Future and its Enemies* and *The Substance of Style*. Postrel is a champion for the everyday benefits of capitalism, from the increased productivity attributable to Wal-Mart to the aesthetic qualities of contemporary toilet brushes.

Postrel's anecdote about cheap flour was read by Brad DeLong, a left-leaning, fully-accredited professor of economics at the University of California at Berkeley. It occurred to DeLong,[39] an authority on the history of economic growth, that flour is unusual in that it reflects continuity with the past. Most goods and services today would not be recognizable to our medieval ancestors (what would they think of a computer or a cell phone?), and many of the implements of the pre-industrial era have no utility in the present. Flour can be used to make connections across the gap of time.

DeLong's analysis starts with the fact that in 1500 the average family lived not far above subsistence. They could do little more than feed themselves with their labor—DeLong estimates that three-fourths of what the medieval economy produced was foodstuffs. If 7500 calories represents subsistence for four people for one day, then it can be inferred that it took roughly three days for the family to work to produce that amount of calories, which are contained in one five-pound bag of flour.

DeLong asks how much one would have to work today in order to obtain one bag of flour. He then notes that if today's family of four in the United States earns an average of $100 a day, then a day's pay can purchase roughly 145 bags of flour, which should be multiplied by three to obtain what could be produced with three days' labor.

I like to put it like this: in 1500, if you were the average laborer who worked three days, cashed your paycheck (so to speak), walked into the local Safeway (so to speak), and emptied your wallet, you could have walked out with one five-pound bag of flour. Today, if you work three days, and you spent three days' pay on flour, you could walk out of the grocery with 430 five-pound bags.

What was it that enabled us to get from the point where we had to work three days to produce one bag of flour to the point where three days' work yields 430 bags of flour? The best answer, to a first approximation, is that we *learned* how to do it. We learned how to grow wheat more efficiently, how to use machinery to harvest, how to build railroads and trucks to transport grain, how to use electric power and automation to manufacture flour, and how to manage logistics and inventories to deliver flour to the shelves of stores.

With this cumulative knowledge, we freed people from the farms. As recently as 200 years ago, over half of the

American labor force was in agriculture. Today, just 2 percent of the population can produce enough to feed the rest, with food leftover for export.

From roughly 1800 through 1950, the excess agricultural labor pool came to the cities, where it became the manufacturing workforce. For the past fifty years, another labor migration has been taking place—out of the factories and into services, such as marketing and middle management. As with food, we continue to produce manufactured goods, but with fewer workers—the fraction of the population on the production lines has fallen dramatically.

The rest of this chapter looks at more issues concerning this growth process. How do economists measure economic growth, and what do these measures show about economic history? Where can we observe economic growth taking place today? What is the outlook for economic growth going forward? Why are some countries so backward? These are among the questions that will be tackled in the sections that follow.

Chapter 9

Growth Across Time

"Ultimately, long-run economic growth is the most important aspect of how the economy performs. Material standards of living and levels of economic productivity in the United States today are about four times what they are today, in say, Mexico because of favorable initial conditions and successful growth-promoting economic policies over the past two centuries. Material standards of living and levels of economic productivity in the United States today are at least five times what they were at the end of the nineteenth century and more than ten times what they were at the founding of the republic"—Brad DeLong[40]

Economic growth is defined as the change in output per capita. To measure output, we take the total value of the goods and services produced by an economy in a year, called Gross Domestic Product (GDP). Then we divide by population to get the average standard of living. Alternatively, we can divide output by the size of the working population in order to measure labor productivity. We use either of these measures of output per capita to compare economic performance across time or across countries.

Historical Perspective

Here is a table (taken from DeLong)[41] showing estimates

of the growth in world population and average output per person from ancient times to the present.

Year	Population in millions	GDP per person in year-2000 dollars
5000 BC	5	130
1000 BC	50	160
1 AD	170	135
1000 AD	265	165
1500 AD	425	175
1800 AD	900	250
1900 AD	1625	850
1950 AD	2515	2030
1975 AD	4080	4640
2000 AD	6120	8175

A few remarks about the table:

1. Measuring the value of output historically is very tricky. There were goods that were very important at some points in time (such as covered wagons) which did not exist in earlier times and which are obsolete today.
2. Through 1800, average output per worker was less than $1 a day in today's terms. Nearly everyone lived in what we would call a state of poverty. The middle class is a very recent phenomenon.
3. Most of the growth in the average standard of living has taken place in the past 100 to 150 years.

Other evidence that corroborates this GDP-based perspective includes the following:

Height and Longevity

According to Ward Nicholson,[42] around the time of

LEARNING ECONOMICS

Christ, the average height of males was 171.9 centimeters and the average lifespan was 41.9 years. In 1400-1800, these figures were 172.2 centimeters and 33.9 years, respectively. Even by 1900, longevity had not reached 50 years. Today, the figures are 174.2 centimeters and 71.0 years, respectively.

Food

According to DeLong (p. 440-441), 2,000 years ago, at least 90 percent of the populace had to be employed in agriculture in order to produce enough food. By 1800, this proportion still was over 50 percent. In the United States today, the proportion stands at around 2 percent.

Destructive power

According to Niall Ferguson,[43] "between the seventeenth and twentieth century, the capacity of war to kill rose by roughly a factor of 800."

Mechanical power

According to data cited in a paper by DeLong,[44] the conversion from steam engines to electric motors helped to increase the total mechanical power in the United States by a factor of 40 in the seventy years from 1869 to 1939.

Computational power

In the article cited above, DeLong notes that the exponential increase in the instructions performed per second by a computer chip, along with the growth in the number of computers, implies a *million-fold increase* in total computational power in the last forty years.

Projecting the improvements in computing power into the future, Ray Kurzweil makes this astonishing claim in *The Age of Spiritual Machines*:[45]

"*Our most advanced computers are still simpler than the human brain—currently about a million times simpler (give or take two orders of magnitude depending on the assumptions used). But... Computers... are now doubling in speed every twelve months. This trend will continue, with computers achieving the memory capacity and computing speed of the human brain around the year 2020.*"

A Perspective from Anacostia Park

These quantitative indicators of cumulative exponential growth are significant. However, it may be easier to grasp the dramatic nature of growth by comparing the life of a particular rich man one hundred years ago to our lives today.

High atop Anacostia Park, a rundown, working "poor" section of Washington, DC, sits the mansion of Frederick Douglass, the great nineteenth century orator and agitator for the rights of women and African Americans. Douglass, although born a slave, became a wealthy newspaper publisher. He came to Washington late in his life, as a U.S. Marshall in 1879. His 21-room mansion was on a 15-acre site and employed three servants. A reasonable guess is that he was in the top one or two percent of the wealth distribution at that time.

The Douglass mansion has been preserved today as a museum in its condition as of 1895, when he died. Below is a partial list of the appliances that can be found there, compared with their modern equivalents.

Item in the Douglass mansion, 1895	Modern equivalent
Rug beater	Vacuum cleaner
Chamber pots	Flush toilets
Ice box (one cubic foot)	Refrigerator/freezer (16 cubic feet)
Washboard	Washing machine
Clothes wringer	Dryer
Irons	No-iron clothes
Indoor well	Plumbing
Kerosene lamp	Electricity
Dry sink	Dishwasher

Today's residents of Anacostia Park, although many would be considered poor by today's statistical measures, have all of the modern conveniences on the right hand side of the table. In addition, they can drive to work, while Frederick Douglass had to walk five miles to his job in the Capitol building. They have radios, televisions, and many other goods that the wealthy Douglass never possessed.

Future Growth

Since 1500, economic growth has accelerated. The main elements of this acceleration have been:

1. The "demographic transition," toward fewer children, so that population growth places less pressure on the food supply.
2. Modern science and technology, which has vastly improved our ability to grow food, use machinery in

place of human labor, and harness information to use resources efficiently.
3. Modern democratic states, which encourage individual freedom and promote economic growth.

All of these elements promise to contribute to economic growth in the future. The "demographic transition" has begun in the underdeveloped countries of the world. Science continues to open new frontiers in biotechnology and nanotechnology (manipulating matter at the molecular level), while innovation continues in computing and communications. Most economists believe that we can achieve growth of at least 1.5 percent per year.

Over the next fifty years, average income would more than double if real growth were just 1.5 percent per year. This is an example of the power of compounding, or exponential growth.

What this sort of economic growth means is that in fifty years the average person will have an income that today would be considered upper middle class. Although some people will have less income than others, absolute poverty is something that can be eliminated by economic growth and policies that assist those who are mentally and physically disabled.

A difference in growth rates that might seem small—say, 2 percent vs. 1 percent—is one that economists would deem to be very important, because of the cumulative effect over many years. We would argue that such a difference is large enough to affect the outlook for many major social concerns, including:

- our ability to continue to reduce poverty
- our ability to deal with an aging population, with its impact on Social Security
- the quality of the environment

Ten years from now, the outlook for these issues will be brighter if economic growth averages over 2 percent than if economic growth averages less than 1 percent. If we have more growth, then the poor will enjoy a higher standard of living, social security will be solvent, and our ability to maintain clean air and water will be greater. If Kurzweil and other optimists are correct, then economic growth will accelerate much beyond 2 percent per year. The economic scenario that this implies is difficult to capture outside of science fiction: goods that we now think of as expensive would be as cheap as the bag of flour that we described in the introduction to this chapter. I spell this out further in the chapter "Asymptotically Free Goods."

Chapter 10

Progress and Displacement

Nostalgia can take remarkable forms. Naomi Klein, author of the anti-globalization manifesto *No Logo*, decries the loss of blue-collar factory jobs in her neighborhood. Who would have thought that someone would mourn the demise of Dickensian drudgery?

Every step forward in economic development involves displacement of an old way of life. New industries are fed by the resources that are released as old industries become more productive. For society as a whole, this represents progress. However, for individuals who wish to continue using outmoded methods, economic growth is an outrage. Wal-mart's efficiency is seen as unfairly boxing out local merchants. Amtrak's advocates see competing forms of transportation unjustly railroading it out of business. Loan sharks resent the intrusion of "subprime" lenders fishing around for low-income consumers. Etc.

Music Industry Blues

These days, the music distribution industry is singing the displacement blues. As Joni Mitchell might put it, the starmaker machinery is trying to drag its feet to slow the circles down.

In 2002, the *Washington Post* featured an op-ed column by Stan Bernstein,[46] whose record store had gone out of business.

LEARNING ECONOMICS

"I opened a record store . . . I was just 20 and still a student, and I couldn't think of a better way to earn a living than by bringing music to my friends and neighbors.

More than three decades later, I still can't. But . . . that store is now history . . .

As the sign I left in the window explained: 'Morninglory Music is closed for good in Isla Vista, due to lack of business. (There was no way to compete with free downloadable music and CD burners).'"

Bernstein concludes with this warning:

"The same forces that killed my small store now threaten a major segment of our economy—creative industries such as music, movies and publishing. What future do they have in a world in which books, films and music are simply passed around rather than purchased?

Copyright laws have helped the creators and producers of information and entertainment contribute greatly to this country and its economy. If we want to continue receiving those benefits, it's time for the government to enforce the law."

Bernstein and others who see the legal system as the salvation of the older way of life in the music industry need to face up to the following facts:

1. **The amount and variety of music being created and recorded today is expanding.** There is no sign that musicians and composers are finding Internet file-sharing a deterrent to creative activity. On the contrary, there seems to be a blossoming of independent talent. At least one veteran artist, Janis Ian, has pointed out the advantages that Internet-based distribution gives[47] to the vast majority of musicians who are not superstars.

   "In the hysteria of the moment, everyone is forgetting the main way an artist becomes successful-exposure. Without exposure, no one comes to shows, no one buys CDs, no one enables you to earn a living

doing what you love. Again, from personal experience: in 37 years as a recording artist, I've created 25+ albums for major labels, and I've never once received a royalty check that didn't show I owed them money. So I make the bulk of my living from live touring, playing for 80-1500 people a night, doing my own show. I spend hours each week doing press, writing articles, making sure my website tour information is up to date. Why? Because all of that gives me exposure to an audience that might not come otherwise. So when someone writes and tells me they came to my show because they'd downloaded a song and gotten curious, I am thrilled!

Who gets hurt by free downloads? Save a handful of super-successes like Celine Dion, none of us. We only get helped."

2. **Copyright enforcement cannot protect record stores.** Even if people had to pay for the music that they download, many would still find this more convenient than going to a store. Record stores are inherently more costly, because they require land, space, labor, and inventories. Regardless of how the copyright issue plays out, the future of music distribution is online, not record stores.

3. **If CD burners were banned, the recorded-CD industry would not be saved.** Moore's Law says that computer storage capacity is increasing and costs are decreasing. This means that people can afford to own more music than they could in a world where the only storage option is a CD. Furthermore, Moore's Law is leading to the expansion of broadband Internet access, which means that distribution of music over the Net is more efficient. To survive, the music industry must repackage its

services (see chapter on "Listen to the Technology") to take advantage of the new technology.

What is happening in music is a tremendous increase in the productivity of music storage and distribution, which will benefit consumers and music creators. By the same token, record stores and CD manufacturers will be displaced by this new technology. However, rather than express their resentment as nostalgia for outmoded business practices, the industry incumbents couch the issue in terms of copyright and intellectual property.

Nostalgia for Inadequate Health Care

Another peculiar case of resentment over displacement comes from political and business leaders who argue that the United States devotes too much of its resources to health care. As David Cutler and Jonathan Gruber remind us,[48] concern over rising health care spending was a major factor shaping President Clinton's ill-fated "reform" proposal, one of the goals of which was to freeze or roll back the share of GDP going to health care.

Nobel laureate Robert Fogel offers an economic historian's perspective[49] on displacement and health care spending.

"The greatest opportunity of the 21st century is to add as many years to life expectancy as we did during the 20th. Life expectancy in the rich countries at the beginning of the 20th century was about 45 years. At the end of the century, it was maybe 77. By the end of the 21st century, it could be close to 100 years.

. . . In 1910, 95 percent of all Americans who lived to 65 had severe chronic conditions on average, six or seven chronic conditions. Today, less than half of all 65 year olds are chronically ill."

Fogel goes on to say,

"In the United States in 1800, it took five people working on the farm to support one person working off the farm. Today, 2 percent of the labor force not only feeds—and overfeeds—the United States, but another 300 million people around the world . . .

That sort of transformation is going to solve our health care problem. We can afford to spend not only the current 14 percent of GDP on health care, but considerably more: I forecast the figure will rise to 21 percent. That's because the production of food, clothing, shelter and consumer durables is becoming incredibly cheap."

Conclusion

Economic progress marches on, and with it comes displacement. Higher productivity in music distribution is releasing resources that can be better utilized elsewhere. Today's record store employees may be tomorrow's providers of better health.

CHAPTER 11

RATIONAL EXUBERANCE

The ultimate irony of the stock market decline of 2000-2002 is that it occurred at a time when long-skeptical economists have come around to the view that the "new economy" story that fueled much of the preceding rise appears to be true. Using Moore's Law,[50] leading professional economists are painting an optimistic picture of economic growth in the coming decade.

In 1987, Robert Solow wrote an article in the *New York Times Book Review* in which he said, "You can see the computer age everywhere but in the productivity statistics." For over a decade, this view held up within the economics profession.

Recently, however, the consensus has moved in the opposite direction. Brad DeLong writes, in a paper called Productivity Growth in the 2000's,[51] that "[economists] nearly all agree that the causes of the productivity speed-up of the 1990s lie in the information technology sector."

What happened between 1987 and 2002 to change professional economists from skeptics to believers in the new economy? Why did computer-driven productivity growth become apparent in the late 1990's when it was not visible earlier?

A Bigger Deal

The answer is that in fifteen years, computers have become a much bigger deal in the economy as a whole.

Information technology investment relative to GDP grew from less than 2 percent in 1987 to 6 percent in 2002. Also, keep in mind that in 1987 the state-of-the-art microprocessor was the Intel 386. In fifteen years of progress[52] from 1985 to 2000, the standard microprocessor went from the 386 with 275,000 transistors to the Pentium 4 with 42,000,000 transistors.

Economist William Nordhaus even says that Moore's Law may understate the progress of computing.[53] His measures suggest that since 1980 the cost of computing has fallen at an average rate of 80 percent per year.

This tremendous increase in computing power, combined with the sharp increase in spending on information technology, coincides with a doubling of the rate of productivity growth, from 1.3 percent in 1973-1995, to 2.7 percent since then. A reasonable estimate is that something like half the increase in productivity growth can be attributed to information technology investment.

The Case for Optimism

It is not 1987 any more. The information technology sector is significant today. Starting from today's high baseline of computing power, further extrapolation of Moore's Law leads to remarkably optimistic forecasts. For example, Nordhaus predicts that by 2025 we will see "'petacomputers,' tiny machines with memory, storage, and computing capacities that are roughly a million times greater than today's personal computers and cost $1 or less. Such devices will be intelligent, essentially free, essentially weightless, and small enough to fit unnoticeably into your shoe or under your skin."

DeLong says that with the high rate of information technology investment and the continued operation of Moore's Law, the only way that we can see a productivity slowdown is for the social return on information technology investment to drop to zero. In other words, as long as we do not become completely unable to figure out new uses for better computing technology, the power of that technology will be felt in future productivity growth.

In fact, DeLong argues that there are reasons to expect the social return on information technology investment to remain high, or even to increase. He cites economic historian Paul David, who studied the impact of the introduction of the electric motor. David, who found that most of the productivity gains came decades after the technology was developed, theorizes that it takes time for knowledge of technology to spread widely enough so that technology is used effectively.

As long as inventors and entrepreneurs can come up with new uses for information processing power, we can be assured of a high rate of productivity growth, which is the key variable in the economy. The case for an optimistic economic forecast is compelling.

What Could Go Wrong?

DeLong's analysis indicates that the biggest potential threat to this "new economy" scenario would be for a large sector of the economy to become "productivity resistant," meaning that it is unable or unwilling to take advantage of better information technology. I think of the music industry as a potential example (see chapter on "Listen to the Technology"). Obviously, growth will not take place if you have the power to outlaw innovation.

DeLong points out that the institutional underpinnings of the information economy probably will differ from those of an industrial economy, just as the institutional underpinnings of an industrial economy differed from those of an agricultural economy. He points out that "Optimistic views of future macro productivity growth assume that government will—somehow—get these important micro questions right."

It could be that the corporation as an institution is not as economically useful as it was 50 years ago. In that case, even though GDP will grow, the share of GDP accounted for by corporations could decline. If so, then people who try to participate in the new economy by investing in corporations could be disappointed.

Rational Exuberance?

Economists did not buy the "new economy" story in 1996. It was economist Robert Shiller who coined the term "irrational exuberance." Even today, some economists continue to expect price-earnings ratios for stocks to revert to low historical levels. DeLong appears to be among these, even though his economic catch-phrase is "slouching towards utopia."[54]

However, the "new economy" story is that price-earnings ratios should be higher than historical averages, because those averages cover periods of lower economic growth. The "new economy" story justifies higher price-earnings ratios, and the cumulative impact of Moore's Law has made that story plausible to economists.

Although there are downside risks to the new economy scenario, there is upside potential as well. Nanotechnology and/or biotechnology could become even more important sources of growth than Moore's Law. The stock market may be depressed, but economists are veering toward rational exuberance.

CHAPTER 12

THE ELASTIC ECONOMY

"For years I thought what was good for our country was good for General Motors and vice versa. The difference did not exist. Our company is too big. It goes with the welfare of the country."—Charlie Wilson,[55] 1953

In the fifty years since "Engine Charlie" made those remarks at a Senate hearing, The United States economy has become more diverse and more robust. We are better able to withstand shocks, minimize concentration of economic power, and sustain growth without being hampered by resource constraints. This can be summarized by saying that the economy has become more elastic.

In the ordinary use of the term, "elastic" means able to stretch. When we describe something as elastic, we mean that it can be bent, twisted, or expanded without breaking.

In economics, "elastic" has a technical meaning. It measures the power of substitution, as consumers and producers respond to changes in prices by changing the quantities demanded and supplied. The greater the response of quantity to a given price change, the greater the elasticity. If a small increase in the price of Coke causes a large shift by consumers toward other soft drinks, then that is high elasticity. If a small increase in the price of cigarettes causes only a small decline in smoking, then that is low elasticity.

Consumer choice is not the only source of elasticity in the economy. Producers provide elasticity by varying the methods and inputs used in production, as well as by introducing new products.

The ordinary definition of elasticity and the technical economic definition are closely related when we talk about an economy as a whole. For the economy as a whole, the more that quantities can adjust in response to prices, the more likely it is that the economy will "bend" rather than "break" when it is stressed. For example, a disruption in oil supplies will be handled more easily by an elastic economy than by an inelastic economy.

Causes of a More Elastic Economy

There are several factors that have caused the economy to become more elastic. They include product diversity, globalization, the Internet, and increased innovation.

Increased diversity of goods and services increases the elasticity of the economy by providing consumers with more ways to satisfy their wants. For example, fifty years ago telecommunications services consisted of telephones and telegrams. Today, those services include cellular phones, faxes, and emails. If the price of one service increases, people can shift to using other services.

Fifty years ago, people generally either prepared meals using time-consuming methods at home or dined at expensive restaurants. Those options are still available. In addition, today's substitutes include convenience foods, microwave cooking, and a variety of fast-food and moderately-priced restaurants.

Globalization has made the economy more elastic in a number of ways. It has contributed to the diversity of products and services available. It has provided opportunities for American firms to manufacture products abroad, substituting foreign labor for domestic labor. It has enabled the U.S. economy to rely on imports for some products, allowing resources to shift into other products and services.

The Internet has also made the economy more elastic in a number of ways. It has enabled consumers to be better informed of the characteristics and prices of products, so that they can substitute more intelligently. It facilitates international trade in services, so that U.S. companies may obtain computer programming services, clerical transcription, and other services in India or Eastern Europe.

Finally, the increased pace of innovation makes the economy more elastic. Inventory management, energy production and distribution, and other basic economic activities can now be addressed by methods that were not available twenty years ago.

One way to describe the elastic economy is that it has become more complex. Human wants continue to be relatively simple and basic. The fundamental resources, such as land and labor, are the same. However, there has been an explosion in the variety of ways of converting the fundamental resources into products and services that satisfy basic human wants. There are a large number of paths leading from resources to satisfaction, and just as with the Internet, a variety of paths diminishes the dependence on any one path, making the system as a whole more robust.

Consequences of a More Elastic Economy

With a more elastic economy, the markets for goods, labor, and resources look very different than they did fifty years ago. This has implications for the role of government policy and regulation.

With an elastic economy, the importance of any one product or any one company is reduced. No one product is as important to the economy as was the automobile fifty years ago. No single company today is as important to the economy as General Motors was in 1953. I would argue that even Microsoft's role in computing is less significant than was General Motors' role in transportation. Microsoft has an overwhelming share of computer software used for office work. However, they have never been the dominant company in other uses of computing, such as servers, games, communication switches, and—more recently—personal digital assistants and cell phones.

With an elastic economy, labor competition is worldwide. One of the most important phenomena of this decade is likely to be the movement of service industry jobs offshore.[56] As Zimran Ahmed pointed out,[57] "most people thought globalization had improved their lives but also thought it threatened their job security. This was held up as a contradiction, but in fact it's *exactly right*: free trade improves peoples lives by lowering the price of goods and services (making people richer) but also makes jobs less stable as domestic industries keep restructuring in line with technological change abroad."

Another irony is that although the overall economic outlook for the next two decades is exuberant (see chapter on "Rationally Exuberant") the outlook for most existing industries may be depressing! People can expect to have to adapt much more than in the past to new skills and new work environments. Twenty years go, could anyone have predicted employment in a call center, or as a web programmer, or for a company like Amazon or AOL? In a world of progress and displacement (see chapter on "Progress and Displacement"), in twenty years many people are going to be working for companies that as of now have not yet been started, doing jobs that as of today do not exist.

In an elastic economy, resource constraints are less binding. Environmentalists need to understand this, or they will fail to address Bjorn Lomborg's analysis, (see chapter on "Substitution, Technological Change, and the Environment").

The more elastic the economy, the more erroneous will be those environmentalists who ignore substitution.

Finally, in an elastic economy, as the market becomes more robust, government regulation becomes more clumsy. Price controls become more damaging, as the California energy crisis of 2001 illustrates. Regulatory mandates, such as CAFE fuel economy standards, deliver poor benefits relative to compliance costs. Labor market rigidities become even more dysfunctional, as is shown by the dismal performance of France and Germany.

Overall, the developments that lead to an elastic economy are extending the advantages that the U.S. has over more socialized countries. Centralized bureaucracies become less functional as the economy becomes more elastic. On the other hand, the private sector has become more chaotic but more robust.

CHAPTER 13

WHAT CAUSES PROSPERITY?

"I had a friend once and he was asked to chair a commission, an international committee, and the title of it was What Causes Poverty. He declined. He said I will do it but on one condition. The condition is that we change the title and I'll chair a committee on What Causes Prosperity. The reason he said that was, the title What Causes Poverty leaves the impression that the natural state of the world is for people to be prosperous and that for whatever reason there are prosperous people running around making people poor . . . He looked at the world the other way. He said the natural state of people is to be relatively poor and that there are certain ways and things that can be done that can cause prosperity."— Secretary of Defense Donald Rumsfeld, Nov. 11, 2002[58]

What are the things that can be done that cause prosperity? Because prosperity depends on growth, economists want to understand how to improve the performance of low-growth countries. However, our knowledge is frustratingly incomplete. Certainly, there is no simple, one-dimensional answer.

There is a counter-example to every generalization and an exception to every simple rule. Are a stable currency and an influx of foreign capital the answer? Don't tell that to Argentina, which collapsed after a decade of a "hard peg" to the dollar and large capital inflows. Is privatization a panacea?

Don't tell that to Russia and the other republics of the former Soviet Union. Is a high propensity to save a source of economic strength? Not if you look at Japan's lost decade. Is democracy necessary? Not if China's recent success is any guide. Are trade barriers the major impediment to progress? Not if you go by the relatively high growth rate in India, where tariffs are among the highest in the world.

In spite of these counter-examples, I would advise a country that wants to improve economic performance to stabilize its currency, encourage foreign capital, privatize government enterprises, aim for a high rate of national saving, adopt democratic institutions, and reduce tariffs. The counter-examples merely illustrate that none of these policies, individually, is decisive.

Fundamentally, I believe that there are two reasons that economists are unable to develop a fool-proof program for economic growth. The first issue is that growth is what I might term a nonlinear feedback process. The second issue is that economic policies themselves are only one ingredient in the recipe for growth.

A Game with Nonlinear Feedback

I suspect that economic growth is one of those processes that provides nonlinear feedback. When the feedback process is linear, we can grope our way toward an answer fairly systematically. However, when the process provides nonlinear feedback, learning what works is more difficult.

Imagine that you needed to turn the lights on in an auditorium, and you had to deal with about 15 switches. Moreover, suppose that a perverse architect had rigged it so that some of the switches have to be up and some have to be down for the lights to come on. Finally, the architect set things up so that unless all 15 switches are positioned correctly, the lights will not come on.

There are millions of combinations of switches for you to try, and only one will work. Moreover, you get no feedback at all until you happen to land on exactly the right combination. That is an example of nonlinear feedback.

It would be much easier if every time you flipped a switch the auditorium became a little darker or a little lighter. That would be linear feedback, which you can use to determine relatively quickly the combination of switches that will brighten the room.

The example with the perverse architect and nonlinear feedback is a metaphor for complex processes that are difficult to understand and control. Cancer is more complex than smallpox, which is why we have eradicated the latter but not the former. Education is complex, in that educational outcomes depend on a combination of factors. Even though one particular factor, such as small class size, may be very important, changing that factor by itself may have almost no impact.

Growth as a Complex Process

It is probably the case that economic growth requires a combination of policies and conditions. No single policy choice can produce significant results in terms of economic growth.

Some of the most difficult choices include:

- Fixed vs. flexible exchange rates[59]
- Policies for dealing with financial crises[60]
- Immigration policy[61]

Although the standard economic prescription calls for privatization, in many prosperous countries governments are involved in a number of industries. In the United States, for example, government is significantly involved in agriculture, education, telecommunications, banking, transportation, and housing. For a developing country, it must be challenging to assess which of these various interventions should be imitated, which ones are counterproductive, and which ones are irrelevant.

The wide array of policy choices can be particularly challenging when it is combined with the problem of nonlinear feedback. A country may fail to see positive results from good policies, because other policies are not well chosen.

Growth Ethics?

The other major difficulty in arriving at policies to achieve prosperity is that cultural and political factors may be involved. I myself do not claim to have "cracked the code" for growth and prosperity. However, based on my reading of the works of economists, including DeLong, Parente and Prescott, de Soto, Easterly, and Barro, as well as non-economists such as Robert Kaplan and Ralph Peters, I have formed some hypotheses about the issue.

What I believe is that to achieve prosperity, a country must foster three "ethics."

1. A work ethic.
2. A public service ethic.
3. A learning ethic.

The work ethic will exist if and only if people feel that work is fairly rewarded. If instead it becomes evident that rewards accrue to those who steal, deal in black markets, or serve a warlord or clan leader, then those behaviors will be more widespread than work.

My guess is that one reason that privatization performed less well than expected in the former Soviet Union is that the work ethic had been too badly undermined. Suppose that employees are used to stealing from their state-run government enterprises to sell into the black market. When privatization takes place, the black markets are still functioning, and old habits may linger. Before the enterprise can get on its feet, it fails.

A public service ethic is something that we take for granted in the United States. If you want to open a restaurant, you may find the paperwork and regulations irritating. However, at least you can count on the public officials to process your application in a reasonable time without requiring a large bribe. In many other countries, the conduct of state employees ranges from routine petty corruption to organized extortion.

The learning ethic has at least three dimensions. First, education must be valued and accessible to all demographic groups. Second, the scientific method must be understood and appreciated, overcoming superstitions and traditions. Finally, mistakes must be recognized and corrected.

Dictatorships do not seem conducive to recognizing mistakes. Faced with a failing state enterprise, the natural tendency has to be to prop up the troubled institution[62] rather than allowing the firm to go out of business. In fact, I surmise that one reason that the United States has been able to rebound from financial scandals more rapidly than Japan is that we have a competitive two-party democracy. The Japanese elite closed ranks around its troubled financial firms, keeping capital tied up in failing enterprises and prolonging the crisis. In contrast, our political leaders have felt obliged to distance themselves as much as possible from the Enrons and the Worldcoms.

Given the importance of the learning ethic, I have difficulty sharing the enthusiasm of George Gilder[63] and others for China. Instead, I am inclined to agree with Ralph Peters,[64] who writes:

"In China, the situation regarding the state's attempt to control information and the population's inability to manage it is immeasurably worse. Until China undergoes a genuine cultural revolution that alters permanently and deeply the relationship among state, citizen, and information, that country will bog down at the industrial level. Its sheer size guarantees continued growth, but there will be a flattening in the coming decades and, decisively, China will have great difficulty transitioning from smokestack growth to intellectual innovation and service wealth.

China, along with the world's other defiant dictatorships, suffers under an oppressive class structure, built on and secured by an informational hierarchy. The great class struggle of the 21st century will be for access to data, and it will occur in totalitarian and religious-regime states."

Limits of Economic Policy

Even if my hypotheses are correct that prosperity can be achieved if a country develops a work ethic, a public service ethic, and a learning ethic, that only begs the question: how are those ethics fostered?

Standard economic prescriptions, such as letting the incentives of free markets operate, are only part of the answer. Free markets are particularly helpful in maintaining a work ethic. However, without a public service ethic, governments will undermine property rights rather than protect them. Without a learning ethic, economic activity in agriculture, manufacturing, and services will stagnate rather than evolve.

Should we be surprised that the so-called "Washington Consensus" or "neoliberal" recommendations for deregulation, financial liberalization, and privatization have not brought rapid prosperity to countries that lack some of the necessary ethics?

On the contrary, I would say that in retrospect we should be surprised that anyone had high expectations for success under such circumstances.

However, even though "neoliberal" policies have not always received high-scoring feedback in the game of cracking the code of prosperity, that does not mean that they are bad guesses. As Brad DeLong somewhat forlornly put it,[65] "The hope is that privatization and world economic integration will in the long run help create the rest of the preconditions for successful development. But we are playing this card not because we think it is a winner, but because it is the last one in our hand."

CHAPTER 14

THE STATISM TRAP

"*Being a modern country, Japan has not allowed its banks to fail.*"—Paul Krugman,[66] Sept. 30, 2001

"*The Japanese Government agreed at the weekend to use taxpayers' money to shore up the nation's fifth-biggest bank after executives said its capital had fallen below legally required levels.*"—Associated Press, May 18, 2003

Paul Krugman believes that the Japanese experience has lessons for the United States. I would agree, except that Krugman has learned the wrong lessons. He thinks that the bank bailouts are a good thing, that Japan's problem is a "liquidity trap," and that the U.S. also could fall into a liquidity trap.

In my view, Japan's bank bailouts are a policy mistake, the liquidity trap is irrelevant, and Japan's trap is its statist economic model. I hope that the United States can avoid falling into the statism trap.

What Liquidity Trap?

Theoretically, there is a point at which interest rates are so low that they cannot go any lower. That lower bound is around zero, because would-be lenders would hold cash rather than lend money at a negative interest rate. At that point, the monetary authority would appear to be helpless. Injecting additional money will not reduce interest rates, and therefore it will not stimulate the economy. That is what Keynes called the liquidity trap.

In 2001, Krugman was prepared to argue that the United States was in a liquidity trap, because the overnight lending rate that the Federal Reserve manipulates was close to 1 percent, which is dangerously close to zero. He wrote,[67] "those of us who worry about a Japanese-style quagmire find the global picture pretty scary."

However, in the real world, as opposed to economics textbooks, there is more than one interest rate. Most interest rates in the U.S. economy are far from zero. At the time Krugman wrote his column, the ten-year Treasury yield was 3.3 percent. Accordingly, I was not persuaded that we were in a liquidity trap. On the other hand, I do believe that in an elastic economy (see chapter on "The Elastic Economy") the key interest rates are not necessarily subject to Fed influence (see chapter on "Can Greenspan Steer?").

Long-term interest rates in Japan are below one percent. But otherwise, Japan does not behave much like a country in a liquidity trap. In a liquidity trap, the loss of effectiveness of monetary policy is mirrored by increased effectiveness of fiscal policy. You can run big budget deficits in a liquidity trap without raising interest rates, so that Keynesian stimulus should be really effective. That has not been the case in Japan. In Japan, both fiscal and monetary stimulus have been ineffective.

Japan's Statism Trap

There are many conceivable explanations for Japan's economic woes. For example, as Australia's Ken Henry[68] succinctly pointed out, the aging of Japan's population was bound to reduce its growth rate. There is even a case to be made that Japan suffers from another Keynesian malady, the "paradox of thrift," in which increases in saving fail to add to investment and instead stall the economy. However, I think that the most convincing overall explanation for Japan's long decline is that its centralized, bureaucratic industrial policy ran out of steam. Brink Lindsey, in his book *Against the Dead Hand*, writes that even at its peak, Japan was a "deformed 'dual economy'—a vibrant and dynamic international sector that all the world envied and feared, and a much larger, but largely stagnant, domestic sector that the world all but ignored."

It is misleading to evaluate statism on the basis of the government's ability to produce winners. In fact, I think history shows that it *is* possible for states to fund successful enterprises. On the other hand, where statism falls apart is in its inability to cut its losses when the government makes a bad bet. The difference with the private sector is that the government is almost totally incapable of winnowing out losers. In the long run, heavy government involvement inevitably leads to suffocation, as "zombie" businesses backed by the government suck all of the oxygen out of the economy. That is what Japan has been experiencing for the past decade.

In his analysis of the sources of economic underperformance around the world, Edward Prescott[69] found that much of the problem in Japan comes from inefficient use of inputs. His measure of "total factor productivity" shows a large shortfall relative to the U.S., with a notable decline in recent years. He points a finger at Japan's state-controlled financial sector.

"The candidate mechanism by which centralized financial systems adversely affect productivity is as follows. Inefficient producers are subsidized in order to preserve jobs. This has the perverse effect of lowering productivity and decreasing overall employment in the economy. Japan is [a] depressed country with a highly centralized financial system controlled by the state. Perhaps

this accounts for the 17 percent decline in its productivity factor in the 1991-2000 period."

About Those Banks...

In Krugman's demand-oriented analysis of Japan's economy, propping up the banks, which in turn prop up zombie enterprises, has been a positive factor. Other economists, presumably including Prescott, would view the ongoing bank bailouts as part of the problem rather than part of the solution.

It is true that when banks are fundamentally solvent but temporarily illiquid, it can be helpful for the government to step in and prevent a bank "run." Deposit insurance performs this function automatically.

However, it is not true that banks should not be allowed to fail. What the Japanese government has done has amounted to trying to cover up and paper over that country's version of our corporate accounting scandals or the 1980's savings and loan crisis.[70] Instead of writing off bad assets and re-allocating capital to efficient uses, the Japanese have effectively remained in denial about bad loans, so that they kept pouring their abundant savings into bankrupt companies and insolvent banks.

The U.S. and Japan

Krugman's story of the liquidity trap is meant to suggest that the United States could end up like Japan. However, in my view our economy will not fall into a Depression because of price deflation, a liquidity trap, or any other demand-side bogeyman. What we have today is an economy whose capacity is growing very rapidly, because of high productivity growth, with demand failing to keep up. I am persuaded that this calls for more fiscal and monetary stimulus, but I don't think we ought to confuse this with a Depression.

If we should worry about becoming like Japan, that is because we cannot be completely confident that we will be able to stay off the road to statism. There are plenty of politicians who believe that we "need" a crash program on energy, a national broadband initiative, and/or single-payer health insurance. Even without such programs, we may slide toward statism if we fail to phase out Medicare (see chapter on "Phase Out Medicare").

I hope we remain a capitalist country. If nothing else, I think it would be desirable to maintain diversity.[71] Different countries should try different approaches to policy problems. Methods that work should be adopted, and methods that fail should be discarded. The United States should be the country that stays furthest away from the statist trap.

Chapter 15

Substitution, Technological Change, and the Environment

Economists are not well thought of these days by environmentalists. Or so it seems from Edward O. Wilson's book, *The Future of Life*.[72] He characterizes economists as narrow, myopic environmental ignoramuses.

"*The bottom line is different from that generally assumed by our leading economists... The economist's thinking is based on precise models of rational choice and near-horizon timelines. His parameters are the gross domestic product, trade balance, and competitive index... The ecologist has a different worldview. He is focused on unsustainable crop yields, overdrawn aquifers, and threatened ecosystems.*"

It's true that economists have trouble with the views of many radical environmentalists. But this just reflects our frustration with the ecologists' use of the most naive and inappropriate economic models and assumptions in their forecasts and policy prescriptions.

That's why Bjorn Lomborg's book *The Skeptical Environmentalist* is such a distinctive, rare, and important work. In addition to sharing the ecologist's concerns about aquifers, sustainability, and global warming, Lomborg accepts the economist's paradigm. By combining economics with ecology, he comes up with a rational, balanced analysis. Unfortunately, environmentalists' denial of the validity of economic analysis runs through much of their criticism[73] of Lomborg's work.

Doing Economics Badly

To understand the threat to environmentalists posed by Lomborg and his ideas, it's important to recognize that the economic theory implicit in the traditional environmentalist position is flawed in the following ways:

1. It ignores the crucial phenomena of substitution and technological improvement.
2. It rejects any finite measure of the cost of environmental damage.
3. It fails to appreciate the role played by interest rates in providing a logical connection between the future and the present.

(Here, I focus on the first issue. Separately, I have written about the other two.)[74]

Environmentalists tend to assume a constant relationship between inputs and outputs. If you are going to produce X tons of grain, then the acreage of land required will be X/Y, where Y is the average yield of an acre of land. Economists call this the "fixed-coefficients" model, because the relationship between acreage and grain is governed by the coefficient Y. Simply put, this is not a realistic model. In practice there are always a variety of production techniques that use different combinations of inputs to produce the same output.

The fixed-coefficients model applies, if at all, only in the very short run. In the long run, there is substitution and technical change. Substitution means that producers will vary the inputs used in production, depending on changes in the cost of various inputs. For example, if land becomes more expensive, producers will substitute capital, labor, fertilizer, or other resources in order to utilize the most efficient combination.

The other long-run factor is technical change. As we accumulate knowledge, we come up with ways to produce more output with fewer resources.

The fixed-coefficients model has a built-in implication that society will "run out" of resources. If you assume that each additional unit of output requires a fixed amount of some resource, then it is mathematically certain that at some level of output you use up all of that resource.

But economists don't believe that we will "run out" of any important resource. As a resource becomes scarce, its price will go up, and people will substitute away from that resource. In addition, the processes of research, accumulation of knowledge, and technical change enable us to reduce the resources needed to produce valuable goods and services.

For example, if you believe in fixed coefficients, then at some point we will run out of oil. But if you take into account substitution and technical change, then you expect that as the price of oil rises we will substitute alternative forms of energy. If you believe in fixed coefficients, then it may seem possible or even likely that we will run out of fresh water. But if you take into account substitution and technical change, then you expect that as the price of fresh water rises we will use it more carefully, and eventually desalination of seawater will be economical.

It is not economists who are ignoring the long run. It is ecologists who are applying short-run thinking (the fixed-coefficients model) to long-range analysis and coming up with predictions that are wrong.

The Wager

The difference between an economic model that assumes fixed coefficients and a model that allows for substitution and technical change was tested in a famous bet between economist Julian Simon and ecologist Paul Erlich. In 1980, Simon allowed Erlich to select a set of five minerals that were supposed to become scarce. Simon then bet that the prices of those minerals would fall rather than rise in ten years. By 1990, the relative prices of all five minerals had declined, and Simon won the bet. If the fixed-coefficients model were correct, then population growth and rising standards of living should have enabled Erlich to win the bet.

In an interview, inventor Ray Kurzweil extrapolated[75] the tendency to substitute human knowledge for material resources in creating wealth.

"[T]he knowledge component of products and services is asymptoting towards 100 percent. By the time we get to 2030 it will be basically 100 percent. With a combination of nanotechnology and artificial intelligence, we'll be able to create virtually any physical product and meet all of our material needs."

In other words, at the rate that we are enhancing human knowledge, we can satisfy all human wants without any physical resources becoming scarce! Although Kurzweil may be overly optimistic, his characterization of long-run economic dynamics is much more reasonable than the fixed-coefficients model that is the basis for ecological doomsayers.

Which Economic Model?

There is an inevitable component of economics to the science of ecology, because it speaks to the relationship between environmental resources and human consumption. Many environmentalists choose the fixed-coefficients model for this component. But as *The Skeptical Environmentalist* demonstrates, changing to a more reasonable model leads to vastly different assessments and predictions for the state of the environment.

The fixed-coefficients model is manifestly inappropriate for long-run analysis, and its empirical failure is well demonstrated. That, rather than professional incompetence, is what explains why economists stubbornly resist ceding our professional judgment to environmentalists. It also explains why, despite the rhetorical scorn heaped on Lomborg by many environmentalists, his approach provides a much better foundation for discussions of public policy.

Chapter 16

Nonlinear Thinking

"It takes a long time to recognize a change in a long-term trend."—Alan Blinder[76]

In 2003, I attended the Pop!Tech[77] conference, an annual event that looks at technology and culture. The conference exemplifies what I would call nonlinear thinking.

The term "nonlinear" has been misused and abused by pundits, to the point where it has degenerated into a fuzzy, feel-good (or feel-cool) expression. I want to use it here in a more well-defined sense.

Points, Lines, and Curves

Try this brain teaser: suppose that we have a petri dish with some bacteria. The amount of bacteria doubles every minute. After exactly one hour, the petri dish is full of bacteria. When was the petri dish half full?

The answers generally fall into three different groups. The first group consists of people who say, "Don't you need to know how many bacteria you started with?" I call this group the *point* people. They are not comfortable with abstract mathematics, so they see the world in terms of points. They think that what makes this problem difficult is that you have not provided them with a precise starting point.

The second group consists of people who say, "I'm not sure, but I guess it was maybe around half an hour or maybe a little later." I call this group the *linear* people, because they try to use a linear approximation to solve the problem. If the petri dish is full after an hour, then if it had been almost empty to begin with and the bacteria were growing linearly, it was half full after half an hour. Often, linear approximations work well, but in this case it is completely wrong.

The third group of people actually gets the answer. As a hint, ask yourself this: if the petri dish is half full after 30 minutes, and the bacteria population doubles every minute, how long will it take until the petri dish is full? If that does not help you know the answer to the original question, then ask yourself: if the petri dish is half full after 25 minutes, and the bacteria population doubles every minute, when is it full? Keep trying this for different times until you see the right answer to the original question.

The people who get the right answer are the *curve* people, the nonlinear thinkers. They are able to comprehend the nonlinear, exponential relationship between bacteria and time, which on a graph would show an increasing curve.

Environmentalists as Point People

My sense is that environmental radicals tend to be point people. This makes their long-term forecasts particularly suspect. For long-term forecasting, nonlinear thinking is best. Linear approximations may work well for forecasts one or two years ahead. Point-based thinking is rarely accurate for more than a few months in today's dynamic economy.

For example, an environmentalist might take the ratio of oil consumption to world GDP as one point and the forecast for world GDP in 50 years as another point. The environmentalist might then conclude that we will not have enough oil in fifty years.

Robert Solow showed what was wrong with this type of thinking thirty years ago. At that time, the "Club of Rome" had what they claimed was a complex, nonlinear model which forecast environmental catastrophe. However, because their analysis took no account of prices, technical substitution, or technological change, it was no better than a point-based tool for forecasting. One of the speakers at this year's Pop!Tech, Geoffrey Ballard,[78] pointed out that every prediction made by the Club of Rome has been false.

Economists as Linear People

Most economists are good at math, so my guess is that they would have handled the brain teaser quickly and correctly. Moreover, economists know that many of the processes that are important in our field, such as compound interest and economic growth, are nonlinear. But the economics curriculum in graduate school is focused on training students to make linear approximations. Studying economics at a leading graduate school involves loading techniques for linear approximations into your analytical tool kit. Naturally, these are the techniques that you use when you do professional research.

Economists also shy away from nonlinear forecasting because it is risky. As the *New York Times*' Katie Hafner reminds us,[79] George Gilder's nonlinear forecasts for bandwidth demand were off target. In fact, a lot of the telecom bubble can be described as a forecast for Internet growth of 10x per year when in fact it was closer to 3x per year. If you build capacity for three years ahead using the 10x model, you will multiply capacity by 1000x, when the 3x reality means that demand only increases by 27x. That is a lot of excess capacity.

However, the odd thing about nonlinear forecasts is that they can be wildly wrong in the quantity dimension without being far off in the time dimension. Even at 3x growth, demand will catch up to capacity within a few years. One can argue that the telecom industry's mistake was not so much the amount of capacity that they built as the high-leverage way in which it was financed. High leverage only works if you can predict the quantity demanded accurately at a given point in time. High leverage is a good idea in a relatively linear world, but not a good idea in a nonlinear world.

Alan Blinder's lament about the difficulty of picking up long term trends is a result of over-reliance on linear thinking. The trend that he was talking about was a pickup in the rate of economic growth. This pickup was best anticipated by a nonlinear thinker coming from outside the economics profession—Ray Kurzweil.

In *The Age of Spiritual Machines*, Kurzweil focused on the implications of Moore's Law.[80] One way to think about his thesis is to imagine that we add up the total intelligence on earth by summing up the amount provided by human beings and the amount provided by computers. Today, the proportion supplied by computers might be much less than 1 percent. Yet Kurzweil would be confident that the proportion supplied by computers will be 99 percent by the middle of the century. That is because the capability of a typical computer is doubling about every two years, while the capability of the typical human grows more slowly.

Kurzweil might project that a computer will have the same mental capacity as a human in the year 2020. If the computer only has 1/8 the capacity of a human at that date, you might think that he is spectacularly wrong. However, if computer intelligence doubles every two years, then the computer will catch up six years later—and once it catches up, it will zoom past.

The implications of the increase in computing power for economic growth are large. However, economists have been slow to catch on. One of the first economists willing to adjust economic forecasts for Moore's Law was Brad DeLong.[81] I tried to sketch out the thinking of DeLong and other economists in my essay on rational exuberance (see chapter on "Rationally Exhuberant").

Nonlinear Lifespans

The speakers at Pop!Tech tried to identify important issues on which to focus over the next decade or more. Given the rapid pace of technological change, this requires nonlinear thinking.

As it turned out, many of the speakers were pleading for the audience to pay attention to a particular idea, because it required monetary investment or regulatory relief to succeed. Examples included global public health, therapeutic cloning, ocean exploration, wireless broadband, hydrogen fuel cells, and livable urban architecture.

One of the more interesting proposals was for a "war on aging." Rather than try to eradicate diseases one by one, Aubrey de Grey[82] believes that we can look at cell damage as occurring in a limited number of ways. Once there is a way to prevent or undo each of these modes of damage (he claims that there are only seven), we can extend a *healthy* life indefinitely—a veritable fountain of youth. He believes that this might be feasible in twenty or thirty years.

Longevity has been increasing fairly rapidly for the past hundred years, from about 45 years at the beginning of the 20th century to close to 77 years at the beginning of the 21st. However, if we reach the point where longevity increases at a rate greater than one year per year, then from that point on people will live forever.

For example, suppose that when you reach the age of 80 the "war on aging" has progressed to the point where longevity is 100. At that point, scientists have another twenty years to come up with new ways to extend life. This might take you to the age of 130, which gives scientists another thirty years... and you live forever.

It seems reasonable to assume that, as with all new technologies, the best anti-aging techniques will go through a period during which they are unproven and expensive. What this means is that there could be a relatively short window—five to ten years—such that people who die before the start of that window just miss out on immortality, people who naturally live just after the end of the window will all be immortal, and the fate of people who would naturally die during the window will depend on luck. During this "window," longevity will go from, say, 85, to infinity. That is nonlinear!

Inconsistent Predictions

Some of the nonlinear predictions made at Pop!Tech 2003 were mutually inconsistent. For example, geologist Peter Ward[83] sketched a number of catastrophic scenarios for planet earth, many of which were only likely to occur after hundreds or thousands of years. He said that we need to start worrying about these contingencies.

When I asked Christine Peterson[84] about Ward's concerns, she scoffed, "In a thousand years, we won't need the earth." Her area of focus is nanotechnology, which she believes will produce remarkable results in the middle of the century. Where this leads is that over the next few hundred years we will develop the technology to engineer our environment and to travel in space.

One question that produces inconsistent predictions is that of energy supply and demand. Ballard sees a future in which hydrogen replaces gasoline as a means for storing and transporting energy. Since hydrogen is not a primary energy source, he believes that another source of power must be developed. He speculates that we will have to return to nuclear power as the solution.

I wonder whether some other approach to the energy issue will come to fruition more quickly. Nanotechnology and computers might facilitate conservation and continued innovation in the internal combustion engine. Biotechnology might be used to engineer plants that can efficiently convert solar energy to human use. In a nonlinear world, a technological substitute for fossil fuels that is only a concept today could still be far away in ten years and yet be an established solution in twenty.

What Great Race?

Hearing the nonlinear thinking of Pop!Tech helps to soften my concern about the future of Social Security. When economists make predictions about Social Security or Medicare, we use linear approximations. Those approximations do not take into account nanotechnology or a successful war on aging or other scenarios that were spun out at Pop!Tech. What I call The Great Race (see chapter on "The Great Race") seems to pale by comparison. Instead, what is uncertain is the continuity of the *human* race (see chapter on "Moore vs. Plato").

Chapter 17

Hayek, Stiglitz, and Michael Powell

Everyone thinks that they are smarter than Michael Powell. The Chairman of the Federal Communications Commission is at least as mis-underestimated as the man who appointed him, President George Bush.

Michael Copps, a Democrat on the FCC, routinely defies Powell, and on several occasions has succeeded in embarrassing him. Kevin Martin, appointed to the FCC by George Bush, deserted Powell on an important vote on telephone deregulation. The House of Representatives voted overwhelmingly to overturn a seemingly minor loosening of media ownership restrictions.

Following the House vote, a front-page story in the *Washington Post* described Powell as beleaguered. "It would be impossible in Washington to have so much controversy over a public figure without some raising the possibility that he will soon step down. Some published reports have stated that Powell has discussed the issue with his staff."

Messy Competition

The FCC oversees industries in which competition is messy. Broadcasting and telecommunications do not resemble the economist's model of "perfect competition," in which there are no economies of scale or network effects or information asymmetries or dominant firms. In spite of all of these deviations from the ideal of perfect competition, Powell favors reducing the weight of the hand of government.

By defending markets even when competition is messy, Powell is being Hayekian. Friedrich A. Hayek, awarded the Nobel Prize in economics in 1974, viewed Competition as a Discovery Procedure.[85] He wrote, "market theory often prevents access to a true understanding of competition by proceeding from the assumption of a 'given' quantity of scarce goods. Which goods are scarce, however, or which-things are goods, or how scarce or valuable they are, is precisely one of the conditions that competition should discover."

Powell's opponents are Stiglitzian. Joseph Stiglitz, awarded the Nobel Prize in 2001, wrote,[86] "But information economics does not agree with Hayek's assertion that markets act efficiently. The fact that markets with imperfect information do not work perfectly provides a rationale for potential government actions."

Hayek would have the government tolerate messy competition. His point is that with the optimal outcome unknown, government resolution of issues shuts off the learning process that market competition provides.

Stiglitz sees the messiness in real-world economies, and he claims to have the right solution in every case. Even Berkeley economist Brad DeLong, who—like Stiglitz—served in the Clinton Administration, wrote that[87] "I'm reading Joseph Stiglitz's brand-new *Globalization and Its Discontents*, and having trouble with it. It seems as though Stiglitz switches back and forth between different positions at blinding speed." Stiglitz's outlook is that markets are imperfect, but he is not. Where Marx offered dictatorship of the proletariat, Stiglitz would give us dictatorship of the Nobel Laureate. Between the two, we might be safer with Marx.

In Washington, the conventional wisdom is Stiglitzian. People do not run for office or seek appointments to high-level regulatory positions out of humility and respect for market processes. It is not surprising that the Beltway views Powell as at best eccentric and at worst a heretic.

The Broadband Issue

Perhaps nothing illustrates better the contrast between Powell's Hayekianism and his opponents' Stiglitzianism than the issue of broadband—the deployment of high-speed Internet connections. Powell is willing to let the market decide the outcome, with messy competition among cable companies, telephone companies, as well as underdogs and upstarts ranging from electrical power lines to wireless networks. Most important, he is willing to leave the decision of how much to spend on broadband up to the consumer.

Opposing this laissez-faire approach is Reed Hundt, FCC Chairman in the Clinton Administration. At a conference in the summer of 2003, Hundt sketched a proposal for the government to spend $40 to $50 billion to subsidize broadband rollout. In defending this large expenditure, Hundt explicitly invoked economist John Maynard Keynes, saying that it would provide an economic stimulus.

Hundt's proposal is Keynesian indeed. Keynes reportedly said that when there is unemployment, the government might as well pay workers to dig ditches and fill them in again. Under Hundt's proposal, many ditches would be dug to lay more communications cable.

Lukewarm Reception

At the conference, Hundt appeared surprised that his proposal received only a lukewarm reception. This was because many of the conference attendees were geeks who have moved on from Hundt's fixation with fixed-line broadband to the New, New Thing of wireless networks. They are finding Powell surprisingly receptive to their ideas. For example, even as he was proudly pulling a "Re-defeat George Bush" bumper-sticker out of his briefcase, telecommunications consultant David Isenberg was paying Powell the ultimate geek complement on wireless: "Powell gets it," he said.

One of Hundt's arguments against Powell's approach of setting different broadband providers competing against one another is that "somebody is bound to fail." He regarded the failure of a cable firm or a telephone company as unthinkable. However, several months earlier Isenberg co-wrote a column in USA Today saying,[88] "Instead of spending billions of tax dollars propping up the telephone companies and delaying the inevitable, let them fail—and fast."

The geeks are in favor of something called "open spectrum," which would take spectrum licenses away from incumbent owners and free it for wireless applications. Powell is trying to do just that. One recent proposal[89] is to allow a huge swath of spectrum that was previously allocated to religious and educational institutions to be re-sold into the market. Copps, the FCC Democrat, once again stands in reflexive opposition, defending the status quo of FCC command-and-control over spectrum utilization.

Rare Wisdom

In the view of the geeks, Powell is a free-market ideologue, but he happens to understand wireless technology. The way I look at it, the geeks come from a Stiglitzian culture, but they happen to understand Hayekian spontaneous order as it pertains to the Internet.

Congress thinks it knows the optimal fraction of the television market that can be owned by one media firm. Reed Hundt thinks he knows better than consumers themselves how much they want to pay for fiber to their homes. Michael Copps thinks he knows how to manage phone lines and how to allocate spectrum. Unlike his detractors, Michael Powell thinks that he knows less than the market. And in my view, that makes Michael Powell a man of rare and precious wisdom.

PART 3

Moore's Law, Progress, and Displacement

INTRODUCTION

"The way that "Moore's Law" is usually cited by those in the know is something along the lines of: "the number of transistors that can be fit onto a square inch of silicon doubles every 12 months."
... However, it doesn't quite do justice to the full scope of the picture that Moore painted in his brief, uncannily prescient paper. This is because Moore's paper dealt with more than just shrinking transistor sizes. Moore was ultimately interested in shrinking transistor costs."—Jon "Hannibal" Stokes[90]

I was defeated by Moore's Law before I even knew what it was. I used to play in Othello™ tournaments. Othello is a board game sold by Pressman Toys, and like checkers or chess, it is a game of skill that requires looking ahead.

In 1987, I came in sixth in the world Othello championships in Milan, Italy, in which over 30 players from a dozen countries participated. I was no threat to finish in the top four, but I was a reasonably decent player.

About that time, some of the first serious Othello-playing computer programs for PC's were developed. One of the best programs was written by a fellow named David Parsons. However, I could beat his program really easily.

A few years later, I bought a new PC, powered by an Intel 486 processor rather than the 286 that I had been using. I took the disk from Parsons' program, loaded it into my new computer ... and proceeded to lose every game I played against the machine.

What happened was that with its more powerful processor,

my new PC was looking ahead seven to nine moves, compared with just five moves before. With the older processor, a search depth of seven or nine moves would have taken about an hour to return a single move—easily leading to a time default in a tournament game. With the new processor, the computer could make each move in less than a minute.

This increase in power reflected the number of transistors, among other factors. The 286 chip had 110,000 transistors, and the 486 chip had 1,180,000 transistors, or about ten times as many.

Intel founder Gordon Moore had predicted in 1965 that for the next ten years processors would become more powerful. As Stokes points out, his prediction was more subtle and far more complex than is usually described. Readers who want to understand what Moore really meant should consult Stokes' article.

Stokes believes that the simplest approximation of Moore's Law might be,

"The number of transistors per chip that yields the minimum cost per transistor has increased at a rate of roughly a factor of two per year."

Research in computer science has maintained a pace close to that of Moore's Law all the way into this century, and experts seem to expect that this will continue for the next decade or more. What this means in practical terms is that the amount of computing power that you can buy for a given amount of money—say, $2000—doubles roughly every two years.

An economic process that doubles every two years is disruptive. Economists are used to compound growth, but at slow rates. Population might grow at one or two percent per year. Labor productivity might grow at one or two percent per year. Interest in a savings account might grow (after inflation) at a rate of two or three percent per year. Stock market investments might yield a return (after inflation) of four to seven percent per year. Moore's Law describes a process that is growing at 50 percent per year. The cumulative results have been staggering already. What lies ahead is even more astounding.

In the chapter on "Rational Exuberance," I talked about the potential for economic growth to accelerate as computers continue to improve. In the chapters that follow, I look at the potential effect of increased computer power on various individual sectors of the economy.

I no longer play tournament Othello. I am discouraged by the fact that computers are so much better than I am. In the early 1990's, a computer could beat me by looking ahead nine moves. My current laptop can look ahead twenty moves!

I have been displaced in Othello. The issue of progress leading to displacement is one of the mixed blessings of technology. This chapter tries to predict some of the displacement that will take place in the future.

Chapter 18

Listen to the Technology

The future is here. But distributors of music have tuned it out.

Technology has made the CD-centric business model of the music industry obsolete. Fifteen years ago, the CD became the superior alternative medium for storing and transporting music. Today, though, hard disks represent the truly low-cost storage medium, and the Internet represents the low-cost transportation medium for delivering music to listeners. In short, something like Napster was inevitable.

That music has become much cheaper to store and to transport would be good news for the music industry, if they would listen to the technology. Instead, they cannot seem to bear the thought of a transition away from the CD-centric business model. Like the people in a 1960's cigarette commercial, the industry would rather fight than switch.

The music industry's court victory over Napster was symbolic, but no judicial ruling can overturn the fact that downloading songs over the Internet is more efficient than purchasing them as recorded CDs. Rather than adopt the lowest-cost technologies available, the music industry is attempting to raise the cost of using those technologies. From suing file sharers to demanding that "Digital Rights

Management" be incorporated in hardware and software, the industry is inflicting pain on the listening public.

Who Needs CD's?

Let's pretend, though, that the CD didn't exist. How would music makers try to deliver their music today? I believe there would be two modes of distribution.

First, music could come packaged with hardware, much like most software is packaged with computers today. In the past, that might have been too expensive. But in a world with cheap, high-capacity hard disks, any system with stereo speakers could, and should, come complete with recorded music. Not just computers, but all car and home stereos as well. A reasonably priced hard disk can store all the music that you have time to enjoy. With several more iterations of Moore's Law a disk will be able to store everything that has ever been recorded.

With pre-installed music, the music industry would make money like Microsoft. Original Equipment Manufacturers (OEM's) would pay music distributors for licenses to their collections. At first, because hard disk capacity is not unlimited, people would have to choose standard music packages and pay extra for custom collections. Eventually, just as the Evil Empire bundled more and more functionality into the operating system, the standard music packages would include more and more of what has been recorded.

How would the music companies do under such a distribution scheme? Well, suppose that each year in the United States sales of car stereos totaled 15 million units, personal computers for home use totaled 60 million, and home stereos totaled 25 million units. Then, if the music industry collected an average $100 license fee for the installed music on each product—a price well within the range of many consumer software packages—it would have $10 billion in

LEARNING ECONOMICS

annual revenue. This would nearly equal the revenue from CD sales today, but with much lower production and distribution costs.

A second method of music delivery would be through third-party developer licenses. The software industry has learned that open systems that encourage third-party developers are more profitable than closed systems. I would argue that Microsoft and Apple are where they are today because Apple did less to encourage third-party developers. (Not that I want to plunge into the Apple-Microsoft debate here.)

Tim O'Reilly made an important pronouncement[91] about the need for Internet companies, such as Google and Amazon, to create open interfaces to their data that would allow third-party developers to add value. Both companies soon adopted such an approach. For example, Google is giving third-party developers licenses to access Google's catalog. Eventually, for high-volume licenses Google will charge a fee. Presumably, the high-volume applications will have revenue models attached to them.

Suppose that, like Google, a music distributor published an interface to its catalog, so that anyone could download music. Any third-party developer could obtain a license to access the catalog to create a play list, operate a radio station, create an algorithm to match people to music that suits their taste, or other value-added services. The developers would pay a license fee based on the intensity with which they access the catalog.

Subscription services, with revenue shared among third-party developers and music publishers, would be another revenue stream for the music industry. Consumers might pay low annual fees in order to be able to download a small number of songs. Third-party developers with high-volume services would pay higher fees. All in all, one can imagine 60 million subscribers paying $60 a year, plus 10 million subscribers paying $150 a year for premium services (more download privileges, custom music recommendation services, priority for concert tickets), for another $5 billion a year in revenue.

What about the Individual?

Suppose that the CD were to disappear and be replaced by these alternative revenue models. What does this scenario mean for individuals? The music consumer would be paying flat fees for unlimited use. When you obtain a stereo with music installed, you pay a one-time fee embedded in the cost of the stereo. When you subscribe to a music service, you pay an annual fee for unlimited use of the service. I think that most music-lovers would gladly pay these modest flat fees in order to save on CD purchases and to enjoy the convenience of listening to whatever music they want whenever they want to listen.

Musicians and composers still would need to get paid. I am assuming that they would continue to be paid by the intermediaries in the music industry. Music distributors would pay musicians in order to keep their catalogs popular.

Of course, the nature of intermediation could change. Anyone who obtains the rights from artists and sets up a hosting service with a catalog and an interface could play the role of a music publisher. The third-party developers could access this catalog. Those developers might turn out to be the critical intermediaries, and they could end up paying musicians.

I suspect that fear of this sort of industry change—and the potential loss of control—is what is driving the behavior of the music industry today. However, eventually they will have to listen to the technology.

CHAPTER 19

THE DEATH OF NEWSPAPERS

The newspaper business is going to die within the next twenty years. Newspaper publishing will continue, but only as a philanthropic venture.

On Friday, June 28, 2002, the *Wall Street Journal's* James Taranto, who edits "Best of the Web Today,"[92] appeared at a conference called Inside the Blogosphere[93]. He disagreed with me about the grim outlook for newspapers. He pointed out that newspapers are a superior technology, because you can read them while sitting on the toilet.

Notwithstanding this strategic relationship with routine bodily functions, newspapers are in trouble based on demographics. For example, consider this analysis[94] for the Newspaper Association of America.

The analysis looks at spending on newspapers by age group. Relative to the average for the entire population, the highest spending comes from older people, and the lowest spending comes from younger people. The best demographic for newspaper spending is the 65-74 year-old age group, which buys newspapers at a rate of 136% of the national average. The worst demographic is 18-24 year-olds, who buy newspapers at a rate of only 25 percent of the national average. In fact, all groups under the age of 45 have newspaper spending rates that are below the national average.

When I raised the issue of the low rate of newspaper readership among young people, Taranto was dismissive.

"People subscribe to newspapers as they get older," he sniffed.

It is true that we have to disentangle life-cycle effects from cohort effects. If people tend to change their newspaper purchasing over the life cycle, then you need to compare young people today with young people in previous years.

To try to sort out the cohort effects from the life-cycle effects, I emailed Peter Francese. Francese is the founder of *American Demographics Magazine*, a highly regarded[95] publication that unfortunately appears to lack its own web site. Francese replied,

"Arnold, You're in luck. I just finished a project on that subject. According to my calculations 63 percent of households 25 to 34 years old bought any newspaper product in 1985. By 1995 that figure had slid to 56 percent. But by 2000 it was down to 35 percent."

Vin Crosbie summarized a series of adverse trends in newspaper readership.[96] Among other data, he cites a projection that in 2010 only 9 percent of 20-29 year olds will read a daily paper.

On a cohort basis, newspaper readership among young adults has fallen by over 50 percent in fifteen years. Taranto and the *Wall Street Journal* have plenty to worry about. In an industry that depends on economies of scale to overcome high fixed costs, a decline in volume that approaches 50 percent is going to be fatal. These demographic effects will slowly but inexorably kill the newspaper business.

Not the Best

In the age of the Internet, when competition is one click away, being good at a lot of things is not as effective as being the best at one thing. Newspapers, with their attempt to provide content in many categories, are poorly positioned.

People will not turn to newspapers for updates on professional sports, because specialized web sites do that better. The same goes for business, weather, and hot news stories. On the web, focused competitors have stolen these markets from newspapers.

The most economically damaging competitor to newspapers is eBay. Classified ads, with their high profit margins, represent half of the net income of newspapers. As that franchise migrates to eBay (and to other web sites that focus on real estate, employment, and so forth), the newspapers will lose a precious revenue source.

"But you *need* us"

Newspaper professionals cannot envision a world without newspapers. They will argue passionately that we need newspapers for at least two reasons:

1. To employ reporters to do the legwork to gather primary news.
2. To employ editors who will ensure accuracy, objectivity, and trustworthiness of stories.

I am not convinced that either of these "needs" is valid. Many newspapers rely more on feeds from news services than on their own primary reporting. My guess is that a web-based network that relies on those sources could survive on a far lower subscription price than newspapers, while paying news services enough in fees to make up for the departure of the newspaper business. Ultimately, news junkies may pay $5 or $10 a year to a web-based network, rather than $150 a year for a newspaper subscription.

As to editorial judgment, people who read topical weblogs are experiencing a phenomenon of distributed editing. It does not work exactly like traditional centralized editing, but the end result is that people are finding help in sorting out fact from rumor and important from trivial.

Where Is the Economic Model?

The subject of weblogs raises the issue of an economic model. Today, newspaper editors and reporters have an advantage over webloggers if for no other reason than the fact that editors and reporters get paid, while webloggers do not. If this condition were permanent, I would predict that weblogs will decline and traditional newspapers will win in the end.

In fact, what will happen is that old models will break down and new models will emerge. For example, in the music industry today, an established music star does better by going with a major label. However, assuming that music distributors fail to heed my advice (see chapter on "Listen to the Technology"), new musicians are going to find that they are better off using alternative distribution channels. Eventually, a "tipping point" will occur: alternative channels will become sufficiently popular that even the stars will find those channels superior.

Similarly, I believe that webloggers and other new entrants in journalism will come up with alternative revenue models. One idea is a broad-based club (see chapter on "The Club vs. the Silo"). However, this is a difficult project to get started.

I am becoming increasingly convinced that what Dan Kohn calls Micropatronage[97] will be significant. Because information wants to be free but people need to get paid, various charitable donation models may hold sway.

The "tip jars" that webloggers use are one form of micropatronage. However, I am more persuaded by a model in which content producers are subsidized by corporate

LEARNING ECONOMICS

philanthropy or non-profit foundations. As Kohn points out, some magazines today are funded by this model. Indeed that is the model for TechCentralStation.com, where many of the chapters of this book first appeared.

In the future, it may very well turn out that both independent journalists and newspapers will require philanthropic support in order to operate. At that point, newspapers, with their high overhead, will be less likely to survive than independent journalists. However, I am sure that the *New York Times* and a few other newspapers will have sufficent nostalgia value in the eyes of some future wealthy mogul to ensure ongoing funding. Maybe James Taranto's newspaper will be among those fortunate enough to find a generous patron.

Chapter 20

The Internet Packet Express

This chapter articulates a vision for the architecture of electronic communications. It describes a relatively simple vision for the future, compared with our messy present. The vision is by no means original with me. My understanding of it owes much to Reed, Frankston, and friends.[98]

Eventually, the electronic communications environment will consist of two types of components. Not being an engineer, I think of these components as:

1. The Packet Express, an all-purpose communication network; and
2. Thingies, which translate the communication streams into useful applications, such as telephony or television

The Packet Express is the network that delivers Internet packets. When I was acquiring my first clues about the Internet, almost a decade ago, I read Ed Krol's *The Whole Internet Catalog*. He described the Internet as sort of like the Pony Express. Data gets put into virtual envelopes, called packets. The envelopes have addresses, called headers, giving instructions for where they should be delivered. Think of these envelopes as being given to a rider, who takes them to the next rider, and the next, until finally they are delivered to their destinations, where the recipients open the envelopes.

The Packet Express consists of communication lines (including radio spectrum) and routers. Until recently, there has been considerable uncertainty about the optimal architecture for the Packet Express, especially for the connection between the Internet backbone and individual users (sometimes called "the last mile"). There still are arguments among partisans of DSL, cable modems, and fiber-to-the-home about the relative merits of those technologies for the last mile. However, it appears to me that Packet Express is going to consist mostly of the fiber-based Internet core and wireless relay stations. Think of the fiber component as the skeleton and the wireless component as the skin. The wireless solution addresses the fact that people increasingly value mobile communications, and it avoids the high cost of modifying physical infrastructure buried in the nation's streets and front yards.

Thingies are devices that receive digital envelopes from Packet Express and convert the messages into human-usable formats. Thingies will replace telephones (including cell phones), televisions, personal computers, stereos, car radios, and other legacy electronic devices.

We might imagine a scenario in which each legacy device is replaced with an equivalent Thingy. A Thingy whose input-output mechanism consists primarily of a microphone and a speaker would replace a phone. A Thingy consisting primarily of a monitor, speakers, and a remote control would replace a TV. A Thingy with an interface consisting primarily of a monitor and a keyboard would replace a personal computer.

Alternatively, we might see hybrid Thingies. To date, there have been only unsuccessful efforts, such as the Woeful And Pathetic (WAP) interface for using telephones to browse the Web. But these early failures do not mean that the hybrid concept is untenable, or that we are limited to just the form factors that are currently popular.

The simplicity and flexibility of this architecture comes from the fact that Thingies all process the same sort of packets. Packet Express does not need to know whether it is delivering television programs or phone calls in its envelopes. The Thingies that open the envelopes can figure it out.

The ultimate realization of this architecture will mean that Packet Express is ubiquitous, and any Thingy can connect. Wherever you might be, if you have a phone-Thingy, you can make a phone call. If you have a TV-Thingy, you can watch a movie or TV program.

The Economics of the Simple Architecture

No great challenge is posed by the economics of Thingies. People will buy their Thingies, or they may rent Thingies when they are away from home. Manufacturers of Thingies will need to charge more than the cost of production, in order to recover high expenditures for research and development. However, to obtain a reasonable outcome, the existing patent system interacting with market competition probably will suffice.

Packet Express presents a challenge, because firms must either have duplicate infrastructure or be able to share infrastructure. There are some existing mechanisms for dealing with this. Suppose that Packet Express consists of the Internet backbone plus wireless relay stations. The companies that own different parts of the backbone have "peering arrangements" that allow traffic to flow between them. Similarly, companies that own some wireless relay stations could have "roaming arrangements" that make it possible for consumers to connect from anywhere.

As a consumer, I will pay a monthly subscription fee that allows me to connect all of my Thingies to Packet Express. How will my subscription fee be calculated? By the number of people in my household? By the number of Thingies I own? By the number of packets I send and receive? Economic theory does not say much about which mechanism is best.

The subscription fees should satisfy two criteria. From an average cost perspective, the fees in the aggregate should cover the cost of operating and maintaining the network. From a marginal cost perspective, the fees should provide some incentive for the individual not to put excessive pressure on the network to expand capacity. However, usage fees should not providing an arbitrary disincentive to use the network.

Charging by the packet probably is overly punitive at the margin. My use of the network presses on capacity only if I try to send packets at times when the network is congested. Some form of "peak-load surcharge" can address this issue. For example, with my local electric company, I am signed up for a program that charges me lower rates all year round, but allows the company to selectively shut off my air conditioning for 15 minutes at a time when demand is high. Similarly, Packet Express access providers might charge a lower monthly fee to people who agree that when congestion is high the packets that they send and receive can be delayed a few seconds more than normal.

My guess is that pricing for Packet Express will wind up looking something like cell phone subscription plans. For $10 a month, you will get up to a certain volume of packets. For $20 a month, you will get up to a higher volume. A plan may include one volume of "peak-time" packets and a larger volume of "off-peak" packets.

Chapter 21

The Wireless Last Mile

At Longbets,[99] people make long-term forecasts, and they put their money where their mouths are. Andy Chapman, founder of Narad Networks, which offers broadband software for cable companies, predicts that at least one local telephone company will require a government bailout to avoid bankruptcy by 2007. I think he is somewhat aggressive about the date, but in terms of economics, he makes a good forecast.

People say that economic forecasting is difficult. I think that forecasting is easy, as long as you stick to forecasts that are based on Moore's Law.[100] Moore's Law is the most powerful economic discovery since compound interest. In fact, Moore's Law is much like compound interest, in that it is a nonlinear process with large cumulative effects.

As I will explain below, I believe that Moore's Law means that the phone companies will lose the broadband battle. Chapman's view is that once they start to lose, they will collapse.[101]

"Their capital structure insures that... even modest market share losses... will cause them to lose creditworthiness and, thus, access to debt capital."

How Moore's Law Created the Internet

The Internet can be viewed in part as a technology that competes with telephony. The Internet uses packet switching,

LEARNING ECONOMICS

which means that messages are broken up into packets. To get a message from point A to point B, several packets must be sent, each one requiring connections to be opened and closed. In contrast, telephony uses circuit switching. When you make a connection (complete the circuit), you keep the connection open until the message (phone call) is complete. As economists Hal R. Varian and Jeffrey K. MacKie-Mason pointed out in a brilliant early analysis[102] of the Internet, the viability of packet switching depends on the relative cost of lines vs. switches.

- A packet-switched network (the Internet) makes efficient use of lines, but it requires lots of switching. The same line can carry multiple packets, but each packet requires switching operations to enable it to reach its destination.
- A circuit-switched network makes efficient use of switching, but it requires lots of lines. A phone call only requires that a connection be made once, but each phone call uses line capacity, even when people are not talking.

The cost of using switches to open and close connections depends on the cost of computation. Because of Moore's Law, this cost has plummeted. As a result, the cost of operating a packet-switched network has fallen much faster than the cost of operating a circuit-switched network. Without Moore's Law, the Internet might have remained a Defense Department curiosity, because no one else could afford to use it. With Moore's Law, the Internet protocols are poised to take over all communications.

Moore's Law, Wireless Networking, and the Last Mile

Moore's Law is also starting to have an impact on the use of the wireless spectrum. The traditional model allocates spectrum bands to particular users, such as television stations. The new model, advocated by Kevin Werbach[103] among others, is to let many users share spectrum, and let the receivers sort out the messages.

The old model of spectrum allocation allows crude receivers to work, by keeping out signals that the receiver might not understand—what used to be called "interference." The new model says that receivers with sophisticated processors do not need to be protected from irrelevant signals. It says that "interference is in the ear of the receiver." With sophisticated receivers, people can send signals at the same time in the same frequency band and still be understood.

Once again, we have an old model that is designed to economize on computer processors while making inefficient use of transmission capacity. We have a new model that allows a given transmission capacity (in this case, spectrum) to carry more information, but requires more computer processing. Guess which model benefits from Moore's Law?

As Timothy J. Shepard puts it,[104] 50 years ago, no one could have designed a workable system for shared spectrum. 25 years ago, a few engineers might have been able to come up with such a system. Today, many engineers could do so. The possibility has been opened up by Moore's Law.

The Long-Term Architecture

The way I see it, Moore's Law ultimately will favor shared-spectrum wireless as the solution for last mile connectivity. Today, I am typing this outdoors, using a laptop that connects wirelessly to a router in my basement, which in turn connects to the local phone company by DSL. My prediction is that eventually I will skip the DSL part, and instead my wireless connection will go to a local wireless network of some sort, and then ultimately to a transmitter on the Internet backbone. The communication network will have a fiber skeleton and a wireless skin. Telephone landlines will be superfluous.

None of this is going to happen next month or next year. I am not sure it will even start to have an impact soon enough to enable Andy Chapman to win his bet. But Moore's Law will eventually run the local phone companies out of town.

CHAPTER 22

ASYMPTOTICALLY FREE GOODS

"Within 10 or 15 years' time, practically every computer and every handheld device will be online all the time. What many people don't realize, however, is that this visionary network is increasingly up and running today. And it doesn't even require any new technology, business models or significant investment . . . the real wireless Internet doesn't cost $50 a month—it's free. All that's required, really, is openness."—Simson Garfinkel[105]

In the Internet era, many of the most bitter struggles over commerce and policy are being fought because of the potential to offer valuable goods and services for free.

- The Microsoft anti-trust case centers around the decision by Microsoft to distribute the Internet Explorer browser at no charge.
- Napster became the flashpoint in a war over music distribution by offering music-swapping service for free.
- As Garfinkel, David Reed, and others point out, new protocols and receiver technologies make it possible to deliver high-speed wireless Internet service at essentially no marginal cost.

Beyond these immediate cases loom several other issues

of products and services where research and development costs are high, but the marginal cost of the final product or service is low.

- The marginal cost of manufacturing prescription drugs is low. Our traditional policy has been to allow drug companies to recoup their research and development costs by giving them patents that enable them to charge prices for drugs that are far above marginal cost. This policy has come under fire with the AIDS crisis in Africa and more recently with the Anthrax scare in the U.S.
- The bioinformatics revolution promises to bring about medical treatments that have high benefits and extremely low marginal cost, but only after difficult and extensive research.
- The cost of data storage, search, and retrieval keeps falling.
- The cost of food production, which has been falling for centuries, could approach zero with bio-engineering of crops.

As the cost of providing and distributing various types of goods and services is falling, some other costs remain high. For example, Garfinkel writes,

"One of the most surprising things we learned from launching our Internet startup was that providing wireless Internet service is really cheap. What ended up bankrupting the company were all the ancillary services we had to develop—credit card billing, technical support, the corporate Web site and the various security measures we had to put in place to prevent unauthorized use of the network by nonsubscribers."

Garfinkel is suggesting that it costs more to maintain an infrastructure that allows you to charge for the service than it does to provide the service itself. If that is the case, then what these asymptotically free goods and services represent is nothing less than a breakdown in the economic system.

A Precise Definition

I want to try to offer a precise definition of an asymptotically free good. I believe it differs from other concepts that have been used by economists.

Traditional economic goods.

A traditional economic good is one for which the marginal cost is above the average cost. This means that adding another consumer will raise the price required to cover the cost of providing the good. Another characteristic of traditional goods is that I cannot consume the good without taking it away from someone else. If I eat a hamburger, then you cannot eat that same hamburger.

Natural monopolies.

A natural monopoly is a good where the marginal cost is below the average cost. Natural monopolies typically involve heavy investments in capital equipment. This means high costs for ongoing maintenance in addition to expensive initial investment.

For example, consider a ride at an amusement park. The marginal cost imposed by the next rider may be close to zero, even though the average cost is high. If the natural monopoly charges its marginal cost, it will lose money. To recover its average costs, the amusement park might charge an admissions fee. Once you are in the park, your marginal cost of a ride may be small, perhaps zero. (This example is due to Walter Oi, "A Disneyland Dilemma: Two-part tariffs in a Mickey Mouse Monopoly.")[106]

Other examples of natural monopolies include utilities, such as electricity. Much of the cost of providing electricity is fixed costs associated with plant and equipment. The marginal cost tends to be much lower.

Public goods.

A public good is one that I can enjoy without paying for it. National defense is an example. In the absence of government provision of such goods, individuals will have an incentive to hold back and let others provide them, which means that collectively the amount provided will be too little.

Clean air is another example. When I pollute, I suffer only a negligible portion of the social damage that I cause. Thus, I face little disincentive to pollute. Every individual treats his or her own pollution as costless, even though it is costly in the aggregate.

An **asymptotically free good** is a good where almost of all of the cost involved consists of research and development. It differs from a natural monopoly in two ways.

1. In contrast with an amusement park or a utility, the cost of maintaining the capital for an asymptotically free good is relatively low.

Once the research is complete and the idea is proven, the costs are trivial. In the absence of patent protection, there is nothing to stop a competitor from taking the idea and driving the price close to zero. For example, once you have undertaken the research to produce a new miracle drug, the marginal and average costs of producing it are low. To take another example, once devices have been designed and protocols established for a high-speed wireless network, the cost of providing and maintaining the equipment for a network may be low relative to the number of users.

2. Asymptotically free goods are like public goods in that it is costly to exclude someone from enjoying the benefit of an asymptotically free good.

- It is costly to hook someone up to the electric grid. It is costly to keep someone *off* a wireless network.
- The cost of setting up and maintaining a gate at an amusement park is relatively low. The cost of policing the Internet to stop music swapping is enormous.

The Role of Government

Liberals consider the role of government in an environment with asymptotically free goods and see opportunities.

- In the absence of government involvement, one person's research can be appropriated by someone else. This would deny any reward to researchers. The only economic ways to encourage research and development are (a) direct government funding and (b) defining and enforcing patent law. The better job the government does with these functions, the better will be the outcomes.
- It is not efficient for prices to be set far above marginal costs. When the marginal cost of drug therapy or wireless Internet service is set artificially high, there will be pressure on government to do something to correct the mispricing.

Conservatives consider the role of government in this environment and see threats.

- Government is traditionally slow to recognize and shut down failures. The private sector is better at the sort

of trial-and-error learning that is required for applied research.
- Private-sector competition is what allows cost-saving innovations to deliver benefits to consumers.
- Asymptotically free goods are disruptive. In a disruptive situation, government tends to become aligned with the opponents of change. For example, recent legislation concerning intellectual property has strongly favored traditional music and movie distributors at the expense of innovation and consumer benefit.

Conclusion

Asymptotically free goods are a new economic force. Problems are being solved not by throwing capital and labor at them, but by undertaking research and development which, when completed, leads to solutions that cost relatively little in terms of traditional factors of production.

I would not want to own stock in a company that generates its revenue from music distribution on CD's and tapes, from phone service, from selling information retrieval services, or from traditional health care services. For these companies, the present value of future earnings has to be calculated under the assumption that at some point they will be crushed by the steamroller of asymptotically free goods.

Asymptotically free goods also raise issues of public policy that may exacerbate the polarization between liberals and conservatives. For those who tend to view government as an instrument of the public good whenever the free-market outcome may be flawed, asymptotically free goods provide an excuse for more government intervention. For those who tend to see government as providing an instrument by which status quo interests can impede change, asymptotically free goods are a reason for keeping government hands off.

Chapter 23

Legamorons in a Trackable Society

"Do these slayings, or the war on terrorism, put these cameras in a different light? If technology is the only way to enforce a law, any law, is it wrong to use that technology because it's intrusive. Society will have to answer that question."—Dana Blankenhorn[107]

Blankenhorn was referring to the DC sniper case, which frustrated and terrified citizens in the fall of 2002. As David Brin[108] anticipated in *The Transparent Society*,[109] the pressure is building for widespread surveillance. In 1999, Brin predicted that the combination of lower-cost snooping technology and increased threats from terrorism would lead to widespread use of cameras and databases.

Brin focused on the issue of how we can maintain freedom and autonomy in such an environment. His thesis is that the solution is not to try to keep government blind, deaf, and dumb by attempting to restrict its ability to use technology. Instead, Brin's solution is to make sure that ordinary civilians have enough access to surveillance technology and databases so that we can provide a check against abuse by corporations or government.

The Trackable Society

My guess is that the real revolution in law enforcement capability will come from digital radios, rather than from video cameras. Digital radios have the potential to be more pervasive and more applicable to law enforcement in the near term.

Here is what Pat Gelsinger, Intel's Chief Technology Officer, is predicting.[110]

"Imagine being able to integrate all the features of wide-area, local-area, and personal-area networks into a single piece of silicon. What if we were able to add transmit and receive, intelligent roaming, network optimization, and permanent IP connectivity capabilities? And what if we were able combine data, voice, and video services on that same piece of silicon? Pretty cool, right?

Let's take it to the next level. If we can shrink this technology down to where it sits on the corner of a die, then we'll have radio on chip (RoC). Every processor will have integrated multiradio capabilities. The result will be ubiquitous radios that are always connected and seamlessly networked across offices, buildings, and even cities."

Soon, we will have the ability to attach these chip-radios to children's clothing, pets' collars, cars, guns, explosive materials, etc. Combine these radios with Global Positioning Satellites and database technology, and you have the trackable society. In theory such a society would have better defenses against snipers, suicide bombers, and other menaces.

Bear with me, and assume that the trackable society in fact greatly increases the effectiveness of law enforcement. Also, assume that we manage to adopt an acceptable system of checks and balances that keep the systems from being abused. Those are important issues that are far from resolved. However, I want to leave aside the issues of privacy and power, as important as they are in the context of surveillance technology. Instead, I want to talk about the way in which better enforcement technology would disturb the legal equilibrium—an equilibrium which I suggest depends a great deal on the fact that many of our laws can be broken with impunity.

Legal Oxymorons

In fact, I would argue that many laws are the legal equivalent of oxymorons—legamorons, if you will. *A legamoron is any law which could not stand up under widespread enforcement.* Laws against marijuana use are a prime example. Rigorous enforcement of these laws on middle-class college campuses would cause a furor.

There are many other legamorons, where we have become accustomed to low levels of enforcement.

- immigration laws
- laws against sexual harassment
- laws against betting on sports
- speed limits
- software licenses
- laws against music sharing
- laws requiring people to pay social security taxes for household workers

In fact, the entire tax system could be viewed as a legamoron. Congress deliberately underfunds the computer systems and audit department of the IRS. Otherwise, if households and businesses had to get everything on their returns exactly right, the cost of tax compliance probably would eat up the entire Gross Domestic Product, and there would be nothing left to tax.

Better enforcement technology, as in the trackable society, would cause us to rethink our legamorons. For example, the vast majority of drivers get away with speeding much of the time. What would happen if it became possible to detect all of these speeding violations?

In theory, perfect enforcement of speed limits would cause everyone to obey the speed limit. But that would be such a radical development that I doubt that it is desirable. If speeding is widespread, it is very likely that it is efficient from both the individual and social perspective. In fact, we probably want the vast majority of speeding violations to be overlooked.

If we introduced perfect speed-detection technology, then my guess is that we would have to rewrite the traffic laws to say what we really mean. What we really want is for people to drive in a way that does not cause undue risk to other drivers. This is much harder to codify than a speed limit, but if laws are going to be enforced strictly, then they have to be written more carefully.

Is Technology the Culprit?

Many people see the problems with strict enforcement as an argument against technology. For example, Jon Udell reports on a conversation[111] that included Eric Norlin and David Weinberger.

The subject of gays in the military came up. Somebody asked whether, in the transparent world of the NSA where "don't ask, don't tell" is irrelevant, gay employees are not tolerated.

Eric: "There were guys who were gay. But they were good, so people looked the other way."

David: "That's the problem with [Digital Rights Management]. Computers are too stupid to look the other way."

What Weinberger is saying is that casual enforcement helps bail society out of its legamorons. But that strikes me as an odd argument.

I am willing to grant that there are many laws for which better enforcement would lead to a worse outcome. However, I find it difficult to believe that putting a cramp on enforcement capability is the optimum solution. Surely, it would be better to abolish the legamorons and instead write laws that we could enforce to society's benefit rather than its detriment.

There may be valid reasons for not trying to use our most advanced technology to prevent and detect sniper attacks, terrorist attacks, and other threats. However, the possibility that advanced technology might make it harder to sustain an equilibrium of bad laws, selectively enforced, strikes me as a poor rationale to make technology the culprit.

CHAPTER 24

METAPHORS FOR INTELLECTUAL PROPERTY

"Since the Internet has lowered distribution and reproduction costs, bad IP laws are more costly now than they were in the past. 150-year copyright terms just didn't matter much before Napster. A new IP regime needs to understand the economics of production for different types of ideas and tailor the right laws for the right circumstances. Personally, I'd like to see shorter copyright, no patents on business processes or software, and longer patents for drugs."—
Zimran Ahmed[112]

Ahmed's intuition about intellectual property (IP) closely accords with my own. However, it is difficult to provide a rigorous justification for my thinking.

IP as a Metaphor

One tends to use metaphors when talking about IP. In fact, the very term "intellectual property" is itself a metaphor. Physical property is something that you can feel, touch, and take away from someone else. Knowledge has none of those characteristics. So why treat ideas or creative works as property at all?

As James DeLong[113] points out, the philosophy that was influential in America at the time of our nation's birth emphasized "natural rights," including the right of a man to the fruits of his labor. Within that philosophical framework, the effort spent composing a creative work or developing an idea is labor, and the creator has a natural right to a reward for that labor. That remains a morally compelling argument for IP.

Another rationale for IP is purely utilitarian. Taking the existence of a creative work as given, the social optimum is to make it available to everyone, for nothing more than the cost to copy and distribute the work. With the Internet, the marginal cost of accessing digital music and text approaches zero, so that all else equal, creative work ought to be available for free.

However, all else is not equal. If creative works were available for free, there would be no reward for creators, and this would reduce the supply of creative works. Therefore, even if we were strictly utilitarians and had no belief in "natural rights," we might still support the concept of intellectual property in order to ensure the development of creative works.

IP as a Racehorse

Michele Boldrin and David K. Levine[114] developed a theoretical argument suggesting that copyright laws are not necessary in order to protect IP. Douglas Clement[115] provides a nice survey of the controversy surrounding their view.

The Boldrin-Levine argument is couched in mathematics, which makes it a bit unclear what is going on. My understanding of it can be articulated using a metaphor from horse racing.

A couple years ago, Laura Hillenbrand wrote what turned out to be a best-selling book about a racehorse named Seabiscuit. The horse's owner and trainer clearly had to go to considerable effort to evaluate and develop their racehorse.

People attempt to make copies of horses, in the process known as breeding. Because a champion like Seabiscuit is valuable for breeding purposes, the owner is able to earn rewards for selling the breeding services. Thus, the fact that a racehorse can be "copied" enhances rather than detracts from the wealth of the original owner.

The Boldrin-Levine paper makes a similar argument about copies of creative works. They suggest that because the first people to buy a creative work will capture value from copying that work, what they will pay for the first copy will be very high. Thus, copyright is not necessary. The owners of Seabiscuit did not need a copyright in order to capture the breeding value of their horse.

If Seabiscuit, the horse, does not need a copyright, why do we need a copyright for *Seabiscuit* the book? My guess is that the publisher, Ballantine Books, could not be sure ahead of time whether *Seabiscuit* would be a winner or an also-ran. The book was available to be copied before this uncertainty was resolved. Without copy protection, another publisher could wait for Ballantine's full line-up of books to come out, observe how they sell, and then choose to copy only the popular titles.

In contrast, the owner of the horse could wait until the quality of the horse was established before making the horse available to others to make copies. I can see how the Boldrin-Levine mechanism works for horses, but I have a hard time seeing it work for books.

IP as Popcorn

I believe that music publishers should not be entitled to take legal action against file swappers. The metaphor I use for this is popcorn.

When I go to a movie theater, I never buy popcorn there. Even though I can afford the four bucks, I am offended by the price.

There are movie theaters that will not allow you to bring your own popcorn into the theater. Clearly, what they are thinking is that if they forbid you from bringing your own popcorn, then you will buy their popcorn. My reaction, however, is that this is just one more reason not to go to the movies—along with the deafening sound, obnoxious patrons, and Hollywood's predictable story lines.

Music publishers who go after file swappers are like movie theater owners who won't let you bring your own popcorn to the theater. They are simply alienating their customers while trying to protect a revenue stream that they were not going to get, anyway.

IP as a Hitting Technique

Baseball players and coaches always work on hitting technique. For example, a popular current saying is "short to, long through" meaning that hitters should try to drive directly into the ball as opposed to starting with a backswing or looping motion.

Suppose that I had been the person who came up with the concept of "short to, long through." Should Barry Bonds be required to get a license from me in order to use it? If you believe that, then you support the idea of business process patents.

Because business processes, like hitting techniques, depend so heavily on execution, the idea of granting them status as intellectual property is abhorrent. Patents on business processes make a mockery of the game and serve only to create opportunities for lawyers.

IP as Prize

Drug companies go to considerable effort and expense in order to develop pharmaceuticals. The reward for this is a patent on the drug. The patent gives the developer control over the manufacturing license for a fixed period of time. The value of this license is the prize for finding the drug.

An alternative mechanism would be to offer prizes for drug development. There are foundations that are dedicated to dealing with particular diseases, such as breast cancer or diabetes. These foundations could offer prizes for the development of pharmaceuticals that achieve certain objectives. Money from the private foundations could be supplemented by government funding for prizes. My guess is that reducing the role of patents and increasing the role of prizes as incentives for drug research would help to shift resources away from research into solutions for hair loss and erectile dysfunction and toward research into solutions for illnesses that many people would regard as more important to address.

Conclusion

I think that the public policy issues that surround ideas and creative works require more than one metaphor. In fact, for many creative works, my controversial metaphor "Content is Crap"[116] applies. That is, until the works have been sifted by a filter, they have no value.

For me, the overall topic is too complex to be resolved with a single formula or policy. The term "intellectual property" is overly broad. We need multiple metaphors.

Chapter 25

The Club vs. the Silo

"The Americans will always do the right thing . . . after they've exhausted all the alternatives."—Winston Churchill

There is much talk these days of the collapse of Internet news media and other "content sites." In my view, this is not a failure of the new medium. Instead, the problem is that the online news providers have not yet exhausted the alternatives to doing the right thing to arrive at a viable economic model.

One alternative that cannot be exhausted soon enough is banner advertising. I have been eager to see this concept die since it first was introduced in 1995.

Another alternative that I believe should be euthanized is the subscription model for individual periodicals. The marginal cost of distributing the publications online is zero, so subscription models are very difficult to sustain.

Finally, there is the alternative of micropayments, meaning small payments for access to particular slices of information. I am now persuaded by Clay Shirky's argument that the mental transaction costs involved in micropayments are too high to make micropayments workable.[117]

The implausible alternatives all are based on the notion of a content "silo," which is left over from the pre-Internet era. Content is embedded in a silo, such as a traditional magazine or newspaper. This silo is presented to the reader

LEARNING ECONOMICS

in "take-it-or-leave-it" fashion. The funding comes from specific subscriptions and advertising.

Arriving at a viable economic model for content on the Internet requires changing the "silo" mentality. There are a number of things wrong with it.

An Anachronistic Wall

First of all, the "silo" model tries to maintain an anachronistic wall between the content in one silo and content in other silos. In the world of physical magazines, it certainly makes sense that a subscription to "Business Week" does not entitle you to read "Forbes." Clearly, they are two separate physical collections of paper.

On the Internet, however, this distinction is not a physical necessity. Most consumers in fact pick and choose articles from a variety of online magazines. In contrast to the physical world, consumers can engage in extensive content aggregation without imposing meaningful costs at the margin.

A second thing wrong with the traditional silo model is that it ignores a critical component of value. Because of the volume of content available on line, the marginal value of additional articles has gone down. The marginal value of annotation, filtering, and recommendations from other consumers has increased. As J.C. Herz put it in an article in the now-defunct silo *The Industry Standard*, "the digital future is probably in the margins, rather than on the pages."

For example, one of Amazon.com's innovations consists of book lists created by readers. These lists create connections among various books. The lists are an example of value created in the margins.

Instead of trying to stay within the silo structure, online journalism should evolve toward broad content aggregation with the value of annotation and connections. This will maximize the value of the online component.

For an economic model, I continue to recommend the idea of "clubs." A club would provide content aggregation, recommendation, and annotation services. Journalists would be paid by clubs, rather than by individual publications. For a consumer, joining a club will provide access to value-added services relative to online content.

Most of the articles that you are able to read when you join a club may be freely available without joining the club. What your membership fee would give you is better access to individual authors, as well as to indexing tools and cross-reference tools. Some of these tools would be provided by community members, as in the Amazon book lists.

The raw content is not what you are paying for. The haystack is free. But if you want help finding the needle, you have to join the club.

While I would not pay to subscribe to an individual online journal, I might be willing to pay to join a club that gives me access to a variety of journals as well as to helpful annotations. Annotations might consist of Lawrence Lee's recommendations[118] for articles on Internet marketing or Virginia Postrel's comments[119] on articles about policy issues.

A club could offer several different levels of membership. The most expensive membership could entitle you to personal chat time with famous authors. Or it could entitle you to 24-hour response time to inquiries that you submit to human experts. Or it could entitle you to use the most sophisticated indexing and cross-reference tools.

In a silo model, I only get one periodical's content when I subscribe. With the club concept, my subscription includes access to many periodicals. Some of these are in the haystack (that is, available to people who are not club members), but perhaps not easy to search and cross-reference. Other articles might be licensed only to clubs, so that individuals who are not members would not have access (or have access only with a lag).

How would journalists and other content providers get paid? They will be paid by the clubs. They may be paid for writing articles that the club's managers know will be particularly interesting to club members. They will be paid for permitting their articles to be searched by the club's indexing tools. In addition, writers may be paid for making themselves available to club members for chats or responses to questions.

Online content providers are trapped in the offline metaphor of a magazine, which is a separate silo funded by a combination of subscriptions and advertising. When they have exhausted the alternatives associated with the silo model, perhaps they will come around to the idea of a club.

Chapter 26

Equilibrium in the Market for Rock 'n' Roll

Legendary guitarist Ted Nugent wrote an anti-Napster rant[120] in the *Wall Street Journal*. In general, rockers seem to be very disappointed that the Internet is not raising the equilibrium wage rate for their work.

It would be nice if we all could be rock stars. Imagine how neat it would be if all of us could receive recognition and financial rewards for our contribution to rhythm and blues.

In practice, however, the rewards for creativity tend to be disappointing. While there are rich movie stars, there are many actors and actresses who wait on tables.

Talented musicians will find at least two characteristics to lament about the distribution of rewards.

1. Average compensation is low.
2. The distribution of compensation does not seem to match the distribution of talent.

On average, musicians are not paid well. True, a tiny minority of pop stars gets paid an enormous amount. However, this is offset by the low wages paid to the vast majority of bands.

The other problem with the market for creative expression is that the correlation between talent and reward is low. In October of 1999, I wrote an essay called Effective Tournaments,[121] in which I talked about how various processes work to sort out winners and losers.

(My goal in that essay was to suggest that the stock market was not doing a particularly good job of selecting the most promising Internet companies. Today, few would argue with my assessment.)

The question about "effective tournaments" is how well rewards are correlated with ability. In chess or golf, the correlation is very strong. It seems to me to be highly probable that Gary Kasparov was indeed the most talented chess player of his era, and that Tiger Woods is the most talented golfer today.

Compare the professional tennis tournament to the pop music tournament. I think that it is a safe bet that your local tennis pro cannot play as well as Venus Williams. However, it would not be safe to bet that it would be hard to find a local lounge singer who is as good as Britney Spears.

If there were an equation that tried to predict market rewards in popular music on the basis of creativity and talent, it would not work very well. In statistical jargon, the R-squared of that regression would be low, and the residual errors would be large.

My guitar playing would not even get me into a local band. On the other hand, in 2002, I published a book, *Under the Radar: Starting Your Internet Business without Venture Capital*, that falls under the category that publishers call "trade, business." That is, it was targeted at a business audience, and it was distributed through ordinary ("trade") bookstores, rather than as a textbook.

Within the trade business category, the year 2001 was dominated by a particular book. This reigning champion—the Gary Kasparov or Tiger Woods that the rest of us are gunning for—was called *Who Moved My Cheese?* From the description, the book sounds even worse than the title.

Something tells me that the book business is not an effective tournament.

People have a hard time accepting the fact that their creativity is not much valued. For example, most web designers complain that their work is not appreciated. Jakob Nielsen[122] constantly tells Web designers to tone down their sites and make them usable. Instead, web designers continue to show off, to the irritation of consumers.

It is as if Nielsen were telling prospective musicians that their best chances of success in rock would come from building a band around drums, bass, and guitar. Finding this advice too stifling, the creative geniuses attempt to form a group consisting of xylophone, kazoo, and tuba. The market often is unkind to originality.

The Internet and the Role of Distributors

When the World Wide Web hit the scene, many rockers became aware of the Internet. Some thought that the Internet would eliminate distributors, allow musicians to sell directly to the public, and thereby solve the problems that had previously existed with market compensation of creative work.

The theory that distributors are the root of all evil holds that:

- Distributors "rip off" artists.
- Distributors use their control over the market to keep the most creative artists down.
- Distributors create the uneven distribution of income for artists.

If distributors were eliminated, the thinking goes, the musicians would earn more money, and the correlation between quality and popularity would be higher.

It turns out that the Internet is indeed threatening to upset the traditional distribution system for pop music. However, no matter what new system emerges, my guess is that the effect on the equilibrium compensation for musicians is likely to be small.

Fundamentally, there is a lot of supply in the market for pop music. Because there are so many people willing to supply services at a relatively low wage rate, the average wage rate is never going to get very high, regardless of what happens to the distribution system.

The other problem—the poor correlation between talent and commercial success—probably reflects consumer network effects. Much of the reason that my daughters like the groups that they do is because their friends like those groups. As the popularity of a band builds, it starts to feed on itself as more consumers recommend the band to one another. Unless the Internet reduces network effects—and I can think of no reason that it should—the random component in success will continue to be large. Clay Shirky[123] argues that Internet popularity follows a power law, which mathematically describes a very uneven distribution.

What is true in rock 'n' roll is true in many other creative fields. If you are waiting for the Internet to deliver an equilibrium in which creative artists are highly paid and there is a strong, systematic relationship between talent and success, do not hold your breath.

Chapter 27

Moore vs. Plato

"The intellectual is no longer a man without a country. But he may be a man without a future. And if he is not in league with the future, can he be right?"—Merle Kling[124]

Almost 50 years ago, in the shadow of World War II and at the dawn of space exploration, the question was raised whether the future could be comprehended by non-scientists. I will argue below that today the question is whether the future can be understood without grasping the implications of Moore's Law.[125]

The Two Cultures

What was an economist like me doing at a "Socratic Seminar" discussing C.P. Snow's *The Two Cultures*, the mind-body problem, and the philosophy of science? This was a two-day event in 2003 sponsored by the organization that hosts my EconLog[126] site.

The seminar, led by Oxford-trained poet Frederick Turner,[127] had a number of erudite participants. It turns out that fellow bloggers Megan McArdle ('Jane Galt')[128] and Will Wilkinson ('Fly Bottle')[129] can hold their own with the sherry-sipping, repartee-trading, philosopher-name-dropping set. For my part, I was in over my head, sort of like when people are discussing opera, or when everyone else is eating with chopsticks.

The theme of the seminar was the difference in viewpoint, if any, between humanists (professors of literature, philosophy, and so forth) and scientists. It was Wilkinson who provided what for me is a useful way to describe this difference. He said that a humanist arrives at understanding subjectively, through introspection and empathy. A scientist arrives at understanding objectively, through the scientific method.

Of Ghosts and Machines

This distinction led me to think of the psychology of Sigmund Freud, which comes from a humanist perspective. Is that perspective destined to disappear, replaced by neuropharmacology? Even Ronald Bailey,[130] an advocate for biotechnology, says that he still believes that some of Freud's concepts, such as the unconscious, remain insightful.

Indulge in a thought-experiment: two patients are brought in to two psychiatrists. The first psychiatrist, a humanist, after interviewing the patients pronounces that both suffer from Depression. The second psychiatrist, a scientist, after reading brain scans of the patients pronounces that both suffer from chemical imbalance. One patient is then assigned to each psychiatrist for treatment.

For six months, the humanist psychiatrist uses a "talking cure," consisting of sessions in which the patient discusses early childhood memories, dreams, and so forth. The scientist psychiatrist puts the other patient on a regimen of medication.

After six months, both patients once again are examined. The humanist psychiatrist interviews both patients and pronounces, "Their depressions are gone!" The scientist conducts a brain scan of both patients and pronounces, "Their chemical imbalances are gone!"

How would you interpret such a result? Such a result would show a correspondence between the subjective experience (lifting the Depression) and the objective experience (better brain chemistry). In terms of an old metaphor, the internal experience of the Ghost (the conscious mind) can be mapped to the externally-measurable Machine (the physical brain).

Who Is Winning?

In the thought-experiment, the two psychiatrists are equally skilled. The scientist and the humanist appear to be tied.

I think that at any point in time, we tend to see the humanists and the scientists as evenly matched. However, this is because at any point in time we focus on the areas where neither side appears to have an advantage. But, if we look at long-term historical trends, the humanists have steadily given up ground. For example, until relatively recently the humanists had psychology pretty much to themselves.

Humanists will boast that their conception of man has stood the test of time. They argue that Shakespeare's insights have lasted for centuries, while, science keeps changing. Scientists have periodically latched on to false doctrines—Skinnerian psychology comes to mind—with fervor.

However, the evolutionary nature of science is a feature, not a bug. The ability of scientists to sift through ideas has led to great breakthroughs, including Newtonian physics, Darwinian evolution, and the many discoveries of the past century.

Breaking with the Past

Economists, unlike humanists, see the present as almost completely different from the past. As we saw in the chapter, "Growth Across Time," from the age of Plato to the era of Shakespeare, there was almost no improvement in the average standard of living. Since then, the rise has been spectacular. Modern workers earn close to 500 times as much. Even more striking is the rate of acceleration of technical change. Most of the increase in living standards took place within the last century. The humanist believes that we can still relate to the early 19th century by reading Charles Dickens. The economist believes that the poverty of that age is scarcely conceivable.

Gazing into the Future

Technologists see Moore's Law as the driving force of our era. Moore's Law is accelerating the rate of progress and technological change even beyond what was observed in the past century. Prior to Moore's Law, an annual economic growth rate of 1 or 2 percent produced significant cumulative change. Moore's Law itself implies annual growth rates of computer productivity of 20 percent or more, which in turn could lift economic growth to unprecedented levels, perhaps 4 percent or higher. See "Rationally Exuberant."

To a humanist, the attempt to overthrow Saddam Hussein had the potential to be long and difficult. To a technologist, such an outcome was highly unlikely, given the advances that had taken place in computer and communication technology in just the last ten years. In a sense, the war to liberate Iraq demonstrated Moore's Law as powerfully as Hiroshima demonstrated modern physics.

At the seminar, one of the humanists remarked with casual confidence that Plato will last for 50,000 years. Bailey and I rolled our eyes, because we regard it as questionable whether the continuity of the human race is assured for even 50 years, much less 50,000. With genetic engineering, advances in neuropharmacology, and computerized implants, our great-grandchildren will be qualitatively different from us.

The New Classics

From the humanist perspective, the classics of literature are indispensable. The project of understanding human nature from the introspective viewpoint continues to owe much to the writers of earlier eras.

From the perspective of science and technology, the indispensable works are those that are informed by Moore's Law. Our required reading list might include:

- Neal Stephenson's *The Diamond Age*, a work of science fiction that attempts to describe a future that includes nanotechnology as well as advances in computers.
- David Brin's *The Transparent Society*, an extrapolation of the path for surveillance technology implied by Moore's Law, which seems eerily prescient after the 9-11-01 terrorist attacks.
- Ray Kurzweil's *The Age of Spiritual Machines*, a bold, often-irritating attempt to trace through the implications of exponential growth in computer technology over several decades.

The Kling thesis is that the project of the humanists is degenerating into an exercise in archaeology. It is a way to study where we have been. But it does not tell us where we are going.

PART 4

Free Trade

INTRODUCTION

Imagine a conversation on a Sunday morning between a surgeon and her tennis partner. This conversation will have three anecdotes that relate to trade.

1. The surgeon's tennis partner asks what software she uses to do her taxes. The surgeon replies that she does not do her taxes herself. "Mine are really complicated," she explains. "I figure that my accountant has been trained to understand this stuff, and he can do it much faster than I can, with fewer mistakes. Doing my own taxes would be like him doing his own surgery."
2. The surgeon talks about needing to give her house a new coat of paint. Her tennis partner suggests that compared with a typical house painter she probably could do this job better herself. "That's true," the surgeon replies. "I have steady hands, and I work more carefully and efficiently than most painters. But I figured that even though it will take the painters 50 hours to do the house and I could do it in 40, it's still a better use of my time to see patients. I can pay the painters with the money I get from seeing patients for two hours, so in a way I can paint my house in just two hours by sticking to medicine."
3. Finally, the tennis partner says. "My brother-in-law had a kidney stone. I was going to recommend that he come to you, but his doctor said that there is a new pill that dissolves some stones. So he doesn't need surgery."

The first anecdote illustrates the advantage of *specialization*. Because they can trade with one another, the surgeon can specialize in surgery and her accountant can specialize in tax return preparation. Specialization allows people to be more efficient, and in this case trade helps both specialists.

The second anecdote illustrates *comparative advantage*. Although she can paint faster than a contractor, the surgeon is even better than the contractor at doing surgery. We say that her comparative advantage is in doing surgery and the contractor's comparative advantage is in painting. By doing the work that is each person's comparative advantage, both the surgeon and the contractor benefit from trade.

The last anecdote illustrates one of the most subtle benefits from trade. Competition and trade lead to *innovation*, in this case the development of a drug that reduces the cost and risk of removing kidney stones.

Competition and innovation are not necessarily a benefit for the surgeon. The demand for her services falls to the extent that medication can be used in place of surgery.

When people complain about "unfair trade" or "unfair competition," it is usually because of the displacement effect on their own jobs. Most people like the benefits of trade—higher living standards, greater efficiency, etc. But everyone resents competition when it hits them personally.

What happens to jobs that are "lost" to progress, displacement, and trade? New jobs become more important. If we had frozen the economic structure in 1800, America would have many more agricultural jobs than we have today. Had we frozen the economic structure in 1950, we would have more manufacturing jobs. But even though we have "lost" jobs in agriculture and manufacturing, there is enough work to keep the economy pretty close to full employment.

LEARNING ECONOMICS

I think that most people prefer the work that they do to the mind-numbing labor of a factory assembly line or the backbreaking labor of a farm. Work today is less dangerous, less unpleasant, and less dreary than it has ever been. Keep that in mind when people complain about "lost" jobs.

The rest of the chapter restates the argument for free trade in different ways. Understanding those arguments is one of the most basic steps in learning economics.

Chapter 28

Roll Over, Ricardo

"*England may be so circumstanced, that to produce the cloth may require the labour of 100 men for one year; and if she attempted to make the wine, it might require the labour of 120 men for the same time . . .*

To produce the wine in Portugal, might require only the labour of 80 men for one year, and to produce the cloth in the same country, might require the labour of 90 men for the same time. It would therefore be advantageous for her to export wine in exchange for cloth. This exchange might even take place, notwithstanding that the commodity imported by Portugal could be produced there with less labour than in England."—David Ricardo[131]

Is the American middle class in jeopardy because modern communications technology enables U.S. firms to use workers in India for tasks such as call-center staffing and software development? Pundits appear to be divided on this issue. However, if you look closely, you will see that professional economists, regardless of ideology, all disagree with the claim that the American middle class will be impoverished by trade with India. We remain loyal to the analysis first propounded by David Ricardo, who would spin in his grave if he could see the contrarian views of outsourcing espoused 200 years later by policy wonk Michael Lind[132] or columnist Paul Craig Roberts and Senator Charles Schumer.[133]

What accounts for the persistent belief that trade with poor countries will make us worse off? Perhaps evolutionary psychology might provide the answer. Anthropologist Alan Fiske[134] has pointed out that there are four ways in which humans transact: on the basis of authority; on the basis of communal sharing; on the basis of equality matching; and on the basis of market pricing. In the era of small hunter-gatherer tribes in which our brains evolved, only the first three were needed. Market pricing is required once you start to interact with strangers.

My hypothesis is that people are not "hard-wired" to understand market pricing, so that they often fall back on the models of authority ranking, communal sharing, or equality matching to guide them. Thus, people interpret *trade* with India as if it were *communal sharing* with India. It certainly is true that if we share with India, we will be poorer. However, it is *not* true that trading with India at market prices will lower our well-being.

Is Math the Issue?

In his book *The Blank Slate*, Steven Pinker suggested that market pricing is counterintuitive because it involves mathematical calculations. Indeed, Paul Krugman has written that the gulf between economists and noneconomists is due to math phobia on the part of the latter. In 1994, journalist Michael Lind made the claim that American workers were being set back because of international trade. In response, Krugman wrote,[135]

"The question here is not why Lind got these numbers wrong. It takes considerable experience to know where to look and what to worry about in economic statistics, and one should not expect someone who does not work in the field to be able to get it right without some guidance. The question is, instead, why Mr. Lind felt that it was a good idea to make sweeping pronouncements about this subject, when he clearly was unwilling to invest time and energy in actually understanding it."

Krugman's words seem to have had little effect. In the January-February 2004 issue of the *Atlantic Monthly*, Lind writes,[136]

"*the productivity gains in heavily automated, capital-intensive sectors such as manufacturing, agriculture, banking, and other routine services have gone almost entirely to the investors who own the machines and the software, not to the workers who remain, and certainly not to the workers displaced into other sectors.*"

This is exactly the same pronouncement that Lind made in 1994. If it were true, then we would observe a fall in the share of national income going to labor. However, the labor share remains as stable today as it was when Krugman pointed out that this data refuted Lind's claim ten years ago. Stability of the share of income means that as the economy grows, workers are gaining as much in percentage terms as capitalists.

Krugman's essay implies that if noneconomists cannot be taught the theory of international trade then they should learn to shut up. This may sound harsh, but advising an unqualified pundit to lay off international trade theory is not unlike advising a massage therapist to refrain from attempting open heart surgery.

My sympathy for Krugman's position increased earlier in 2004, when I attended The Real State of the Union,[137] an event sponsored by The New America Foundation (a think thank) and *The Atlantic Monthly*. There, Michael Lind was given an equal spot on a panel with Martin Neil Baily, the former Chairman of the Council of Economic Advisers under President Clinton. Baily is a real economist. His remarks reinforced what I wrote in the chapter called "The Balance of Saving," where I argued that the key to increasing net exports is to increase net national saving. Meanwhile, Lind's comments, such as "we need to create comparative advantage," or "low wages are India's comparative advantage," betray a fundamental misunderstanding of economic concepts.

Ultimately, Krugman despaired of explaining Ricardo to math-phobic non-economists. It is true that in the process of attempting to teach students the Ricardian model of international trade, economic textbooks have settled on using equations and graphs. In spite of this evolution, I think that there is hope for the math-phobics, and the rest of this chapter will attempt to get at the economics of outsourcing without resorting to such devices.

Comparative Advantage

Economists use the term "comparative advantage" to describe Ricardo's analysis of trade. It describes relative productivity, and it is to be distinguished from absolute advantage.

Why do doctors use assistants to type up reports, rather than type them up themselves? Even a doctor who can type faster than a secretary will still use a secretary. The doctor uses the secretary because the doctor's time is more profitably spent practicing medicine than doing typing. Even though the doctor may have an *absolute* advantage over the secretary in typing, the doctor has a much bigger absolute advantage in practicing medicine. Therefore, we say that the doctor has a *comparative advantage* in practicing medicine, and the secretary has a *comparative advantage* in typing.

This example—which makes sense to most people—illustrates why there is no need to "create" comparative advantage. As long as two people have different skill sets, there will be comparative advantage. Even if one person has better skills in all areas, there is a pattern of specialization that is more efficient than simply randomly assigning tasks to each person. In baseball, even if Derek Jeter could play first base better than Jason Giambi, we would still say that Giambi's comparative advantage is playing first base.

Comparative advantage is a characteristic that determines the most efficient way to allocate resources. Comparative advantage would exist even on a commune, with no markets and no wages. If the members of a commune rotate all tasks evenly among themselves, there is still comparative advantage—it's just that such a commune fails to exploit the opportunities for efficiency that would come from specialization.

Equilibrium Conditions

Although we may be able to do away with equations, we cannot do away with what the equations keep track of: equilibrium conditions. An equilibrium condition is a stable situation. In physics, a rock that is lying on the ground can be in equilibrium. A rock that is suspended in midair with nothing holding it up is not in equilibrium. As economist Daniel Davies[138] pointed out in a blog post, the mistakes that can arise from forgetting an equilibrium condition are "fearfully easy to make."

One mistake is to posit an economy in which there are overlooked profit opportunities. For example, it is wrong to assume an economy in which workers are paid less than their marginal product, meaning the worker's contribution to the value of what she produces. Paul Craig Roberts made such a mistake quite explicitly at a recent Brookings event[139] devoted to a discussion of the Schumer-Roberts op-ed piece. Roberts claimed that Indian software workers are paid less than their marginal product.

It violates an equilibrium condition to suppose that Indian software programmers are paid less than the value of what they produce. Such an assumption raises questions of what is being overlooked. Why don't firms hire more programmers, since they are getting more in value than what they are paying? If the reason that firms do not increase their hiring is that all of the qualified programmers are already working, then why do they not demand higher wages? Until wages come in line with productivity, there are unexploited profit opportunities.

General equilibrium does not require that Indian software programmers be paid the same salary as American programmers. However, it *does* require that they be paid the same *per unit of output.* If Indian software programmers have one-fourth the productivity of American developers, then the equilibrium wage for Indian software developers is one-fourth the wage of workers in the United States. General equilibrium analysis would say that low wages in India are not a competitive tool; instead, they are a consequence of the productivity differential.

General equilibrium implies that you can have either low wages with low productivity or high wages with high productivity, but never low wages with high productivity. Thus, the non-economist's fear of low-wage countries is misguided. In the essay quoted above, Krugman writes, "In fact, one never teaches the Ricardian model without emphasizing precisely the way that model refutes the claim that competition from low-wage countries is necessarily a bad thing, that it shows how trade can be mutually beneficial regardless of differences in wage rates."

Other equilibrium conditions are trade balance and full employment. To see why trade balance is an equilibrium condition, imagine a barter economy. In a barter situation, in order to pay for Indian software programmers, we would have to provide goods or services to India in exchange. Thinking in terms of barter helps to clarify the symmetry in trade that is an equilibrium condition.

Because of symmetry, as American software programmers are displaced the demand for labor in export industries increases. Wages go up in those industries, inducing more

Americans to work there. Some of these new workers come from the software industry, and some come from other industries which in turn must hire from the software industry to fill in. The most logical outcome with symmetry and comparative advantage is that American workers shift to where they are relatively more productive, which means that their wages go up.

Full employment is another equilibrium condition. In the long run, wages adjust upward in some sectors and down in others, and workers seek the best opportunities relative to the skills that they have or are able to acquire. In fact, that process plays out over time and gets caught up in issues of macroeconomics, which is beyond where I want to go here. These days, an economist might invoke monetary policy rather than equilibrium as the guarantor of full employment.

When people claim that the overall economy has "lost" jobs because of trade, they are ignoring an equilibrium condition and speaking as if there were no symmetry (or no Federal Reserve). That is a fundamental error—the equivalent of ignoring gravity in physics or evolution in biology.

What is true is that the demand for labor can fall in some easily-identified industries while it increases in other industries in ways that are less visible. Baily is one of a number of economists who advocate programs to ease the plight of workers displaced by trade. I myself tend to find the case for government intervention less persuasive. The way I see it, in a dynamic economy there are plenty of ways that new jobs are created and old jobs are made obsolete. I trust individual initiative more than government programs to deal with those circumstances. Still, at least Baily and I (and Krugman, for that matter) can discuss our ideological differences within a reasonable economic framework. With the noneconomists like Lind or Roberts, you cannot get to policy until you first clean up their conceptual mess.

Violating Equilibrium Conditions

In his *Atlantic* article, Michael Lind's thesis is that unless the government steps in, the middle class will disappear as businesses increase productivity through outsourcing and the use of technology. As he portrays it, today's office workers are going to wind up working cash registers at fast food restaurants.

This sort of downward mobility has been forecast repeatedly by noneconomists over the past several decades, and it has yet to occur. Economists see upward mobility as more likely, because it is extremely difficult to obtain Lind's prediction without violating equilibrium conditions. If wages and productivity are linked, and Indian office workers become as productive as American office workers, then Indian office workers will earn American wages, and everyone will be better off. The only way that Indian office workers can continue to earn less than American office workers is if Indian office workers are less productive than American office workers.

The only way that Indian office workers can displace American office workers without being as productive as American office workers is if there is some other industry in which America's productivity edge over India is even greater. In that case, American labor will tend to shift to that relatively more productive industry. That is more likely to lead to higher wages in America than to lower wages.

I cannot go so far as to claim that it is impossible to construct a theoretical example that satisfies equilibrium conditions in which American workers earn lower wages as a result of globalization. I believe that I could construct such an example, but in order to work it requires a very large difference in wage rates between two types of Indian workers—the average wage differential between India and the United States is not the driver. I also do not think that the example would have any real-world relevance, given actual data.

Moreover, I can state with complete confidence that Michael Lind, Paul Craig Roberts, Senator Charles Schumer, and other math-challenged pundits could never in a million years show how their thinking about trade could be made consistent with equilibrium conditions. Giving such commentators credence in discussions of economic policy is like trusting your open-heart surgery to someone who has never so much as dissected a cat.

Chapter 29

Don't Smoot the Weasels

If there were a Hall of Fame for economic policy blunders, then the Smoot-Hawley tariff of 1930 would get in on the first ballot. The consensus among economists is that this protectionist legislation exacerbated and contributed to the Great Depression[140] that held most of the world's economy in its grip for a decade.

Today, with the stock market having suffered its worst collapse since 1929, unemployment high and rising in much of the world, and deflation considered a risk for the first time since the Second World War, the last thing we need is another setback to international trade. It is in that context that I think we should take a sober assessment of the urge to inflict economic punishment on what Scott Ott[141] dubbed the "axis of weasels"—France, Germany, and Russia. The first instinct of the Bush Administration was to not allow those countries to bid on contracts to help rebuild Iraq.

Rebuilding Iraq

I think that Iraqis ought to choose which foreign suppliers to use in rebuilding the country. That choice should be competitive, based on price and quality considerations. Private-sector companies from France, Germany, and Russia should be allowed to compete for Iraq's business, along with other private-sector companies. Even if we have a quarrel with the governments of the Weasels, it is not productive to take revenge on the private sector.

As more countries develop economic ties with Iraq, this will broaden the base of support for the new regime. I think we would like to see other countries with a stake in a stable, prosperous Iraq.

On the other hand, I see no particular need to give the United Nations as an institution an economic role in Iraq. Trading oil for food, for example, does not require a bureaucratic middleman.

Boycotts?

Obviously, people should be free to choose to buy whatever they want for whatever reason they choose. But I hope that the desire on the part of Americans to boycott products from the Weasel countries, and vice-versa, will prove to be short-lived. An economic boycott is the opposite of a JDAM—it causes maximum collateral damage while having little or no impact on the target.

Among the casualties in a boycott of French wine, for example, would be Americans in the import business as well as privately-run French wineries whose owners may have supported our war effort, for all we know. Again, I think that if our quarrel is with the government, we ought not to punish the private sector.

Free Trade Now

What I would like to see the Bush Administration try in the wake of its military success in Iraq is a reverse of Smoot-Hawley. That is, we should undertake a unilateral reduction in tariffs, farm subsidies, and other trade barriers. This would include eliminating the steel tariffs for the Weasel countries and others. The Bush Administration's steel tariffs might not make it to the Hall of Fame, but they were a recession-exacerbating blunder in the tradition of Smoot-Hawley.

After the war in Iraq, the rest of the world views the United States as being extremely powerful, and they are wary of what we will do next. If our next big foreign policy gesture were a dramatic reduction in our trade barriers, this would send a positive message about our values and our role in the world.

It is odd that in international trade we have come to believe that reductions in trade barriers have to come from mutual "agreements." This is not the case. Getting rid of trade barriers unilaterally will make our economy more productive and our consumers better off, regardless of what other nations do.

One of the silliest government positions ever created was that of "Chief Trade Negotiator." There is no need to negotiate—we can do our part for free trade now. The whole concept of trade negotiation is absurd. It is like saying to your spouse, "I'll change my underwear regularly, but only if you'll agree to brush your teeth." We should eliminate our harmful trade barriers, not keep them in place just to have "negotiating leverage."

America's security is enhanced by a strong economy. One way to ensure a strong economy is to open up trade, even if that benefits the Weasels.

Chapter 30

Please Outsource to My Daughter

"Many of us have our shirts laundered at professional cleaners rather than wash and iron them ourselves. Anyone who advised us to "protect" ourselves from the "unfair competition" of low-paid laundry workers by doing our own wash would be thought loony."—Alan Blinder[142]

Phyllis Schlafly is loony.[143] And, as Glenn Reynolds pointed out,[144] she is not alone. The phenomenon of using the Internet to outsource white-collar work has created the latest fad in economic terrors—fear that the United States is about to be run over by that economic juggernaut: India.

As Alan Blinder's observation reminds us, outsourcing is the basis of all economic activity. Every time we trade in the market instead of doing something ourselves, we are outsourcing.

In fact, a good way to attain clarity in discussing the issue of outsourcing is to substitute the phrase "economic activity" for outsourcing:

- There sure has been an increase in *economic activity* with India lately.
- Aren't you afraid that you could lose your job to *economic activity*?

- The Congressman has introduced a bill that he promises will stop *economic activity*.

To put a human face on outsourcing, consider my oldest daughter, Rachel. After she finished her sophomore year in college, in the summer of 2003, she worked for a temporary agency. A medical testing firm outsourced some of its data entry work to the agency, which in turn outsourced some of it to Rachel.

Is Rachel's job vulnerable? Absolutely. No doubt, my friend Prashant[145] would be happy to talk the medical testing firm into using his company[146] instead. The data entry would then be done in India.

Am I concerned? No. Because outsourcing is symmetric. For every job that we outsource to India, India outsources a job to us. That giant sucking sound you hear is jobs being created in the U.S. to meet the needs of Indian consumers. That is guaranteed to happen. The Indians are not just going to smoke the dollars that they get when they are paid by U.S. firms. They are going to spend those dollars, and that spending ultimately will create jobs.

The process is likely to be very convoluted. Maybe the Indian workers will outsource the production of yogurt. The yogurt producers may outsource the production of milk to Australia. The Australians may want beer, which they outsource to Germany. The Germans want drug research, which they outsource to the United States,[147] because we still allow drug companies to profit from research (see chapter on "Quack Economic Prescription"). With low interest rates, thanks to the fact that all of our trading partners want crateloads of U.S. Treasury securities (see chapter on "The Dollar Bubble and the Bond Bubble"), one of our drug companies can finance a new research facility. To build it, the construction company may hire workers who are new immigrants. The new immigrants might want schools where their children can learn to read English. These schools might outsource some of their teaching to Rachel. (Just kidding. The teachers' union will not allow economic activity. And they do not seem to care much for teaching English to immigrants, either. But you get the idea.)

Rachel would much rather work with children than do data entry. I am confident that with enough outsourcing, she will be able to get a better job.

Will Rachel's wage go down because her data entry job is outsourced to India? No. Rachel's wage will depend on her own skills. Presumably, one of the benefits that she will obtain from college is that she will find a career that is more lucrative than a job doing data entry. However, my guess is that there will be times in her life when she needs to change fields or obtain new skills. In a world of Progress and Displacement (see chapter on "Progress and Displacement"), you cannot stand still.

Someone who commented on Glenn Reynolds' article under the pseudonym "Unemployed MBA" clearly is not comfortable with progress and displacement. Maybe he went to a business school where they teach you that having an MBA automatically entitles you to a job with a big salary, and if you do not get it you should blame outsourcing. Unfortunately, business schools rarely teach their students to be entrepreneurial and opportunistic.

When I worked in a big company, I always tried to find somebody who could replace me. I figured that the sooner I could outsource my job, the sooner I could make a move. If I could not move up the ladder, I could at least move sideways and broaden my skill set. So I hired people with an eye toward having them take over my job. That meant that they had to be willing to do whatever work I needed, to be inquisitive, and to learn—all of which tended to rule out MBA's.

Don't waste time calling yourself an unemployed MBA, or an unemployed webmaster, or an unemployed data entry clerk. Instead, position yourself to take the jobs that India inevitably will outsource to us. The best way to get those jobs is to be willing to do whatever work is needed, to be inquisitive, and to learn. That is my advice to Rachel. Assuming she takes it, the jobs that get outsourced to her will be good ones.

CHAPTER 31

MANUFACTURING A CRISIS

"30 years from now, instead of growing a tree, cutting down the tree and building this wooden table, we would be able to just place some DNA in some living cells, and grow the table."—Rodney Brooks[148]

"I want you to understand that I understand that Ohio manufacturers are hurting, that there's a problem with the manufacturing sector. And I understand for a full recovery, to make sure people can find work, that manufacturing must do better. And we've lost thousands of jobs in manufacturing... So I told Secretary Don Evans of the Commerce Department, I want him to appoint an assistant secretary to focus on the needs of manufacturers, to make sure our manufacturing job base is strong and vibrant. In other words, any part of a good recovery for the state of Ohio and other manufacturing states has got to be for the manufacturing sector to come around."—President George W. Bush[149]

As the 2004 election season got underway, apparently the first order of business was to solve the manufacturing crisis. Or to manufacture a crisis for government to solve.

With the announcement above, President Bush appointed one bureaucrat to deal with the manufacturing crisis. Perhaps eventually we will have an entire department—like the Department of Agriculture—doling out subsidies to an ever-shrinking population that claims to be of the manufacturing sector.

The proportion of the work force employed in manufacturing has been declining for decades. Below is a table showing total employment and production workers in manufacturing. The source is the Bureau of Labor Statistics.[150]

Year	Total Nonfarm Employment	Manufacturing Production Workers	Percent of Workforce
1952	48.9 million	12.8 million	26%
1962	55.7 million	12.0 million	22%
1972	73.8 million	13.5 million	18%
1982	89.7 million	12.3 million	14%
1992	108.7 million	12.0 million	11%
2002	130.4 million	10.8 million	8%

What is happening to manufacturing is the same thing that happened to agriculture during the industrial revolution. From 1850 to 1950, resources were released from the agricultural sector to meet new consumer needs—for transportation, appliances to increase the comfort and reduce the work of the household, and electronic entertainment.

In any given sector, when productivity increases faster than demand, employment declines and workers move into other fields. That is what has been happening in manufacturing. As Bruce Bartlett[151] and others have pointed out, manufacturing *output* remains high. However, we can produce the same output with less input, and the workers not needed in manufacturing are going into other sectors, primarily services, where demand is increasing more rapidly than productivity.

What About China?

With the political season upon us, you will hear that we are losing manufacturing jobs to China. The new Commerce bureaucrat will be tasked with looking into this. I wonder how the assistant secretary will decide what is the "correct" number of manufacturing jobs that belongs in the United States. I wonder how he or she will decide which of those jobs China ought to give back. It used to be that China had central planners who would do that sort of analysis. But they did away with central planning in their manufacturing export sector, and that is what enabled them to begin to compete. I doubt that we have anything to gain by turning to central planning—or to any form of government management of trade.

When other countries, including China, try to manipulate trade, they mostly hurt themselves. We should not follow suit.

In the long run, the right number of manufacturing production workers in the U.S. economy could approach zero. If in our lifetimes we witness the disappearance of Dickensian factory labor, would that be such a horrible thing? If my daughters never get to operate a rivet machine or stuff containers with fiberglass, as I did for two summers, will they grow up deprived?

David N. Thompson and Gregory K. Ottosen, of Crossroads Research,[152] have written a book called *The Real New Economy*. They describe the world as consisting of developed countries, cheap-labor competitors (like China), and non-modernizers. They point out that countries like Japan and South Korea have made the transition from cheap-labor competitors to developed countries. They now have to compete, as we do, by coming up with innovative products. Eventually, the authors argue, China's income will rise until it, too, will have to compete on the basis of brainpower.

Thompson and Ottosen believe that as China passes through the cheap-labor competitor phase, the countries that today are non-modernizers will become cheap-labor competitors. When they in turn pass through that phase, some time before the end of this century, we may face a shortage of unskilled labor, so that wages of unskilled workers could rise.

Robotic Nation?

Or maybe unskilled labor will not be scarce later in this century. I doubt that unskilled labor would be scarce in the world envisioned by Rodney Brooks, in which we have the ability to manipulate DNA well enough to grow a table.

In an essay that is based on solid technological analysis but weak economics, Marshall Brain wrote,[153]

"There will be huge job losses by 2040 or 2050 as robots move into the workplace. For example:

- *Nearly every construction job will go to a robot. That's about 6 million jobs lost.*
- *Nearly every manufacturing job will go to a robot. That's 16 million jobs lost.*
- *Nearly every transportation job will go to a robot. That's 3 million jobs lost.*
- *Many wholesale and retail jobs will go to robots. That's at least 15 million lost jobs.*
- *Nearly every hotel and restaurant job will go to a robot. That's 10 million jobs lost.*

If you add that all up, it's over 50 million jobs lost to robots. That is a conservative estimate. By 2050 or so, it is very likely that over half the jobs in the United States will be held by robots. All the people who are holding jobs like those today will be unemployed."

The last sentence is what reveals Marshall Brain's economic ignorance. As James Miller[154] pointed out, the existence of robots is not inconsistent with full employment of humans. On the contrary, it means that we will enjoy high levels of well-being while having jobs that are much less unpleasant to perform.

Bound to Fail

We are in a very effervescent economy. The rate at which skills become obsolete is already mind-boggling. (Just think of how many computer operating systems you have learned to work with.) Going forward, however, the pace of change will accelerate further. The need for skill refreshment will affect a broader spectrum of the work force.

In this dynamic environment, the new Commerce Assistant Secretary in charge of trying to keep production workers on the assembly line is bound to fail. I just hope that he or she does not try too hard.

Chapter 32

The Language Barrier

"There's been a lot of bad news out there in the world economy lately. Supposed economic superpowers like Germany and Japan have fallen on hard times; Asian tigers that thought the future belonged to them suddenly find that it belongs instead to Westerners with ready cash; Latin Americans who thought they had put their past behind them are watching with horror as financial crisis strikes once again. And yet there are also some surprisingly happy economic stories out there. What do they have in common?

... Yes, the common denominator of the countries that have done best in this age of dashed expectations is that they are the countries where English is spoken."—Paul Krugman, That Certain *"Je Ne Sais Quoi"* Of Les Anglophones[155]

Although Krugman's wonderfully-titled essay was written in 1999 and referred to the 1990's, the economic importance of English is likely to increase in the next decade. In the future, the digital divide could turn out to be the language barrier.

In "The View from 2003,"[156] Brad DeLong speculates on the causes and consequences of economic change. An important factor is that the Internet makes possible trade in information-based services, such as software and education. Looking ahead twenty years, DeLong writes, "International trade in white-color jobs is growing as competitive as trade in blue-collar jobs."

If DeLong is correct, then the participants in this new international trade are going to be people who speak English. We already see this with many businesses outsourcing call centers, document transcription services, and data entry to English-speaking workers in India and the Philippines.

The Poor Indian Vs. the Rich Frenchman

In 2003, I had a serendipitous opportunity[157] to hear Nobel laureate Michael Spence give a talk on the Internet and productivity. He, too, argued that the Internet will promote worldwide trade in white-collar work. During the question-and-answer period, I posed the following question:

Take a 15-year old growing up poor in India but learning English. Then consider a relatively wealthy 15-year old growing up in France but learning French. Which one is likely to be better off in 20 years?

My thinking was that over the next twenty years, the Indian who knows English will have an advantage. Spence said that he felt better about predicting that a Chinese would overtake a Frenchman, because China has better infrastructure than India. (This view is shared by Indians.)[158] However, Spence agreed with the thrust of the question.

The Internet is facilitating rapid spread of knowledge and high-speed communication. As Spence pointed out, the global communication network is replacing local mass markets and vertically-integrated firms with international targeted markets and complex, external supply chains. For these purposes, the dominant language, particularly for cross-border Internet activities, is English.

Joel Mokyr, in *The Gifts of Athena*,[159] points out how important the spread of knowledge was for the Industrial

Revolution. He emphasizes the importance of what he calls the Industrial Enlightenment for opening communication between scientists and entrepreneurs.

Nick Schultz, in an essay on Mokyr,[160] pointed out that "entrenched interests" oppose knowledge-driven progress in many ways. Schultz mentioned many conflicts between traditionalism and economic growth, but he may have omitted one of the most important: language. In the era of the English-dominant Internet, to speak another language is to impose a barrier on the fastest-growing component of international trade.

On a visit to Israel in 2002, I happened to run across Sheizaf Rafaeli,[161] Director of the Center for the Study of the Information Society at the University of Haifa. He pointed out that 50 years ago, there were strong arguments—even fisticuffs—over whether to teach high-level technical courses in English or in Hebrew. The proponents of Hebrew won, perhaps to the benefit of Israeli culture but surely to the detriment of its economy. Today, Israelis who develop web sites can either develop for a small audience in their native language or face the necessity of maintaining their web presence in English.

A Dissent from Negroponte

Nicholas Negroponte, of the MIT Media Lab, vehemently disagrees[162] with the thesis that non-English speakers will find themselves on the wrong end of the digital divide. He says, "The content side will not be dominantly English. It unquestionably ten years from now will be Chinese. But more importantly, between language translation and all sorts of things, we're going to see again, a real rise in multilingual systems and of course multilingual, in my opinion, it's not a 100 percent synonymous, but certainly leads to multicultural."

LEARNING ECONOMICS

Negroponte believes that with computer-mediated communication, I can converse in English with someone speaking Japanese. This sounds nice in theory, but in practice the challenges of speech recognition and language translation appear to be too great for the next several years.

For now, the Internet revolution is boosting the economic prospects of the English speakers of the world. This includes the countries where English is the native language, as well as the people in other countries who happen to be educated in English. People who never learn English may be destined to spend their lives on the wrong side of the language barrier.

Chapter 33

Oil Econ 101

My instinct is to oppose any policy initiative that is touted to fight child pornography or the drug menace. It's not that I'm in favor of child porn or drug abuse. However, I am conditioned by experience to expect proposals supposedly aimed at those problems to turn out to be ineffectual while threatening damage to the Internet and/or the Constitution.

But the worst refuge of scoundrels, in my opinion, is the line that "we need to reduce our dependence on foreign oil in order to fight terrorism." When I hear that, my baloney-sandwich detector really starts vibrating. I am ready to reject whatever is on offer, whether it be oil drilling in Alaska, regulations on SUV's, or some new synthetic fuels program.

Oil Is Oil

I teach economics in high school. Here is a good question for an introductory course:

If the United States currently satisfies 10 percent of its demand for oil with imports from Saudi Arabia, by what percentage must the U.S. reduce its consumption in order to be 100 percent independent of Saudi oil?

If you answer "10 percent," you get an F. If we reduce oil consumption by 10 percent, then we will not cut 100 percent of our imports from Saudi Arabia. We cannot arrange to consume only American oil and no Saudi oil. Oil is oil. If we reduce demand by 10 percent, we probably will reduce our demand for Saudi oil by 10 percent, not by 100 percent. (Actually, oil is not exactly the same everywhere. Saudi oil is somewhat cheaper to extract and refine than other oil. What this means is that if we reduce our demand for oil, the impact is likely to be felt somewhat more on other oil, and somewhat less on Saudi oil. Lowering our demand by 10 percent might not lower Saudi oil exports much at all. But we can leave that aside for now. Just keep in mind that oil is oil.)

But what if we passed a law against importing Saudi oil? In that case, the Saudis would export their oil to us via Venezuela. They might not physically use this channel, but if the Venezuelans sell more oil to the U.S. and the Saudis sell more to other customers no longer served by Venezuelans, it has the same effect.

I have received emails suggesting that I should switch brands of gasoline to a company that supposedly does not use Saudi oil. But if we all did that, then the brand that we switched to would run out of non-Saudi oil and have to start using Saudi oil.

The correct answer to the question of how much the United States would have to reduce oil consumption in order to drive our demand for Saudi oil to zero is 100 percent. Only if we stop using oil altogether can we be sure that we are not contributing to the demand for Saudi oil. Oil is oil, so that any demand for oil creates demand for Saudi oil.

Once we recognize that oil is oil, it should be apparent how futile it is to try to reduce Saudi oil revenues by cutting back on our demand. True, if we reduce demand, then total world demand falls, and oil prices and revenues fall, but unless we take truly Draconian steps the effects are likely to be small.

How to Reduce Oil Consumption

I personally do not care much for SUV's, but the way I express my dislike for them is the same way that I express my dislike for cable television. I don't purchase those products. (One could argue that the fact that other people buy SUV's causes me some harm. For that matter, one could make the same argument about cable television. However, those effects are small, below what I would regard as the threshold that might justify regulation.)

As an economist, even if you told me that the policy objective is to reduce oil consumption, I would not opt for regulating the fuel economy of SUV's as my first choice. I would prefer a large gasoline tax (preferable phased in to give people time to adjust). This would give people a clear incentive to conserve, while allowing them to find the most efficient means to do so.

In contrast, regulating fuel economy of SUV's is inefficient. Old SUV's would be exempt from regulation, and they would tend to stay in the market longer. And new fuel-efficient SUV's would cost less per mile to drive at the margin, leading to more miles driven, which would cancel out some or all of the effect on gasoline consumption.

Of course, this still begs the question of why we should be reducing oil consumption below the natural level incented by the cost of oil in the market. One can argue that lower oil consumption would lead to lower pollution, but if fighting pollution is the objective then it is more efficient to tax or regulate pollution than to regulate fuel economy. From a pollution-fighting standpoint, it would be better to have a low-pollution car that gets 15 miles to the gallon than a high-pollution car that gets 40 miles to the gallon.

Just Take the Oil

The issue that leads people to suggest that we need to "reduce our dependence on foreign oil" is the apparent role of Saudi Arabia in funding terrorism. Someone who I love dearly but is a bit naive once said to me, "We've got a powerful army. The Saudis don't have bupkis. We should just take the oil!"

She is naive, because she is not sensitive to the issue of imperialism and world public opinion. To wage a war for oil would be to offend the sensibilities of large numbers of decent, well-educated people.

However, if Saudi funding for terrorism is the crux of the issue, then we have little choice but to confront the Saudis directly. The indirect approach of reducing oil demand is meaningless. Only a worldwide boycott of Saudi oil would effectively cut off their oil revenues. Yet such a boycott would be difficult to orchestrate and would itself be tantamount to war.

The problem with sponsoring terrorism is not that oil revenues are the source of funds. The problem with sponsoring terrorism is that it is grossly immoral. People introduce the connection with oil revenues as a red herring. As we have seen, trying to make a connection between fighting terrorism and regulating SUV's or drilling for Alaskan oil is a violation of Oil Econ 101. At best, it is a way to dodge the challenge posed by apparent Saudi support for terror. At worst, it is an attempt to advance another agenda using terrorism as an excuse.

The real issue is the alleged Saudi funding of terror. No matter how much demand we withdraw from the oil market, the Saudis will have revenue and we have to be concerned with how they use it.

If cutting off funding is critical to winning the war on terror, then we must press the Saudis on that point. We should tell them that we respect their rights as a sovereign nation, but they owe it to the community of nations to not fund terrorists. If that approach does not work, then it is a waste of time to wring our hands over our "dependence on foreign oil." The only fallback position is the one suggested by my wife: just take the oil.

Chapter 34

The Balance of Saving

"Isn't it just a little twisted that the United States, the world's richest country, is on track to borrow more than $500 billion from abroad this year? Isn't it even stranger that this borrowing includes sizable chunks from countries such as India and China, many of whose 2.3 billion people live on less than a dollar or two a day?"—Ken Rogoff[163]

On the subject of the trade balance, politicians and economists do not think alike. As a result, the political solutions to the trade deficit are almost always bad economics.

Politicians think of our trade deficit (the excess of imports over exports, which has reached $500 billion a year or about 4 percent of GDP) as evidence that we have lost a "trade war." They blame enemy tactics, such as low wages, tariffs, or unfair trade rules.

Economists, such as the International Monetary Fund's former chief economist Ken Rogoff, view the trade balance as determined by an equation involving aggregate saving:

Private Saving Plus Government Saving Equals Trade Surplus

Government saving is negative whenever the government runs a Budget deficit, which is typical. Only if private saving is greater than the Budget deficit can a country run a trade surplus. If the Budget deficit soaks up more than the savings provided by domestic sources, then a country must borrow from abroad. When it borrows from abroad, it runs a trade deficit.

One way to see this is to think in terms of currency flows. When we buy goods from, say, China, the Chinese obtain dollars. Those dollars will be used either to buy U.S. securities or U.S. goods and services. When the dollars are used to buy U.S. securities rather than goods and services, we run a trade deficit. Our trade deficit with China reflects the fact that they buy more of our securities than we buy of theirs. It reflects a balance of saving in which China is a creditor and we are a debtor. As Rogoff puts it,

"We save less of our income than any other rich economy. China's citizens save more than 40 percent of their income; the United States would be lucky if its citizens ever decided to save at half that rate. No matter how rich you are, if you continually spend more than you earn, you are eventually going to run into problems."

Think National Saving

By focusing on the balance of saving, economists come up with a completely different set of policy prescriptions than the ones that are popular with politicians. Increasing exports relative to imports is not a matter of beating up on China to live up to its commitments in the World Trade Organization. It is not a matter of prohibiting U.S. firms from outsourcing to India. It is a matter of increasing national saving.

One way to increase national saving is to reduce the government Budget deficit. This may be a low priority while the economy is weak and in need of stimulus, but it will become a high priority as the economy returns to full employment. Some combination of spending cuts and tax increases will be needed during the next Presidential term.

Reduced government borrowing is only part of the

solution. We also need higher private saving. Private saving consists of personal saving and corporate saving. In these areas, it is the obsession with "progressive" tax policies that stands in the way.

Compared with other major industrial countries, we have lower sales tax rates and higher corporate income tax rates. Thus, our mix of taxes punishes private saving more and consumption less than the mix of taxes in other countries. It could well be that this tax mix is the biggest reason that the United States is a debtor nation, with massive trade deficits. If we could stop thinking of taxes on consumption as taxes on "the poor" and taxes on capital income as taxes on "the rich," we could create a tax system with incentives to become the supplier of capital to the rest of the world that Rogoff argues is our proper role. Moreover, the details of the WTO and other microeconomic policies would not matter. If our savings rate were higher, the United States would run a trade surplus, regardless of whether other countries use tactics that are "fair" or not.

The Economists' Solution

The trade deficit is political dynamite. Any moment, demagogues from either party could blow up the world trading system by enacting trade barriers, perhaps causing other countries to "retaliate." (Economists, who think of a trade barrier as a nation shooting itself in the foot, are reluctant to adopt the term "retaliation" to describe responding in kind when another nation punishes itself.)

The economists' optimal solution to the U.S. trade deficit is to try to take the best and reject the worst ideas from supply-side economics. We should try to increase both private saving and government saving.

The best idea from supply-side economics is to use tax policy to encourage work and thrift rather than as a tool to redistribute income. We should change the mix of taxes to favor saving rather than consumption. That would increase private saving.

The worst idea from supply-side economics is to cut taxes without cutting government spending. This increases government deficits, reduces national saving, and increases the trade deficit. If tax revenues are going to be reduced by lowering some tax rates, then either other tax rates must be increased or government spending must be restrained. Otherwise, supply-side economics is just a cover for government deficits, making it the problem rather than the solution for the trade deficit.

PART 5

Macroeconomics and Bubbles

INTRODUCTION

Macroeconomics studies the causes of fluctuations in broad economic phenomena. The most important of these are unemployment and inflation. Inflation is a general rise in the prices of all goods, or a relative decline in the value of currency.

The previous chapter, "The Balance of Saving," illustrates the view held by most economists that the balance of trade is a macroeconomic variable. We see the trade balance as depending on economy-wide relationships between saving and investment rather than on the competitiveness of individual industries.

Macroeconomic theories were developed in response to puzzling episodes in economic history. The most important of these was the Great Depression of the 1930's, which in the United States produced unemployment rates over 10 percent for nearly a decade, with a peak unemployment rate of over 25 percent of the labor force. It was a time of great poverty and misery, even though we clearly had the productive capacity to achieve affluence.

If you are looking for ironclad theoretical reasoning backed by overwhelming empirical evidence, then stay away from macroeconomics. If you make a thorough study of the field, you will find competing doctrines and dogmas, imprecise data, and the inability to conduct repeatable experiments.

To see why macroeconomics is difficult, consider the argument made near the very beginning of this book against the likelihood of a persistent labor shortage. In that section, I pointed out that it would be natural for wages to adjust upward, leading to an increase in labor supply and a reduction in labor demand, which would eliminate the shortage.

This same argument holds in reverse. When there is unemployment, meaning an excess supply of labor, a drop in wages should reduce supply and increase demand, eliminating the unemployment. Many macroeconomists, from John Maynard Keynes to Milton Friedman, believe that this process of downward adjustment of wages works slowly and painfully. If instead the level of demand for output can be maintained so that there is less need for downward wage adjustment, the economy will have an easier time remaining at full employment.

Why does aggregate demand sometimes fall short of the level needed to maintain full employment? My beliefs about this issue are influenced to an unusual degree by Charles Kindleberger, who was not considered a macroeconomist.

Kindleberger was an economic historian, who wrote extensively on the Depression and on historical episodes of speculative frenzy. He noted that these episodes, such as the Dutch Tulip Mania in the 1620's and 1630's or the South Sea Bubble in England in roughly 1710-1720, had common elements. A country achieved wealth as a result of the combination of winning a war and encountering a new market opportunity. Kindleberger called this process "displacement." Displacement resulted in early speculators achieving riches, leading masses of people to join in, resulting in overspeculation. This was followed by a panic, a crash, and an economic recession. This model of fluctuations was laid out by Kindleberger in his book *Manias, Panics, and Crashes*.

Several of the essays in this book apply the Kindleberger model to the Internet Bubble and the subsequent recession. I wrote these essays as events were unfolding. In July of 1999, the Nasdaq composite index, which measures stock prices in a technology-heavy segment of the stock market, was around 2640, and the unemployment rate in the United States was down to 4.3 percent. At that time, I wrote "Arithmetic in a Bubble," in which I argued that the prices of Internet stocks were too high to be sustainable.

By January of 2000, the Nasdaq had climbed further, to 3940, and the unemployment rate had improved to 4.0 percent. I wrote "Briefing the President," in which I suggested that at some point stock prices could plummet, triggering a recession.

The Nasdaq's highest month-end close was in February of 2000, when it reached 4700. In March, it began to fall, reaching a bottom of 1172 in September of 2002. In December of 2000, with the Nasdaq already down to 2471 but the unemployment rate still low at 3.9 percent, I said in "Some Keynes for President Bush" that a large fiscal stimulus would be needed to boost the economy.

In August of 2003, with the Nasdaq at 1810 and the unemployment rate at 6.1 percent, I assessed the state of the economy, in "Labor Force Capacity Utilization." I argued that the recession had been long and deep.

In September of 2003, with the Nasdaq at 1787 and the unemployment rate at 6.1 percent, I assessed economic policy in "The President's Macroeconomic Report Card." While policy had not been perfect, it had been more constructive than I would have expected.

How did I know that the boom in Internet stocks was a bubble? I got involved with the commercialization of the Internet very early, in 1994. I saw its resemblance to the Kindleberger model as early as August of 1995, when Netscape Communications became the first Internet company to sell stock to the general public. The response to Netscape's initial public offering was overwhelming, and this paved the way for many other "dotcoms" to turn their founders into millionaires, even though almost none of the businesses made profits.

Most of the articles in this section are about the Internet Bubble and its aftermath. I believe that the stock market crash of 2000-2001 created conditions that were conducive to another Great Depression. However, several factors cushioned the fall.

1. In contrast with 1929-1933, the Federal Reserve made a conscious effort to avoid a monetary contraction and thus avoided deflation.
2. The Bush Administration's populist economic policies, which expanded the government budget deficit beyond what would have taken place naturally with the recession, represented in the short run—and I should emphasize *only* in the short run—a textbook application of Keynesian fiscal stimulus.
3. Compared with the 1930's, there were fewer impediments to the necessary labor market adjustments. There was no rise in unionism and no attempt by the government to encourage business cartels to keep prices artificially high.

As you read the sections in this chapter, I would caution you not to become too attached to the theories and explanations that you find. Given all of the controversy that exists within the profession about macroeconomics, any one economist's views should be taken with a grain of salt. Moreover, as the economy evolves over time, a macroeconomic model that is accurate for one era may prove erroneous in another. This chapter can by no means provide a definitive account of macroeconomics.

CHAPTER 35

ARITHMETIC IN A BUBBLE

(Written in July 1999) My favorite Internet IPO went off this week.

The concept of www.musicmaker.com is one to which I can relate instantly. Ever since I was a teenager, I have "produced" recordings by making tapes of albums, so that I could mix artists and listen to selected songs. From the tapes that sequenced Jefferson Airplane and Blind Faith to those that included Melissa Ethridge and REM, I have enjoyed making my own favorite blends.

The idea of musicmaker is to let you do that on the Internet. I have not used the service yet, because at the moment their catalog is not as good as mine. I mean, sure, they have licensed more records than I have. But I have more of the records that I want than they do. For example, they have none of the four artists listed in the previous paragraph.

But the concept is not what makes musicmaker my favorite IPO. What makes it my favorite IPO is the price/revenue ratio.

Last year, musicmaker had $75,000 in revenue. That is thousands, not millions. And that is revenue, not profits. They took in enough in sales to pay a secretary with benefits, and now they have gone public. Successfully.

After the IPO, the market capitalization of musicmaker was over $700 million. Dividing this by their revenue gives a price/revenue ratio of nearly 10,000.

Yahoo has a price of about $170 per share and sales of about $1.12 per share, for a price/revenue ratio of only 150.

I am told that investment bankers tend to value Internet companies before they go public at 10 times revenue. They are assuming that they can get more than that when they take the companies public.

If a company had a profit margin of 4 percent, then by definition its earnings would be 4 percent of revenues. If it were expected to grow at the same rate as the economy as a whole, it might have a price/earnings ratio of 25. In that case, its price/revenue ratio would be its price earnings ratio times its profit margin, or 1.

Based on the preceding paragraph, it would seem that 1.0 is a reasonable approximation of a "steady state" price/revenue ratio. By "steady state" I mean the conditions that will prevail once the Internet economy has matured to the point where it grows no faster than the economy as a whole.

Yahoo's current market valuation is about $35 billion. If the steady-state price/revenue ratio is 1.0, then for Yahoo to achieve that ratio means that revenues would be $35 billion. If its revenues were to double every six months, then starting from the latest annual sales of $260 million and holding its stock price constant, it would take well over three years to reach that point.

Yahoo's revenue per page view consistently has been 4/10 of one cent. They have benefited from an increasing interest in e-commerce on the part of advertisers. On the other hand, they have been hurt by a phenomenon that I believe was first noted by Jakob Nielsen: click-through rates (the consumer response rate to the common form of Internet advertising, which in turn determines the value that sponsors place on such advertising) fall by 50 percent a year. If it takes Yahoo 250 page views to get $1 in revenues, then to reach $35 billion in revenues will require 8.75 trillion page views per year, or about 24 billion page views per day. If the world

LEARNING ECONOMICS

population is 6 billion, then on average everyone in the world, regardless of age, language, or access to the Internet, will have to view 4 pages on Yahoo per day.

Another statistical law found by Nielsen is that relative to Yahoo (which is the number one Web site), the page views of other web sites follow a zeta distribution. That is, the number two site gets half of Yahoo's page views, the number three gets one third of Yahoo's page views, etc. Using page views and site rankings for homefair.com, I have found this approximation to be accurate.

Yahoo has a total market value of $35 billion. Assuming that the stock market values Yahoo correctly and that the value of web sites is proportional to page views, then the second most popular Web site would be worth $17.5 billion. To be worth $1 billion, a site would have to rank in the top 35. It should be difficult for any site that is not in the top 100 to go public.

However, this has not proven to be the case. For example, DrKoop.com, which in terms of traffic probably is not even in the top 5000 web sites, has a market cap of over $900 million.

Note: Since this article was first published, musicmaker.com and DrKoop.com stock collapsed. Yahoo's stock valuation also is down considerably from July of 1999.

Chapter 36

Briefing the President

(Written in January 2000) A nonprofit organization called the Internet Policy Institute was formed in 1999 (as of 2003, it was defunct). Its main project was called "Briefing the President," which was described on its web site as "a series of policy memoranda designed to identify and explore the fundamental issues that will affect the development and use of the Internet."

In my opinion, there is one policy issue that is likely to overshadow all others that the Internet might pose for the next President. The issue will be how to ameliorate a long, deep economic slump that results from a collapse of the Internet bubble.

Here are my opinions concerning the probabilities of various events:

- The probability of a stock market crash over the next four years, in which at least 25 percent of all stock market wealth is wiped out, is 90 percent.
- If such a crash occurs, the probability of a serious economic slump is 80 percent.
- Given an economic crisis, the probability that the President's economic advisers will know what to do about it is not better than 50 percent.
- Given that they know what to do about a crisis, the probability that their advice will be followed is less than 25 percent.

LEARNING ECONOMICS

People who know me are aware that I am pessimistic by nature. These probabilities must sound extremely gloomy. However, let me try to make the case that they are reasonable, and perhaps optimistic.

First, consider the stock market. In the January 12, 2000, edition of the *Washington Post*, op-ed columnist Robert J. Samuelson cited estimates that the aggregate price-earnings ratio of the Nasdaq was about 200 as of the end of 1999. I have not confirmed this estimate, and if it happens to be very far off then the rest of this essay will have to be discounted accordingly. However, it comes from a reasonable source, Brian Rauscher of Morgan Stanley Dean Witter.

Let us place an aggregate price-earnings ratio of 200 in perspective.

In 1999, James Glassman and Kevin Hassett published a book called *Dow 36,000*, which purported to justify a higher market price-earnings ratio than has been observed in the past. They claim that investors no longer are demanding the high risk premium that in the past held down the price-earnings ratio. They argued that the price-earnings ratio should be 100. Since the Dow was at 9000 at a price earnings ratio of 25, they concluded that the Dow should be at 36,000. However, they only could justify a price-earnings ratio of 100. Using their logic, the Nasdaq needs to fall 50 percent to be valued correctly.

Most economists believe that Glassman and Hassett commit fundamental errors of arithmetic and accounting. Even if we assume that investors in stocks require no risk premium, economists would argue that the market price-earnings ratio ought to be the inverse of the real interest rate (the interest rate after inflation is subtracted). Today, the interest rate on the Treasury's inflation-indexed bonds is about 4 percent. That means that the risk-neutral price-earnings ratio ought to be 25 for the market as a whole. For stocks whose earnings are going to grow faster than the economy, the p-e ratio can be higher. For stocks whose earnings are going to grow more slowly than the economy, the p-e ratio ought to be lower. If 25 is the right p-e ratio for the Nasdaq, then the Nasdaq needs to fall 87.5 percent to be valued correctly.

Until 1996, the average price-earnings ratio for the stock market was about 14. If that is the appropriate ratio for the Nasdaq, then it needs to fall 93 percent to be valued correctly.

In conclusion, an 85 percent drop in the value of the Nasdaq seems entirely plausible. How would this drop in paper wealth affect the real economy?

According to estimates given in Samuelson's column, the market value of the Nasdaq was $5.2 trillion, out of a total market value of $15.8 trillion for all stocks. Thus, an 85 percent drop in the value of the Nasdaq would reduce stock market wealth by about $4.4 trillion, or over 25 percent of all stock market wealth.

The economic links between stock market wealth and economic performance are somewhat tenuous empirically. We have two important historical examples in which major market meltdowns were followed by slumps—the 1930's in the United States and the 1990's in Japan. However, this does not prove that stock market crashes cause depressions.

There are a number of plausible linkages between wealth and economic activity. Moreover, because stock market wealth today is so high (it is much higher relative to the size of the economy than it was in 1929), even if these linkages are weak, the overall effect could be devastating.

Overall GDP in current dollars is running at a $9.3 trillion annual rate. About two-thirds of this is personal consumption expenditures. Estimates are that consumers spend between 1 and 5 percent of wealth each year. Therefore, a drop in wealth of $4 trillion would lead to a drop in consumption of between $40 and $200 billion.

Business Fixed Investment is just over $1 trillion at an annual rate. A collapse of stock prices would cause at least some of this investment to disappear. If investment were to decline by 10 percent, that would be $100 billion.

One of the most dangerous components of the economy from the standpoint of macroeconomic stabilization is the state and local government sector. This is a very large sector of the economy (almost twice the size of the Federal government in terms of GDP expenditures, although smaller in terms of transfer payments), and it is highly procyclical. When the economy is strong, this sector increases spending, and when it is weak it cuts back. State and local spending is just under $1 trillion at an annual rate. If capital losses in the stock market reduce tax collections by 5 percent, then spending will fall by almost that much, or $40 billion.

It is not difficult, therefore, to envision a drop in GDP of $200 to $400 billion, arising directly from a crash in the Nasdaq market. This would be a decline of 2 to 4 percent, which likely would be extended by multiplier effects. That is, as spending declines, employment declines, spending declines more, etc.

Beyond the straightforward linkages, one should be concerned with the impact of a crash on the psychology of consumers and businesses. For example, the personal savings rate, which averaged 6 percent for most of the post-World War II period, has fallen close to zero recently. What if the savings rate rose back to 6 percent? In that case, consumer spending would fall even farther.

Business investment has consisted of spending on technology and the Internet. What if a stock market crash leads to a general reconsideration of technology spending?

Another psychological issue is the effect of a crash of the Nasdaq and of an economic downturn on the New York Stock Exchange, where stocks that represent most stock market wealth are traded. So far, we have been assuming that these stocks escape unscathed. However, suppose that the prices of non-Nasdaq stocks fall by 25 percent. This would wipe out another $2.5 trillion in wealth, and cause nearly as much damage as the 85 percent decline on the Nasdaq that is assumed to be the trigger.

In short, it seems very plausible that a stock market crash would cause a very deep recession, with real GDP declining at a 5 percent rate or higher for two years or more. Could economic policy overcome this?

I believe that most economists continue to be Keynesians. That is, we believe that government spending and tax cuts, accompanied by stimulative monetary policy, would help to alleviate a slump. However, there is some probability that the economists who advise the next President will not be Keynesians. Or, if they are Keynesians, there is some probability that we are wrong, and that textbook fiscal and monetary stimulus will not work.

Even if the Keynesian prescription is correct, it may be difficult to carry out politically. For example, in an economic crisis the dollar could be falling sharply as foreigners attempt to sell their U.S. assets, and this could put pressure on the Fed to tighten monetary policy. For fiscal policy, the most reliable stimulus would be government spending, but the political pressure may be to use tax cuts and increases in transfer payments, which might go mostly into savings. Also, with the Federal deficit already increasing due to the economic slowdown, it may be impossible to vote for a further fiscal stimulus of more than $100 billion or so. In that case, the stimulus probably would not be sufficient to offset the collapse in demand coming from the private sector.

In the 1930's in the U.S. and in the 1990's in Japan, policy was not particularly successful. Much political energy was expended on "structural reform." In the U.S., this included deposit insurance and securities regulation. In Japan, various forms of financial and business reforms have been debated and, in some cases, adopted. If the Nasdaq crashes, we can expect to see similar energy focused on electronic trading, investor suitability, accounting rules, and other issues which at best will amount to closing the barn door after the horse has gone.

Economic depressions, like personal depressions, are frustrating, frightening events. I certainly hope that we can avoid one. However, it seems to me that such a scenario is at least plausible, and indeed highly probable.

Chapter 37

Some Keynes for Bush

(Written in December, 2000) Last week, our neighbors told us about a frustrating experience shopping at Sears. They were dismayed by the stupidity of the sales clerks and other staff. Although I expressed my sympathy, I remarked, "As an economist, I find your story heartening. It says that times are good. In a recession, you would find college graduates working as Sears clerks."

Times may not be good much longer. In January of 2000, I predicted that the next President would face a recession caused by a stock market crash (see chapter on "Briefing the President"). Also, I predicted that the President's economic advisers might not know what to do about it. Subsequent developments have been along the lines that I feared.

The father of macroeconomics is John Maynard Keynes. Since the 1960's, his reputation has declined steadily, particularly among conservative economists. I continue to believe that Keynes is relevant today. What follows is some elementary Keynesian economics that President-elect Bush is likely to need but unlikely to hear.

1. **Recessions are caused by a shortfall of investment relative to desired savings.**

Keynes viewed the economy as a contest between the "hoarding" instinct and the entrepreneurial instinct. The "hoarding" instinct is to save and to look for conservative investments. The entrepreneurial instinct is to look for promising new business opportunities. Entrepreneurial instincts, or "animal spirits," promote economic activity. The entrepreneur provides a productive outlet for the savings provided by hoarding. When "animal spirits" decline, there is too much desired savings relative to the lower level of investment. As a result, economic activity contracts, and you have a recession.

2. In today's economy, the stock market embodies "animal spirits."

The stock market is a major influence on business investment. Keynesian economist James Tobin argued that when the market value of capital is higher than replacement cost, investment will increase. He focused on the ratio of market value (in the stock price) to the replacement cost of capital. When this value, called Tobin's q, gets over 1.0, even by a small amount, investment is stimulated.

While a value of q of 1.2 would be stimulative, the dot-com mania caused "q" to soar close to 100 for Internet companies. New dot-com stocks were valued at hundreds of millions of dollars, even though it cost only a few million dollars to create a new dot-com company. As a result, the number of new dot-com firms rose dramatically. Investment in the Internet mania was very high.

3. Stock market movements are not always rational, and in the late 1990's the U.S. market was way overvalued.

Keynes did not believe that financial markets behaved rationally. This was one of his most controversial positions.

Robert Shiller, a colleague of Tobin's at Yale, wrote a book called *Irrational Exuberance* that was published just before the stock market peak in March. In fact, the drop in the market that has occurred since the publication of the book has served only to take stock prices about to where they were when Shiller began to write the book. In other words, from Shiller's perspective, so far we have seen only some of the air let out of the bubble. There is still much more room for declines in share prices.

4. Monetary policy has only limited ability to counteract sharp recessions.

Suppose that the stock market continues to decline. This could lead to a major downturn.

Already, we are seeing signs of declining investment. One major venture capital fund returned $1 billion to investors, because the fund managers did not believe that they could invest the money profitably. Other venture capital funds are trying to prop up their earlier investments rather than finance new firms.

There is room for the Federal Reserve to reduce interest rates. However, when firms find that they have excess capacity on hand, a lower interest rate does not stimulate more investment. The main expansionary effect of lower interest rates will be to stimulate exports by reducing the value of the dollar. This is a sluggish and uncertain channel, and even if it works it implies higher inflation because the relative price of imports will increase.

5. Deficit spending is needed to fight recessions.

If there is a deep recession, and monetary policy is not fully effective, then to counteract a downturn the government must use fiscal policy. Expansionary fiscal policy involves moving the government budget toward deficit, with a combination of increased spending and lower taxes.

Unfortunately, in the last several years, the public and politicians have come to believe "surpluses good, deficits bad." In fact, the surpluses have been the result of strong economic performance, not its cause. The proof of this is the fact that when President Clinton's fiscal policies were enacted early in his term, they were forecast to result in continued deficits. The surpluses were unexpected, because the strength of the economy was unexpected.

There is a slight case to be made in favor of budget surpluses. Other things equal, running a budget deficit will worsen the generational imbalance that is embedded in our demographics. That is, as a country we would like to save for the future, when the ratio of retired people to workers will rise sharply.

However, if you ask me to choose between a full-employment economy with a budget deficit and a recession economy with a surplus, I would not choose the surplus. The full-employment economy will help to give more work experience to younger people. That will make them more productive later in life. Ultimately, the best hope for dealing with the demographic crunch is higher productivity, not government savings.

My Recommendation

Overall, if you accept points (1)-(5), there is a case for thinking in terms of turning the Federal Budget in the direction of a deficit. How should this be done?

One approach that would be congenial to President Bush would be a large tax cut. Unfortunately, much of the tax cut that was part of his campaign was "back-loaded," with the larger cuts occurring farther into the future. If anything, we probably need a more front-loaded tax cut.

In addition, some of the tax cuts most popular with Republicans may not be very stimulative, because they are likely to be saved rather than spent. For example, eliminating the "death tax" is unlikely to unleash much spending. I cannot imagine that the marginal propensity to consume out of inheritances over $700,000 (smaller inheritances are tax-free today) is very high.

Another approach to running a deficit would be to increase Federal spending. However, the notion that the first Republican President-plus-Congress since 1952 would go on a spending spree is difficult to contemplate.

An alternative would be to give large grants to state governments—what used to be called general revenue sharing. For example, the Federal government might give each state $1,000 for every person living in that state. This would amount to a $280 billion program.

One impact of a recession is to reduce state revenues. Because they are obliged to balance their budgets, this leads them to reduce spending. The result is to reinforce the downturn. However, with revenue sharing, the states would have less need to cut back.

In conclusion, I believe that a large, temporary revenue-sharing program would be a good approach for fighting a recession. This form of fiscal stimulus would quickly find its way into the economy. Unfortunately, I suspect that there is little chance of any Keynes getting through to Bush. (*Postscript*: the Bush fiscal policies turned out to be more Keynesian than I had expected. See "The President's Macroeconomic Report Card.")

CHAPTER 38

LABOR FORCE CAPACITY UTILIZATION

(Written in August 2003)

"One could instead define expansions and recessions in terms of whether the fraction of the economy's productive resources that is being used is rising or falling (in which case the behavior of the unemployment rate would be a critical guide to whether the economy was in expansion or recession)... [this] might lead to the conclusion that the recent recession lasted much longer than 8 months and that it might not have ended yet."—National Bureau of Economic Research [164]

The NBER's business cycle dating committee officially stated that the latest recession began in March of 2001 and ended in November of 2001. This approach leads to three characterizations of the recession.

1. It was brief.
2. It was shallow.
3. It is over.

All of these statements are false. The recession was deep, it was long, and it is still underway. Economists and others who rely on the NBER and on indicators such as GDP growth,

237

interest rates, or stock prices have been misled. The economy is weaker than many people realize.

Everybody Should Watch LUCY

As the NBER pointed out in the statement quoted above, one approach to evaluating economic performance is to examine measures of capacity utilization. For example, the latest reading of the Federal Reserve Board's measure of capacity utilization[165] in the industrial sector is far below normal.

I think that an even broader estimate of capacity utilization can be constructed by using data from the Bureau of Labor Statistics. My goal is to estimate the extent to which the labor force is working at capacity. We might call this the Labor Capacity Utilization Index, or—using some poetic license with the acronym—LUCY. When LUCY is 100 percent, the economy is running at full throttle. When LUCY is far from 100 percent, the economy is sputtering.

I measure labor utilization as hours worked in the nonfarm private sector, based on the index calculated by the Bureau of Labor Statistics.[166] I measure labor capacity as the sum of men and women aged 16 and over.[167] I took the ratio of utilization to capacity and divided it by its peak value in December of 1999 to get a maximum of 1.0; then I multiplied by 100 to get an index that can be interpreted as percent utilization of labor capacity.

How has LUCY behaved? During the long recovery of the 1980's, labor utilization rose from just under 80 percent to just over 91 percent, but then from June 1990 to March 1992 it drifted down to 87.2 percent. From there it expanded until December of 1999, when it reached 100 percent.

Labor utilization was still as high as 98.5 percent in January of 2001. From March of 2001 through November of 2001—the respective dates for the beginning and the end of the recession, according to the NBER—labor utilization fell from 97.8 percent to 94.5 percent. Since November of 2001, labor utilization has plunged still further, to 90.3 percent in July of 2003. In other words, the drop that LUCY has taken so far during the "recovery" exceeds the decline that took place during the recession. NBER, you've got some 'splainin' to do!

Productivity-Cushioned Recession

Growth in real GDP has been positive in recent quarters, leading pundits to call this a jobless recovery. I think that a better term would be productivity-cushioned recession. That is, although labor demand has been declining, the economy has eked out positive growth in real GDP because of remarkable gains in productivity.

In fact, the most striking feature of today's economy is the strength of productivity growth. Almost a year ago, Brad DeLong pointed out[168] that productivity growth was triple the norm for this stage of the business cycle.

If you did not know that productivity were growing at 4 percent per year, then a growth rate of real GDP of 2 to 2.5 percent would be considered satisfactory. However, taking into account high productivity growth, 2.5 percent GDP growth is terrible. LUCY, the measure of labor utilization, is not thrown off by faster productivity growth. The NBER, which still looks at GDP growth without taking into account productivity, has been fooled.

Policy Implications

LUCY is telling us that we are *not* in the midst of an economic recovery. Labor utilization has declined every month this year. Contrary to the NBER and conventional wisdom, this recession is long, deep, and ongoing.

The first implication of this analysis is that the economy is a long way from potential. Even if a recovery were to begin next month, it would take years to eliminate all of the slack in the labor market. The last time LUCY was at today's level of 91.3 was March of 1994, and it took over two years to reach 95. It was not until the end of 1997 that labor force utilization reached 98 percent. Thus, the soonest that we are likely to see a high level of economic performance is early 2007.

The second implication is that monetary policy probably could be more expansionary. The current thinking at the Fed seems to be to let up on the gas as long as real GDP is rising. However, that means that the Fed is no longer applying stimulus, even though LUCY is low and falling.

The third implication is that we are going to see large Budget deficits for at least three or four more years. Politicians are not going to have the will to cut spending or increase taxes while the economy is in the toilet. Nor would a budget balancing be wise with so much labor market slack.

In general, economists, pundits, and politicians need to adjust their focus on the economy. From the perspective of capacity utilization, the economy is low and still sinking.

Chapter 39

The President's Macroeconomic Report Card

(Written in September 2003)

"The Bush fiscal policy is the worst policy in over 200 years."—George Akerlof[169]

With school starting up again, my mind is on grading. I am going to argue that on macroeconomic policy, President Bush deserves a B+ or an A-, using as a standard the modified Keynesian model that can be found in the high school Advanced Placement economics curriculum, or on Paul Krugman's web site.[170]

I may be the only economist in the country who would make this claim. Conservative economists would reject the Keynesian metric, and instead would grade President Bush on different criteria. This essay is not addressed to them.

Instead, I wish to speak to my fellow saltwater economists (see chapter on "Sweetwater vs. Saltwater"), who accept the Keynesian paradigm. I believe that they would agree with my grade if the President were Al Gore. However, in today's polarized environment, even Nobel Laureates foam at the mouth.[171]

Facts are Facts

Saltwater economists would characterize economic performance since President Bush took office as poor. While there are conservatives who try to put a positive spin on economic news, I share the saltwater view. Facts are facts. Labor market indicators, such as the capacity utilization measure (see Chapter on "Labor Force Capacity Utilization") that I favor, describe a prolonged slump.

However, reasonable economists would agree that President Bush did not cause the recession, and they would agree that the Clinton economic record was partly a matter of luck. As Paul Kasriel and Asha Bangalore put it,[172] "It appears to us that the sweet spot of history that coincided with the Clinton administration has passed ... The economy is now reaping the whirlwind of the largest stock market bubble in the history of this country. The G.W. Bush administration inherited this economic mess."

Outcomes vs. Policies

If macroeconomic outcomes are partly determined by luck, how should economic policy be graded? The problem is tricky, as is illustrated by the data in the table below. It gives the values of two macroeconomic variables as they stood in January of 2001 and July of 2003. The first variable is the ten-year interest rate, as measured by the Federal Reserve constant-maturity Treasury index.[173] The second variable is the seasonally-adjusted unemployment rate.[174]

Variable	January, 2001	July, 2003
10-year Interest Rate	5.16 %	3.98 %
Unemployment Rate	4.1 %	6.2 %

LEARNING ECONOMICS

Let us start with the ten-year interest rate. Suppose that someone were to suggest that the Bush Administration deserves credit for the reduction in that interest rate, and that the Bush tax cuts must have contributed to the decline. My saltwater friends would object strenuously to this interpretation.

Economists of all stripes would agree that the only way to gauge the effect of the Bush tax cuts on interest rates is to compare the performance of interest rates with what those rates would have been without the tax cuts. To perform this analysis, you would use a numerical model of the economy. Some economists favor large computer models, while others prefer "back-of-the-envelope" analysis. In either case, it turns out that most reasonable models would show that the Bush tax cuts caused the ten-year interest rate to be *higher* than it would have been otherwise.

Naturally, the most objective way to assess the effect of the President's tax cuts on unemployment is to use the same methodology. Comparing the results of a macroeconomic model simulated with and without the tax cuts, one would conclude that the tax cuts *lowered* the unemployment rate from what it otherwise would have been. My guess is that the effect is small—probably less than one-half of one percentage point—but it was favorable.

My point is that the economic models that would be used by President Bush's strongest critics would in fact show that his policies helped to ameliorate the slump that he inherited. Their overheated rhetoric is at variance with their analytical framework.

What Would You Have Done?

Of course, if the unemployment rate is 2 percentage points too high, and the Bush tax cuts only reduced the unemployment rate by less than one-half of one percent, then in hindsight, certainly, there is room for improvement. However, even in hindsight, the saltwater economists have only feeble suggestions. They recommend that tax cuts should have been front-loaded and phased out; however, in macroeconomic models, temporary tax cuts are even less stimulative than permanent tax cuts. They also recommend that tax cuts be given to low-income consumers on the grounds that such consumers would be more likely to spend; however, there is little or no evidence that the distribution of tax cuts makes a large difference in their stimulative effect. None of the saltwater critics *today*[175] makes a proposal as dramatic and specific as the one that I made right after the 2000 election (see "Some Keynes for President Bush"): "the Federal government might give each state $1,000 for every person living in that state. This would amount to a $280 billion program."

Saltwater economists are not making any radical proposals for fiscal expansion beyond what has already taken place. That is probably reasonable. After all, if a $480 billion deficit makes only a dent in the unemployment rate, then what do we need—a $2 trillion deficit? The bottom line is that President Bush's critics have no analytical basis for claiming that they could have produced a significantly lower unemployment rate while maintaining any semblance of fiscal responsibility.

Why the Bad Grade?

Orthodox Keynesian policy in a recession would be to cut taxes. The Bush Administration has done that. Orthodox policy would be to increase government spending over what had been planned. The Bush Administration has done that, too. When a student hands in an exam that repeats almost exactly what the professor was saying in class, but the student still gets a low grade, then one can only conclude that the professor has something personal against the student.

I believe that, if pressed, Akerlof and the other economists who spoke out so vehemently would say that they are giving their bad grade to the Bush Administration on the basis of the *long run* path implied by tax cuts, taking the path of spending as given. They would have to admit that over the near term their differences with the Bush fiscal policy are almost immaterial.

The economists who worry about long-run fiscal policy may be right. I think that the structure of Medicare is a larger source for concern than the Bush tax cuts, but if the former is not changed then the tax cuts may have to be reconsidered in a few years.

However, one bright spot in the economy is that recent productivity performance continues to shine.[176] If this reflects a long-term increase due to Moore's Law, then the economy is winning what I call The Great Race (see chapter on "The Great Race"). Should that prove to be the case, then by the end of this decade the Budget will be well into surplus and Akerlof will be viewed as the worst grader in over 200 years.

Chapter 40

The Great Displacement

"The high rates of investment in street, highway, water, and sewer capital literally helped pave the way for the postwar suburbanization boom."—Alexander J. Field[177]

If I were in charge of the high school curriculum, I would have one semester of a history course devoted entirely to the 1930's. Students would be required to read from *The Gathering Storm* by Winston Churchill and from *Reflections on the Great Depression*, by Randall E. Parker.

I keep coming across parallels between the 1930's and the present day. An impassioned pacifism swept the western intelligentsia. In England in February of 1933, the Oxford Union passed a resolution declaring that "this House will in no circumstances fight for its King and Country." Similar petitions were popular on elite college campuses in the United States. Meanwhile, of course, 1933 was the year that Adolf Hitler consolidated his power in Germany.

Myths of the Great Depression

Parker's book is a collection of interviews with famous economists who lived through the Great Depression. Thus, it combines first-hand memories with professional expertise.

The economists span the ideological spectrum, but they are surprisingly in agreement on many important points. For example, as Parker notes in his overview, "all of the individuals interviewed, most to a greater extent, attribute the ending of the Depression to the onset of World War II."

The economists agree that the New Deal mixed some harmful programs, such as the National Recovery Administration (a central planning board with the objectives of restricting industrial output and raising prices) and the Agricultural Adjustment Act (which pursued the goal of raising farm prices using policies that included destroying crops) with some successful financial reforms. Milton Friedman, a conservative who opposed the expansion of government under the New Deal, nonetheless praises "the series of monetary measures that Roosevelt took, including the bank holiday, the going off gold, the program to purchase gold, the silver purchase program." James Tobin, whom many regard as the foremost exponent of liberal Keynesian economics, nonetheless says that "When I got to college I began to realize that the NRA and the AAA were very bad ideas . . . Roosevelt was very lucky to get out from under the NRA." (The NRA was declared unconstitutional by the Supreme Court.)

A number of myths that are popular in conventional histories of the Depression are punctured in Parker's book. For example, the *Wikipedia* echoes many textbooks in saying,[178] "A fundamental misdistribution of purchasing power, the greatly unequal distribution of wealth throughout the 1920s, was a factor contributing to the depression." None of the economists interviewed by Parker cites this so-called causal factor.

Another myth is that the New Deal rescued the country from the Great Depression. The economists agree that the economy expanded from 1933 to 1937, but this expansion was tepid in relation to the collapse that had taken place. In 1937, with unemployment still at double-digit levels, the economy contracted once again. National output finally regained its 1929 level in 1941, which may explain why the economists are unanimous in attributing recovery to the Second World War.

A Parallel with Today's Economy

The current recession (or recent recession if you believe the NBER chronology rather than mine—see the chapter on "Labor Force Capacity Utilization") is unlike earlier post war recessions. In a widely-cited article, Federal Reserve economists Erica L. Groshen and Simon Potter[179] describe the difference as "the predominance of permanent job losses over temporary layoffs and the relocation of jobs from one industry to another."

In the typical "inventory recession" of the postwar period, excess inventories led to temporary layoffs of workers, who were re-called back to their same jobs once stockpiles had been brought down to normal levels. Our current labor market instead is dominated by permanent job losses. Productivity has been soaring at unprecedented rates of 5 to 6 percent, which means that GDP growth of 2 or 3 percent is insufficient to require the available labor resources.

Today's labor market could be described in terms of progress and displacement. In some sectors, notably manufacturing, productivity is growing faster than demand, creating excess labor. Eventually, workers will find their way to other industries, in which demand is growing faster than productivity (in the chapter on "Progress and Displacement", I suggested home health care as an example). However, this process requires a number of adjustments—wage changes, worker retraining, worker relocation, etc.—that take a while to work out. Above all, we no longer have an irrationally exuberant stock market creating the impression that everyone can be productively employed doing business development for a Dotcom. People have to find real jobs, which is more difficult.

What I had not realized until I read Alexander Field's article is that the Great Depression was also an era of high productivity growth. Field argues that the 1930's were also a period in which technological innovations were being exploited to increase productive efficiency.

The Depression certainly was an era of displacement. In fact I have borrowed the very term "displacement" from the late economic historian Charles Kindleberger, author of *Manias, Panics, and Crashes* and one of the eminent economists interviewed by Parker. Kindleberger's theory of manias, such as the Tulip Mania, the South Sea Bubble, or the Internet craze, is that they are triggered by a major change in the economic or geopolitical environment. The change creates new opportunities and sudden wealth, leading to greed and overspeculation. Kindleberger views the 1929 stock market boom and subsequent crash as a classic example of this theory. The geopolitical realignment following World War I, and the rapid growth of industries in automobiles and electronic communications, created displacement.

The development of motorized transportation must have affected every sector of the economy in the second quarter of this century. It permitted efficient farms located away from population centers to replace inefficient farms located close to cities and towns. It allowed people to enjoy the comfort and relative low cost of living in the suburbs while continuing to work in central cities. It allowed factories to relocate out of expensive central cities and into outlying areas and smaller towns.

Until World War II, however, the labor released by the progress of the 1930's was unemployed. The war brought full employment. After the war, to the surprise of most economists, the economy did not sink back into another recession. Instead, overall demand was high enough to absorb the nation's work force.

Have We Learned Our Lessons?

If today's economy shares some characteristics with that of the 1930's, then perhaps we should be worried. Will the economy pull out of its current slump, or will we suffer another long, stubborn period of high unemployment?

So far, we are doing much better than in the 1930's, and I am optimistic that we will continue to do so. First of all, monetary and fiscal policy are much more expansionary today than they were then. In fact, monetary policy in the Great Depression was so bad that most economists regard the contraction in the money supply as the primary cause of the severity of that episode. Fiscal policy, in spite of Roosevelt's willingness to experiment and Keynes' advocacy of deficit spending, was feeble or even perverse by modern standards. Current policies certainly deserve a higher grade (see chapter on "The President's Macroeconomic Report Card").

Another reason that I am optimistic is that we are less likely to try some of the more dubious experiments of the New Deal, such as the central planning of the National Recovery Act. Thus, if Harold L. Cole and Lee E. Ohanian[180] are correct in attributing the slow recovery of the 1930's to the *adverse* impacts of the New Deal, then we are likely to be spared a similar fate.

Among economists, at least some of us have been worried about a repeat of the Great Depression since the days when the Dotcom bubble was at its height. As one of the worriers, I believe that our handling of the crisis has been better than expected, although not perfect. If you go back and read the chapter on "Briefing the President," you will see that my predictions for economic policy were overly pessimistic. Today, my hope is that the worst is behind us.

Chapter 41

Can Greenspan Steer?

(Written in August 2002) At the beach where we vacation every summer, my daughters like to ride the bumper cars at an amusement park called Funland. One thing I notice is how weak is the link between the steering wheel and the direction of the car. Often, it seems that while the girls are spinning the wheel frenetically, the change in heading that they purchase is slight.

This flimsy steering mechanism strikes me as an apt metaphor for monetary policy. Federal Reserve Chairman Alan Greenspan can spin his steering wheel (the Federal Funds rate), but the correlation between those actions and the direction of interest rates in general is weak and inconsistent.

Consider which of the following statements best characterizes the recent trend in interest rates.

a) Interest rates have been unchanged since December of 2001, the last time the Federal Reserve cut its key rate.
b) Interest rates have fallen sharply in the past three months and are significantly below last December's levels.

As any consumer with a mortgage or any corporate treasurer managing her company's debt knows, the correct answer is (b). Only people who are fixated on Greenspan and the Fed would answer (a).

Economists Paul Krugman and Brad DeLong are Fed-fixated. In a *New York Times* column, Krugman wrote that

"*The U.S. economy's 'potential output'... what it could produce at full employment... has lately been growing at about 3.5 percent per year, thanks to the productivity surge that began in the mid-1990's. But according to the revised figures released a couple of weeks ago, actual growth has fallen short of potential for seven of the last eight quarters...*"[181]

And yet the Fed chose not to cut rates on Tuesday. Why?"

DeLong, writing in the *Financial Times*, agreed that "*the Federal Reserve's failure to cut interest rates so far this spring and summer is very puzzling. If 1.75 percent was the appropriate interest rate last winter, when stock indices were 20 percent higher than they are today, it is hard to see how 1.75 percent can be the appropriate interest rate today. If 1.75 percent was the appropriate interest rate last winter, before the shock of revelations about corporate accounting began to drive a larger wedge of uncertain size between the terms on which the government can borrow and the terms on which private businesses can raise capital, than 1.75 percent is unlikely to be the appropriate interest rate today.*"

Output Gap

Krugman and DeLong make an important point that is not widely understood, which is that economic performance should be measured relative to potential growth. There is an unfortunate tendency, in the press and even among professional economists, to write as if the benchmark for economic growth is zero. This means that only negative growth constitutes a recession, and it implies that growth of one or two percent per year is acceptable.

Given Krugman's estimate that potential GDP is increasing at a rate of 3.5 percent per year, any shortfall relative to that in economic growth represents underperformance. What DeLong and Krugman recommend using as an indicator is the output gap, the difference between actual and potential GDP. According to DeLong, that measure currently stands at four percent.[182]

It is particularly important to set the correct growth benchmark in an economy where potential output has been super-charged by Moore's Law (see chapter on "Rationally Exhuberant"). Because of Moore's Law, DeLong forecasts accelerated growth in productivity.[183] That means that Krugman's estimate of 3.5 percent annual growth in potential GDP may be conservative.

Taking into account the effect of Moore's Law on potential growth, actual economic performance in the past two years has been dismal. Krugman's admonishment to "mind the gap" is well founded. To close the gap in one year, the economy would have to grow by 7.5 percent (3.5 percent potential growth plus 4 percent to close the gap). We certainly should not settle for growth of 2 or 3 percent when Moore's Law is in effect.

Who Needs the Fed?

With the economy slumping, DeLong and Krugman say that we need the Fed to lower interest rates. Where their argument loses force is when we examine what is happening in the bond markets. We already have lower interest rates!

As DeLong's *Macroeconomics*[184] textbook says, "The interest rate that is relevant for determining investment spending is a long-term interest rate." The ten-year Treasury rate, which rose to 5.21 percent in April and 5.16 percent in May, has fallen below 4.30 percent recently. This is a dramatic decline, which among other things has fueled a drop in mortgage interest rates.

The drop in long-term rates does not reflect fears of deflation. In fact, Morgan Stanley's Richard Berner and David

Greenlaw see little change in the market's expectations for inflation.[185] They point out "The yield on the 3% 10-year TIP [Treasury security indexed for inflation] that was auctioned a month ago has fallen sharply, by 50 basis points, or roughly the same decline as that in comparable 10-year notes."

Since May, the real or inflation-adjusted interest rate, as measured by the yield on TIPs, has fallen from over 3.5 percent to 3 percent. Thus the long-term real interest rate has declined by 20 percent! (Again, this was written in August, 2002.)

One of DeLong's concerns is that the drop in Treasuries could simply reflect a flight from corporate bonds into safer securities. In that case, the drop in Treasury yields would not be matched by a reduction in private-sector borrowing costs. However, corporate bond rates also have declined. The average interest rate on Corporate bonds rated Baa by Moody's has fallen from 8.09 percent in May to 7.52 percent recently.

In short, looking at the unchanged Federal Funds rate gives a false picture of how interest rates have behaved recently. While Greenspan and company stood pat, the bond market dramatically lowered the cost of borrowing in the ways that matter most to consumers and businesses.

Bond Market Vigilantes

Over a decade ago, Wall Street economist Edward Yardeni coined the term "bond market vigilantes" to describe the phenomenon of private investors exercising interest rate policy independently of the Fed. At the time, he noted a tendency for long-term interest rates to rise whenever investors caught a whiff of inflation, regardless of what the Fed might have been doing at the time.

When the Fed last cut interest rates, in December of 2001, the bond market vigilantes were not buying it. The ten-year rate actually was higher in December and January than it was in November. The bond market vigilantes were implicated in April[186] when the ten-year rate rose again.

Thus, the verdict on last December's rate cut would be that it was ineffectual. On the other hand, this summer, key interest rates plunged without any action on the part of the Fed. The Fed's ability to steer interest rates is looking a lot like a child's ability to steer the bumper cars at Funland.

In our large, sophisticated financial markets, the Fed is only one player, and its significance may be less than is commonly assumed. Even if they spun their steering wheel much harder, it is doubtful that they could get market rates to turn any more in the desired direction.

Chapter 42

The Bitterness of Supply-Siders

For die-hard hippies, it is always August 1969 and "I'm goin' on down to Yasgur's farm." If you suggest that we are no longer Woodstock Nation, they get very bitter.

Supply-side economists present a similar profile. They challenged the establishment, and for one shining moment in 1981, they had their Woodstock, as President Ronald Reagan managed to push through a major tax cut. However, like the hippies, supply-side economists have either been co-opted or marginalized over the years. In 2003, they could be found carping about the appointment by President Bush of Harvard's N. Gregory Mankiw as Chairman of the Council of Economic Advisers.

As the New York Times reported,[187] the supply-siders that Mankiw once derided in a textbook as "charlatans and cranks" were certainly cranky. Think-tankers Martin Anderson and Stephen Moore are quoted as hostile to Mankiw.

The Wall Street Journal's Susan Lee is not re-fighting the battles of the 1980's. Her objection to Mankiw is current. She complains that "his best-selling textbook argues that deficits or government debt pushes up interest rates." (Susan Lee may not know this, but Glenn Hubbard, Mankiw's predecessor as CEA Chairman, also has a textbook, which says the same thing.)

What was Supply-side Economics? Anyone? Anyone?

If you missed Ben Stein's lecture in *Ferris Bueller's Day*

Off, you can find some explanations that are almost as good on the Web. James D. Gwartney[188] writes, "Supply-side economics stresses the impact of tax rates on the incentives for people to produce and to use resources efficiently." Raymond Keating[189] writes, "in the supply-side view, the size of government generally takes precedence over concerns about, for example, the size of a nation's budget deficit."

In the 1980's a *bona fide* supply-sider believed that cutting tax rates would lead to higher tax revenues. As Brad DeLong describes it,[190] supply-side economics was used to deny the inconsistency between the goal of tax reduction and the goal of deficit reduction. While DeLong, no friend of supply-side economics, acknowledges that its proponents take a different view of history, my memory coincides with DeLong's.

Supply-side Economics and Deficits

In 2003, supply-side economists are no longer suggesting that cutting tax rates will increase government revenue. On the contrary, Milton Friedman[191] and Gary Becker[192] are saying that cutting tax rates is a way to put downward pressure on government spending, presumably by reducing revenues.

The new "litmus test" for supply-siders appears to be the belief that government deficits do not increase interest rates. Susan Lee is accusing Mankiw of heresy in that regard.

In making the case that larger government deficits do not lead to higher interest rates, Lee gives several somewhat mutually inconsistent arguments:

1. Ricardian equivalence

According to this hypothesis, as individuals we "see through" the Budget and realize that deficits now will lead to higher taxes later. Therefore, we save now in order to pay those taxes. I do not know anyone who makes their savings decisions by looking up the government Budget data. So you have to argue that somehow people are factoring in the government Budget implicitly without being aware of it. Although as an economist I believe that people can solve complex optimization problems intuitively if they have enough practice, there is no way for people to "practice" making long-term saving decisions—you only go around once in life.

Lee says that "most" economists "work with some form" of Ricardian equivalence. That sentence is true, if by "work with some form" you mean "are aware of but dismiss."

2. International Capital Flows

Lee's next line of defense is that "any left-over pressure will be absorbed by global capital markets." It is true that if private net saving does not increase to match an increase in the government Budget deficit, then the gap must be met by foreign capital inflows. However, the mechanism by which this occurs is that higher interest rates attract foreign capital. Thus, although foreign capital attenuates the effect of the Budget deficit on interest rates, it does not eliminate it. Moreover, when deficits get large enough, foreign capital can turn around and go the other way. See Argentina.

3. Small Change

Lee's other argument is that deficits are small, so that the increase in outstanding debt is negligible. She writes, "Global credit markets are enormous—around $40 trillion—and the U.S. government deficit represents a small share. In fact, next year's deficit of some $300 billion is truly a drop in the bucket."

This is true. A *one-time* Budget deficit of $300 billion is not large in comparison with GDP, total credit flows, or other appropriate metrics. Of greater concern is the outlook in the years ahead. The Committee for Economic Development[193] forecasts that over the next ten years the cumulative deficits will be $2 *trillion*. That is not small change. As Everett Dirksen might have put it, a trillion here a trillion there and pretty soon you're talking about real money.

Conclusion

The supply-siders are bitter with Greg Mankiw and the rest of us. However, we are the ones who ought to be bitter, because supply-siders are weakening the conservative position.

The real debate in this country should be over the appropriate size of government, particularly the future of Medicare (see chapter on "Phase Out Medicare"). Those are topics on which conservatives hold at least some (I would say a lot) of the intellectual high ground. Instead, the supply-siders would make their stand on the proposition that tax cuts can be sustained without spending cuts, using theories that rest on intellectual quicksand.

CHAPTER 43

WOULD KEYNES CHANGE HIS MIND?

"Practical men, who believe themselves to be quite exempt from any intellectual influence, are usually the slaves of some defunct economist. Madmen in authority, who hear voices in the air, are distilling their frenzy from some academic scribbler of a few years back."—John Maynard Keynes[194]

I recently characterized the United States as an elastic economy (see chapter on "The Elastic Economy"), meaning that there are more opportunities for substitution and adaptation in response to economic shocks. As I will explain below, John Maynard Keynes described an economy that is *inelastic* in several key respects. Does this mean that government attempts at macroeconomic policy reflect an outdated distillation of Keynes' own academic scribbling?

Keynes vs. Elasticity

In the 1930's, the United States experienced persistent rates of unemployment of 15 percent or more. This would be impossible in an economy in which the assumptions of classical economics hold. So Keynes broke with some of those assumptions. One way to describe Keynesian economics is that it includes several important inelasticities.

One feature of Keynesian economics is that the labor market behaves as if the demand for labor is highly inelastic in comparison to the supply of labor. Inelastic labor demand means that when a firm suffers a drop in demand, only a dramatic reduction in wages would allow it to maintain the same level of labor input. Workers will not accept such wage reductions, and the result is a drop in employment. During the Depression, this phenomenon occurred in many industries at once.

Keynes argued that both saving and investment are inelastic with respect to the interest rate. He viewed saving as being determined by a basic hoarding propensity, which does not depend on interest rates. He viewed investment as being governed by "the state of long-term expectations." He would have described the dotcom boom as a case of "animal spirits" on the part of venture capitalists and Wall Street speculators, with the current situation as being one of pessimistic long-term expectations. Changes in interest rates are not sufficient to offset these mood swings.

The Elastic Economy Meets Keynes

Today, the economy is more elastic than it was in the 1930's. Today's recession is a far cry from the Great Depression of the 1930's. Of course, some of this may be due to a difference in the severity of the shocks in the two periods (making that comparison would be a difficult task). And much of it is due to a better policy regime, particularly relative to money and banking. But I believe that some of the credit belongs to the more elastic economy.

Labor demand seems to be more fluid than was the case in the 1930's. The economy is less concentrated in the manufacturing and agriculture sectors. Firms are more adaptable, and the employment base is more diverse in terms of types of work and variety of industries.

The Internet and increased foreign trade contribute to the elasticity of labor demand. The ability to shift production overseas enables firms to reduce wages for some jobs. With the Internet, the work that can be relocated now includes computer programming, customer support, and clerical functions.

In fact, these days labor supply may be less elastic than labor demand. A reader of EconLog wrote this comment:[195]

"I was talking with the Executive Director of my alumni association this afternoon. He notes that none of the current class of computer science graduates has a job offer as yet. In contrast, each of the Petroleum Engineers has an average of seven. The school has a 4-6 year pipeline for graduates in each department. Students tend toward those departments that have good offers for their graduates when the students enter the program.

This would indicate at least several years worth of lag in responding to a changing labor market."

When it is labor supply that is inelastic, and there is a mismatch of skills with needs in the labor market, economists refer to this as structural unemployment. (Note, however, that there is still a question of why these mismatches cause unemployment as opposed to adjustments in relative wages.) Structural unemployment is a supply-side issue, not necessarily amenable to Keynesian demand-side policy intervention.

Even though the stock market continues to be at the mercy of the "state of long term expectations," overall saving and investment do respond to interest rates. Lower long-term rates stimulate the demand for housing construction. Moreover, homeowners who do not buy new homes can refinance their mortgages, giving them the ability to increase consumer purchases.

One of the mechanisms for balancing the supply and demand for capital is international trade in goods and assets. Even if domestic saving and investment were not responsive to a drop in interest rates, a decline in rates here relative to overseas would cause a decline in foreign investment in the U.S., which in turn would lead to a weaker dollar and a lower trade deficit. Lower interest rates can increase the demand for domestic output through this channel.

The Policy Challenge

The good news is that the elastic economy is more resistant to economic downturns, because labor markets, asset markets, and capital markets have become more complex and more diverse. The bad news is that by the same token the elastic economy is more resistant to economic policy. Any given amount of fiscal or monetary stimulus will have less "bang for the buck" than in the past.

For monetary policy, the problem is the high elasticity of supply and demand for long-term financial assets. As a result, the Fed can manipulate short-term interest rates without necessarily having any effect on mortgage rates, corporate bond rates, or other interest rates that affect saving and investment. The ability of conventional monetary policy to affect real economic decisions is weakened. See the chapter on "Can Greenspan Steer?"

I suspect that fiscal policy, too, is less effective. My guess is that as labor markets become more complex, they tend to follow their own dynamic. An increase in spending or a cut in taxes provides less of a "quick fix" when unemployment is a varied mix that includes hotel workers, telecommunications managers, and web programmers, with some industries in cyclical slumps and others in secular decline. It was probably easier for stimulus to work when unemployment consisted of laid-off auto workers ready to return to the assembly line.

For the elastic economy, the options for dealing with our current unemployment problem appear to be these:

1. Increase the dosage of fiscal stimulus. The disadvantage of this is that it would put taxpayers deeper in the hole in the long run.

2. Increase the dosage of monetary stimulus. Even though the Federal Funds rate is already less than 2 percent, we are not in a liquidity trap where there is no room for rates to fall farther. Instead, as Federal Reserve Governor Ben Bernanke has pointed out,[196] the Fed has available to it the option of buying long-term Treasury bonds or even mortgage-backed securities. The disadvantage of this is that it might prove to be destabilizing, because we do not have any experience with which to calibrate the degree of novel forms of monetary intervention.
3. Wait for the private sector to right itself. The disadvantage of this is that it has become politically unacceptable to "do nothing" about recessions.

No doubt there are demagogues out there who will claim to offer a risk-free, pain-free way to restore full employment. But to me, all of the options appear to have down sides.

Perhaps even Keynes would tell the public today that the Federal government is less well positioned to solve the problem of unemployment than are the individual decision-makers operating in a decentralized, elastic economy. After all, it is Keynes who reportedly once remarked,[197] "When the facts change, I change my mind—what do you do, sir?"

CHAPTER 44

WHAT'S YOUR MARGIN OF SAFETY?

(Written in October 2002, which turned out to be close to the bottom for the stock market.)

"The margin of safety is always dependent on the price paid. It will be large at one price, small at some higher price, non-existent at some still higher price."—Benjamin Graham[198]

Are stocks cheap, or are they still overpriced? The answer depends on how large a margin of safety one requires between the intrinsic value of stocks and the price that one is willing to pay.

For an example of someone with a very high margin of safety, consider Pimco's Bill Gross. In *Dow 5000*,[199] Gross uses a standard method for arriving at intrinsic value. The intrinsic value of the Dow Jones Industrial Average is the price for which the dividend yield plus the real dividend growth rate equals the real rate of interest.

Gross suggests that the real interest rate is the rate on ten-year inflation-indexed securities (TIPs) issued by the U.S. Treasury, which is 3.0 percent. That inflation-adjusted yield is a target for stocks. Furthermore, he assumes that real dividends will grow at 2.0 percent per year, which is reasonable, because this is a good estimate for the inflation-adjusted growth rate for the economy as a whole.

The required dividend yield for stocks is the difference between the real interest rate and the real dividend growth rate, or 3.0 - 2.0 = 1.0 percent. The ratio of the dividends on one unit of the Dow Jones Industrial Average to the level of the Dow should be one percent. Gross estimates that one unit of the Dow yields $185 in dividends. If the dividend yield were 1.0 percent, then the intrinsic value of the Dow should be 18,500.

Why is the Dow not at 18,500? Because of the margin of safety. Nobody wants to pay the intrinsic value for stocks. They want to pay less than that, in order to have a margin of safety. Graham himself sometimes spoke of a 50 percent margin of safety, meaning that if the intrinsic value is 18,500 one might be willing to pay 9,250.

Graham's "margin of safety" plays the role in stock market valuation that economists usually assign to something called "the risk premium." However, this is a case of bad economic jargon driving out a useful practitioner's concept. There is no way for most economists, much less ordinary investors, to have intuition about what is a reasonable risk premium. But anyone can grasp the concept of a margin of safety.

Gross expresses his argument for a Dow of 5,000 in terms of a risk premium. But it is easy to convert his risk premium to a margin of safety. Since he says that he would find the Dow a buy at 5000, and his own figures give an intrinsic value of 18,500, he is only willing to pay 27 percent of intrinsic value for the Dow. His margin of safety is 73 percent.

Incidentally, venture capitalists—who advertise themselves as the riverboat gamblers of the investment community—use a margin of safety of 90 percent. A venture capitalist wants a rate of return that is a "ten-bagger," or 1000 percent, which means that if they put $10 million into a company they think that the shares they are buying are really worth $100 million.

What Does the Market Think?

The market value of the Dow does not depend on any one individual's margin of safety. It depends on the margin of safety of the entire market of investors. Relative to the market, if you have a comparatively large margin of safety, stock prices will seem too high to you. If you have a relatively small margin of safety, then stocks will appear to be cheap.

If Bill Gross is serious about his 73 percent margin of safety, but most other investors are willing to live with a smaller margin of safety, then the Dow will never drop to his target level. He will miss out on earning a rate of return that is considerably higher than the 3 percent he could get by buying TIPs.

On the other hand, if you buy the Dow at 8000 and the market permanently adopts Gross' margin of safety, it would take you a very long time (several lifetimes, in fact), for your returns to outperform TIPs. In the less-than-very-long run, changes in the market margin of safety dominate changes in intrinsic value as a source of the variation in stock market returns. Or, as Gross puts it, over the past hundred years,

"Ninety percent of the market's real return then came from factors other than earnings growth."

Stocks will always be priced below intrinsic value. How much below depends on the market's margin of safety. If the margin of safety gets larger, then prices will fall and returns will be low. If the margin of safety gets smaller, then prices will rise and returns will be extra-ordinarily high.

What Do Economists Know?

As an economist, I feel qualified to have an opinion about the elements that go into the calculation of intrinsic value. In fact, I think that the intrinsic value of the Dow is higher than

18,500, because I believe that Gross is using an unrealistic indicator of the real interest rate. The market for TIPs is very thin, and I suspect that they are underpriced. (Putting my money where my mouth is, I have a lot of TIPs in my portfolio.) If TIPs were priced higher, then their yield would be lower, and this indicator of the real interest rate would be lower. This would raise the intrinsic value of the Dow beyond 18,500.

I also think that there is some potential for real economic growth to exceed 2 percent, which also would boost one's estimate of intrinsic value. Nonetheless, I would be willing to use 18,500 as a benchmark.

On the other hand, I feel quite unqualified to predict what the market's margin of safety will be. If the Dow is at 7600, then the margin of safety is around 60 percent. Gross thinks that it belongs at 73 percent, so that you should be able to buy stocks for 27 cents per dollar of intrinsic value. My personal margin of safety is closer to 50 percent, but I cannot claim to speak for the market.

I cannot rule out the possibility that the market's margin of safety could reach 73 percent, or even go higher. However, the fact that the margin of safety *might* for a period of time get as large as 73 percent is not an argument against buying stocks today. Buying stocks is a mistake only if the margin of safety expands to 73 percent *and remains stuck there*. As long as the margin of safety does not increase *permanently*, buying stocks will pay off.

For what it's worth, my reading of the historical record is that the market margin of safety is very unlikely to get permanently stuck at the level that Gross is advocating. I use the ratio of nominal GDP (in billions of current dollars) to the Dow as a crude indicator of the margin of safety. Suppose that Gross is right, and that the right level for the Dow is 5000. In that case, the ratio of nominal GDP to the Dow

LEARNING ECONOMICS

would be just over two. That means that a ratio of two corresponds to Gross'margin of safety of 73 percent.

Since 1959, the ratio of nominal GDP to the Dow has been less than two from 1959-1974 and from 1992 to present, which suggests that the market margin of safety was lower than 73 percent. However, the ratio was more than two from 1975-1991, which suggests that during that period the market margin of safety was higher than 73 percent. Based on that, one might say that for the majority of the past forty years the market's margin of safety has been less than what Gross is recommending.

The way I read the data, the chance that the market will *permanently* adopt a margin of safety of 73 percent or higher is close to nil. In fact, I believe that the chances are remote that the market's margin of safety will always remain as large or larger than the current 60 percent. At some point, the market's margin of safety will recover to lower levels, and that would mean that investors who buy today will enjoy superior returns.

Chapter 45

The Dollar Bubble and the Bond Bubble

"The Teflon-like resistance of the US dollar is yet another manifestation of this pervasive sense of denial. Currencies, of course, are relative prices. And in a synchronous global recession everyone gets hurt. Yet if a US-centric world tumbles into recession, goes the logic, the dollar is still viewed as the 'tallest pygmy.'"—Steve Roach[200]

Morgan Stanley's Steve Roach is one of many economists to have noticed what might be called the "dollar bubble." The dollar is overvalued relative to fundamentals. The manifestation of this is the large U.S. trade deficit. Net investment from abroad (the difference between U.S. assets purchased by foreigners and foreign assets purchased by U.S. investors) is rising. As a result, foreign investors are accumulating an ever-increasing amount of U.S. assets relative to our GDP.

For some nice charts and alarmist analysis of the relationship between foreign investment and the trade deficit, by a blogger named billmon,[201] use the link provided in the footnote. I think that billmon is using the standard liberal forecasting model, which predicts disaster based on the following logic: *America is bad. George Bush is a doo-doo head.*

Just watch. Bad things are going to happen to America. Regardless of how that forecasting model turns out, I think that billmon's charts are accurate.

At some point, foreign investment in the U.S. will slow down. This will cause a decline in the value of the dollar (in fact, the dollar did slip in 2003). At some point, our trade deficit will start to diminish. If the dollar falls far enough, we might even enjoy a trade surplus.

Screwed Either Way

Even though the dollar is overvalued, it is impossible for the United States to suffer a currency crisis of the sort experienced by Asian countries in the late 1990's or Latin American countries seemingly once a decade. The reason is that the United States has the luxury of having its debts denominated in its own currency.

When another country—say, Argentina—builds up a large foreign debt, that debt is denominated in dollars. Therefore, when the crunch comes and Argentina's peso declines in value, the cost of the debt increases. Argentina's borrowers, who can no longer afford to pay in dollars when their earnings come in pesos, are screwed.

On the other hand, when the United States suffers a currency decline, it does not affect the domestic value of our debt. We can still afford to pay in dollars. Foreign lenders, who find that they have lost purchasing power when they convert our payments to local currency, are screwed.

The beauty of having dollar-denominated debts in a world of currency fluctuations is that the United States is fairly insulated. If the foreign currency crashes, forcign borrowers take the hit. If the dollar crashes, foreign lenders take the hit. Foreigners are screwed either way.

The Safe Haven

Why do foreign investors invest so heavily in dollar-denominated assets and bear the risk of a decline in the dollar? Personally, I think it is because they are stupid. But that is not an appropriate answer for an economist to give.

If I were forced to pick an economic theory to explain the dollar bubble, it would be the theory of the safe haven. In a world of political and economic turmoil, America's securities represent a stable store of value. Are you a Saudi worried about the viability of the regime? Buy U.S. securities. Are you a citizen of a former Soviet republic trying to keep the criminals and kleptocrats away from your savings? Buy U.S. securities. Are you a European who is pessimistic about the prospects for the welfare state? You get the idea.

Foreigners, like our own domestic liberals, talk about the U.S. as if it were going to hell in a handbasket. But when they make decisions with their money, it turns out that they are even more worried about the prospects in their own countries, including the leadership of their own doo-doo heads. Like Steve Roach, they concede that the American economy is the "tallest pygmy."

The Bond Bubble

The safest of all of the save havens would be U.S. Treasury securities. Otherwise, it becomes difficult to explain how long-term interest rates in this country have continued to decline. This is the opposite of what the critics are saying should be happening, given those enormous, irresponsible tax cuts and big deficits and all.

The mystery is why there is so little expected inflation built into the yields on long-term bonds. In 2003, J. Huston McCulloch,[202] an expert at extracting the term structure of implied expected inflation by comparing the yields on ordinary (nominal) bonds with inflation-indexed securities (TIPS), reviewed a survey of inflation forecasts and concluded, "10-year TIPS therefore have a higher expected return, in either real or nominal terms, than nominal notes of similar maturity, for every one of the 34 forecasters polled. At the same time, the indexed notes are essentially risk-free to their respective maturities, while the inflation risk on 10-year nominals is considerable. This is what is known in the economics literature as second order *stochastic dominance*. This means that no informed rational risk-averse investor with these inflationary expectations should be investing in the nominal notes when the indexed notes are available at current rates."

Translated from academic-speak, McCulloch is calling investors stupid for buying nominal Treasury securities. If "stupid" is too strong a word, we could use the euphemism "foreign," which is reasonably accurate, as "billmon" shows in his charts.

Implications

If you are a speculator, then the dollar bubble and the bond bubble represent interesting opportunities. I think that there is a lot to be said for over-weighting your portfolio in favor of TIPS and in favor of securities denominated in foreign currency. A real risk-taker might play the interest-rate or foreign-currency futures markets (you would short the dollar and short long-term U.S. bonds), but then even if I'm right about the bubbles you could face the gambler's ruin problem: before the markets return to the levels that I believe are consistent with underlying fundamentals, you could have gone bankrupt.

If you are waiting for a financial-market disaster to come crashing down on the evil Americans and their evil Republican Administration, I would not hold your breath. If the dollar bubble bursts, it will reduce our wealth a bit (because of the rise in the cost of foreign goods), but the improvement in our trade competitiveness will help to increase output and employment.

Bursting the bond bubble would lead to higher interest rates on Treasury securities. For that to happen, something has to occur to revive concern about inflation. Concerns about inflation will rise when the economy has settled into a solid recovery, which would alleviate another silly doomsday scenario—deflation.

Robert Solow, in an excellent article[203] about the incentive of economic pundits to forecast improbable disasters, concludes, "If the economy recovers next year of its own accord, it is a fair bet inflation will soon be the panic of the month." I think that a recovery and a revival of inflationary expectations is something to worry about if you are a bond investor. But it would not be bad news for the Administration.

PART 6

Social Security, Health Care, and Education

INTRODUCTION

When you hear the phrase "big government" what comes to your mind? Anti-poverty programs that lavish benefits on the poor? Millions of lazy clerks doing meaningless jobs? Overpriced military hardware? In fact, none of these stereotypes explains where your tax dollars are going. Most government spending goes to programs that are popular with the middle class—public education, Social Security, and Medicare. Collectively, I refer to those areas as the Welfare State.

It is impossible to reduce the size of government without making some basic changes in the Welfare State. We can have permanent tax cuts only if we change the Welfare State. If we keep the Welfare State as it is, we will have to pay more in taxes in the future to maintain it.

Many economists would support increased taxes to pay for the Welfare State. However, I believe that the Welfare State works poorly. Rather than focus on alleviating poverty, the Welfare State reshuffles money among various middle-class constituencies. Many of the beneficiaries are better off than the people whose taxes pay for the Welfare State. The Welfare State also does a poor job of promoting learning and saving—the most important factors in economic growth.

The rest of this chapter looks at the Welfare State. I start with a radical alternative that I call "bleeding-heart libertarianism." I then look at the problems with each of the components of the Welfare State: Social Security; Medicare; and public education.

CHAPTER 46

BLEEDING-HEART LIBERTARIANISM

"I am a bleeding heart libertarian. Because I'm a nice guy and want to address society's problems and I want disadvantaged people to become better advantaged. By instincts and experience I believe that government seldom delivers the benefits the "bleeding heart liberals" and "big government conservatives" always seem to hope for. In many cases government only makes things worse. As with technology and prose, less is often more. I'm not one of those doctrinaire Big-L Libertarians who want to eliminate government. My aim is to improve government by making it smaller. The most important part of this process is to persuade our fellow citizens to demand less of our government."— Stefan Sharkansky[204]

Of the roughly $3 trillion that government in the United States at all levels collects in taxes of all kinds, close to two-thirds goes to pay for Social Security, education, and health care. This is the Welfare State.

The conventional wisdom is that the intent of the Welfare State is to reduce the disparity between the unfortunate and the well-off. The Welfare State supposedly redistributes income and reduces poverty. In fact, I believe that **the Welfare State redistributes poverty and reduces income.** As Karl Kraus once said of psychoanalysis,[205] the Welfare State is the disease which it purports to cure.

The Bleeding-Heart Libertarian Approach

To contrast with the Welfare State, let me offer the Bleeding-Heart Libertarian approach to income redistribution. Conceptually, it would involve abolishing public education, all forms of free or subsidized health care, and Social Security. It would abolish all forms of taxation other than a tax on personal consumption. All consumer spending, including spending on education and health care, would be subject to tax. To assist the poor, there would be a negative consumption tax, somewhat like the negative income tax[206] that was originally proposed by Milton Friedman.

The entire Bleeding-Heart Libertarian Welfare State can be summarized by the equation

$$T = .4C^* - \$7000$$

where T is the total taxes that an individual would pay and C^* is the person's consumption expenditures including spending on education and health. $7000 is a constant term that creates a personal exemption of $5000.

For a family of four, the equation would be $T = .4C^* - \$28,000$. Because there are four people, the constant term gets multiplied by four. Below is a table that shows how a family of four would be taxed assuming that it spends *exactly 100 percent* of its disposable income.

Income	Spending	Taxes
$0	$20,000	-$20,000
$14	$30,000	-$16,000
$28	$40,000	-$12,000
$42	$50,000	-$8,000
$56	$60,000	-$4,000
$70	$70,000	$0
$84	$80,000	$4,000

$98	$90,000	$8,000
$140,000	$120,000	$20,000

I chose the parameters in order to redistribute as much income as the current Welfare State, and also to collect enough additional taxes to fund the remaining functions of government. In the aggregate, personal consumption spending plus spending on education and health care amounts to roughly $8.5 trillion. Multiplying (.4) times $8.5 trillion gives $3.4 trillion in gross taxes, which is roughly what is collected today. Multiplying $7000 per person times a population of 280 million gives roughly $2 trillion in total exemptions. Thus, the net tax take of this system is about $1.4 trillion, which is close to the amount needed to fund that part of the government that is not the Welfare State.

If we had a larger exemption, we would have a more generous bleeding-heart welfare state, but we would not have enough money to fund the rest of the government. Another way of saying this is that the table above is indicative of the most redistribution that can be accomplished with a marginal tax rate of 40 percent.

Remember that in the table it is assumed that a family consumes all of its income. Suppose instead that a family with $90,000 in income spends only $70,000. Because the family would pay taxes only on its spending, such a family would pay no taxes. If they spent $80,000, the family would pay $4000 in taxes.

Some liberals would object that this consumption tax is "regressive." People with high incomes who choose low consumption would pay less in tax than people with low incomes who choose high consumption. However, I think it is a misnomer to call this "regressive." As an economist, I view consumption as the more reasonable indicator of well-being. There is no reason to tax people on the income that they save—to do so reflects only dogmatic anti-capitalist prejudice.

Winners and Losers

A low-income family of four would have quite a struggle. Remember, under the bleeding-heart libertarian approach they have to pay for schooling for their children. Also, they have to pay for health insurance. There is no Medicaid, and no freeloading at the hospital emergency room. There would be no food stamps or other forms of assistance. Only cash in the form of the negative consumption tax, plus the family income. For example, with an income of $14,000 supplemented with $16,000 from the government, such a family would have to afford food, shelter, education, health care, and everything else on a budget of $30,000.

Does the bleeding-heart libertarian approach seem harsh? Actually, the Welfare State is worse. The Welfare State targets much more of its largesse to people who are less needy. Medicare pays for hospital bills for everyone over 65, including millionaires. The school districts with the highest per-pupil spending rates tend to be those with the wealthiest residents. Many of the elderly who receive Social Security are well-to-do.

Where does the Welfare State get the money to fund benefits for the non-needy? Mostly, it comes from the working poor. Families with incomes in the range of $15,000 to $40,000 face effective marginal tax rates of 100 percent, or even more. That is because as their income increases, they lose eligibility for housing subsidies, food stamps, Medicaid, and so on; at the same time, their tax burdens rise, primarily because of the payroll taxes that fund Medicare and Social Security. In the bleeding-heart libertarian model, a family with an income of $28,000 would receive a supplement of $12,000 from the government. Under our current system, such a family would receive very little government assistance, apart from the "benefit" of a bottom-of-the-barrel public school. Moreover, it would be subject to payroll taxes, property taxes, sales taxes, and state income taxes.

The bleeding-heart libertarian approach systematically redistributes resources to people in need. The Welfare State arbitrarily creates winners and losers among people with similar income and spending circumstances. Compared with the bleeding-heart libertarian model, in today's Welfare State:

- Well-off elderly who spend a lot on health care are winners. So are people who choose not to buy health insurance but instead receive free care at emergency rooms. The working poor who have health insurance and pay taxes for Medicare are the losers.
- Among people who can afford to save for retirement, those who choose *not* to do so are rewarded with Social Security benefits. Those who do save are punished with taxes on their investment income.
- Children who live in school districts located where there is a lot of high-priced real estate are subsidized. Children who live in rural areas and small towns, or children whose parents pay for private school, are penalized.

To put it succinctly, the Welfare State makes losers out of people who want to get ahead through hard work, thrift, or education. Those are precisely the activities that produce economic growth and social wealth, and they are hit particularly hard by Welfare State redistribution.

Politics and the Welfare State

The Welfare State certainly has well-organized constituencies. The winners, such as the AARP and the teachers' unions, know who they are. The losers—the working poor, children stuck in low-quality school districts—have much less political clout. The Welfare State has friends in both parties, as evidenced by the move to add a prescription drug benefit to Medicare.

As the Baby Boomers age, longevity increases, and new medical technology is developed, the cost of the Welfare State is going to rise. Economists agree that in another generation the share of GDP required by the Welfare State will exceed the share of GDP of total tax revenues today. The outlook for the working poor and other Welfare State losers is decidedly grim.

The Bush Administration is undermining the Welfare State by trying to limit taxes as a percent of GDP. However, no one in either party is willing to talk plainly about the failures and inequities of the Welfare State. Those failures and inequities are the crazy aunt that politicians of both parties try to hide.

Suppose that the Welfare State is abolished or curtailed, and no redistribution mechanism is erected in its place. In that case, I am not certain what would happen to poverty. It certainly would be redistributed: some current beneficiaries would lose, while some who are trapped in poverty by the current system would escape. With overall economic growth higher, we might very well see a decline in overall poverty.

However, the scheme I outlined above would provide a better alternative. If it were adopted, there would be improved overall living standards, as a result of encouraging the activities that lead to growth. Overall higher living standards, combined with the efficiency of the redistribution mechanism, would drive out poverty. The working poor would see their effective tax burdens plummet. Thrifty people would live very comfortably in their retirement. Access to a good education would be more equal.

All things considered, it seems to me that the risk involved in embarking on a course to abolish the current Welfare State is actually rather small. I think that there are much better alternatives available, along the lines of the bleeding-heart libertarian model. Committing ourselves to the Welfare State as it exists today amounts to robbing the poor.

Chapter 47

A Social Security Policy Primer

In his book *Hard Heads, Soft Hearts*, Alan Blinder formulated Murphy's Law of economic policy, which states that economists gain attention only when they take unreliable, controversial positions. When most economists agree on a well-supported idea, such as free trade, the media pays them little heed.

Social Security is an issue where the media debate is dominated by unreliable demagogues on both sides. The media serves as a megaphone for partisan think tanks, drowning out mainstream economics.

Social Security and the Baby Boom

Social Security is a system in which payroll taxes on young and middle-aged workers are used to fund benefits to retirees. This "pay as you go" model would not be an issue if population cohorts were constant. However, the Baby Boom and secular increases in longevity can play havoc with the system.

The table below presents a simple numerical illustration of the Baby Boom phenomenon. We have a population of seven people. There are three generations—young workers, middle-aged workers, and retirees. In a steady state, there might have been just six people—two in each generation. However, because of the Baby Boom, in the year 2000 there are now three middle-aged workers, and in the year 2025 there will be three retirees. Each worker produces $40,000 of output. Each retiree consumes $10,000 of output from Social Security transfers (he or she might consume more out of personal savings).

The Baby Boom and Social Security: An Illustration

	As of year 2000	As of year 2025
Young Workers	2	2
Middle-Aged Workers	3	2
Retirees	2	3
Total Workers	5	4
Total Output	$200,000	$160,000
Consumption of Retirees	$20,000	$30,000
Percent of Output Consumed by Retirees	10%	18%

The whole Social Security issue boils down to the last line of the table. The portion of total output consumed by retirees soars from 10% when the Boomers are working to 18% when the Boomers retire. Social Security has to find the money to pay those benefits. (For actual demographic data, Asymmetrical Information[207] recommends a paper by Maureen Culhane.)[208]

Don't Fret About Grandma

One conclusion that leaps out from the table is that grandma (someone who is retired in 2000) has nothing to worry about. Unless she lives another 30 years, the taxes needed to fund her Social Security are not onerous. The only reason to bring up the subject of cutting benefits to current retirees is to try to make a demagogic attack that consists of falsely accusing a political opponent of threatening to throw grandma out of her wheelchair.

What *is* up in the air is how the Baby Boomers' benefits will be paid for. Assuming that this consumption is paid for out of taxes on workers, we need a big honking tax increase in 2025. A concern that I have is that the tax increase required will be so big that it will discourage some people from working, which will lead to still higher tax rates, and still fewer workers, until the whole scheme implodes.

An Artificial Problem

If the Baby Boomers were to postpone their retirement, the problem would go away. There would be more workers producing output, and there would be fewer retirees to absorb Social Security taxes. In our numerical example, if only half of the Baby Boomers were retired in 2025 (think of them as working half time), then output would be $180,000 and Social Security payments to retirees would be $25,000. The proportion of output used to fund Social Security would be less than 14 percent, which would be much more manageable.

It is fair to conclude that the Social Security problem is largely an artifact of the retirement age. Raising the retirement age to something like 73 would make Social Security quite manageable. This increase in the retirement age does *not* need to affect anyone currently over the age of 50 (remember—don't fret about grandma). In other words, the higher retirement age would not take effect for more than 15 years. By that time, continued improvements in health should make work a viable option for most Baby Boomers.

Of course, no one would be forced to work. People who are too unhealthy to work would still be eligible for disability. People who are healthy but want to retire before age 73 would have to finance their early retirement out of their own savings.

It is important to recognize that we are not necessarily doomed by demographics to suffer a reduced standard of living in 25 years. (It is even more important to recognize this in Japan and Europe, where, as Culhane's paper shows, populations are aging faster than in the United States.) A lower standard of living comes from demographics *combined with* the strict retirement age, which provides a strong disincentive for the elderly to work. There are mainstream economists on the left and on the right who agree that reducing the distortion caused by the retirement age is the single most powerful policy tool that we have available for addressing the Baby Boom Social Security issue.

Alternative Bailouts

Changing the retirement age would resolve the Social Security problem. There should be no need to look for alternative ways to bail out the system. However, we must examine alternative bailouts, because changing the retirement age is not yet on the table politically.

One possible bailout is productivity. Under a rather optimistic scenario in our numerical example, output per worker could double between 2000 and 2025, giving us $320,000 of output to distribute. As it happens, however, Social Security benefits are indexed to wages, which means that they too would double if productivity were to double. That would raise benefits to $60,000, which is still 18 percent of output. If instead Social Security benefits were indexed only to prices (meaning that benefits stay constant in inflation-adjusted dollars rather than increasing with productivity), then benefits would be $30,000, and the proportion of output going to retirees would actually *fall* under the optimistic productivity scenario.

Looking at the actual Social Security System (as opposed to my numerical example), and looking at a far less optimistic productivity scenario, John F. Cogan and Olivia S. Mitchell[209] argue that changing from wage indexing to price indexing would resolve the outlook for Social Security. Unfortunately, they do the analysis in terms of Social Security's "actuarial shortfall," which in my opinion is an artificial and understated measure of the Social Security problem.

Regardless of whether price indexing would completely eliminate the Social Security problem, it would permit productivity growth to go a long way toward bailing out Social Security. Replacing wage indexing with price indexing is a way of reducing benefits in a manner that is fair and gradual.

Another possible bailout, which recently received a lot of play on Asymmetrical Information[210] and other blogs, was suggested by Michael Boskin.[211] Under the Boskin Scenario, as the Boomers withdraw savings from tax-advantaged accounts, such as IRA's, the tax payments that they make will be sufficient to cover Social Security. He argues that this is a large tax increase that is overlooked in the forecasting models that are currently used to project government receipts in the long term. One might argue that this form of a big honking tax increase would not be so bad, because it would not fall on younger workers and it might not lead to major reductions in work, thrift, or other helpful activities that taxes usually discourage.

The Savings Bailout

The Boskin Scenario illustrates another way to bail out Social Security. If we save a lot now, then we can afford to pay for retirement later. The Boskin Scenario works because Boomers' savings accumulate, giving rise to tax payments that the government can use to pay for the Boomers' Social Security benefits.

As the Boskin Scenario exemplifies, **it does not matter whether the private sector or the public sector does the saving.** Confusion over this point accounts for a lot of spilled ink and distorted arguments, particularly over the effect of the Bush tax cuts on Social Security.

Think of the tax cuts as shifting revenues from government to the private sector. Which sector is more likely to save those revenues? Assuming that tax cuts go to "the already satiated," as Robert Solow[212] put it, the marginal propensity to spend might be on the low side, say 1/2. That is, for every dollar that people get in tax cuts, they spend fifty cents. If the government's marginal propensity to spend is higher than that, then overall national saving—and our ability to pay for Social Security benefits in 2025—will actually *increase* as a result of the Bush tax cuts. Of course, if we assume that the government has a marginal propensity to spend of zero and the tax payments would have been used for debt reduction, then the tax cuts almost surely serve to reduce national saving and to make it more difficult to pay for Social Security in the future.

Stock Market Scenarios

Bailouts that I find particularly misleading[213] are based on what I refer to as stock market scenarios. The standard assumption in such scenarios is that the inflation-adjusted returns on the stock market will be 7 percent. Because this is far above the growth rate in the overall economy, which is likely to be more like 2 to 4 percent, it leads to highly distorted conclusions.

For example, if you assume that the government issues a large volume of debt and uses that debt to purchase shares in stock mutual funds, then with 7 percent returns the stock market generates more than enough money to repay the debt *and* fund Social Security. Obviously, the same thing happens if we substitute "privatization" for government buying of mutual funds. Thus, the stock market scenario allows think tank partisans, such as Peter Ferrara,[214] to concoct privatization plans that appear to be a "free lunch," causing the Baby Boomer problem to disappear by magic. The stock market scenario makes an appearance in Cogan and Mitchell's discussion of privatization and also in the Boskin Scenario.

In the stock market scenario, the economy is assumed to grow at 2 percent per year, but the stock market is predicted to provide returns of 7 percent per year. This disparity is expected to last for fifty years or more.

To see the flaw in the stock market scenario, start with the algebraic fact that the ratio of the value of common stocks (P) to the total economic output of the country (Y) is the product of the price-earnings ratio of the stock market as a whole (P/E) and the share of corporate profits in economic output (E/Y). That is,

$$P/Y = (P/E)(E/Y)$$

If stock prices grow at 7 percent per year while the economy grows at 2 percent per year, then the ratio of stock prices to GDP (P/Y) fifty years from now will be more than ten times what it is today. How could that happen?

If the price-earnings ratio of the stock market (P/E) stays constant, then in order for P/Y to increase tenfold, the ratio of earnings to GDP (E/Y) has to increase tenfold. However, corporate profits are over 10 percent of national output today, so that if the ratio increases by tenfold, then corporate profits will be more than 100 percent of national output. That is impossible.

Alternatively, suppose that the ratio of corporate profits to national output stays constant. Then we need the P/E ratio to increase by tenfold in order to get a tenfold increase in P/Y. So, if the P/E ratio today is about 25, then in fifty years it will be 250. That would require investors to almost ignore risk and the time value of money in valuing stocks. No one believes that this is possible.

Historically, investments in the stock market have yielded 7 percent. That is because early in the twentieth century price-earnings ratios were in single digits. Over the course of the last century, the stock market went from being dramatically undervalued to being valued fairly, and along the way investors earned extraordinary returns. This idiosyncratic past cannot be extrapolated into the future.

As I see it, there is a plausible scenario in which stocks yield a 7 percent return for many years going forward. That scenario is one in which Moore's Law, biotechnology, and nanotechnology prove fruitful. In such a scenario, the *economy* will see growth closer to 7 percent than to the 2 percent commonly forecast, and that growth will in turn provide enough earnings to fuel a comparable rise in stock prices. If such a techno-utopian scenario plays out, then the question of how to finance Social Security will seem trivial—our wealth will be abundant. This is a nice scenario for daydreams, but not one which anyone would suggest as the basis for conservative planning.

I happen to like the idea of privatization. It appeals to my values of personal responsibility and "right-sized" government. But I am completely turned off by the severe demagoguery and counter-demagoguery on both sides of the privatization debate.

Fighting Murphy

Almost all aspects of the public discussion of Social Security appear to be dominated by Blinder's "Murphy's Law" phenomenon. The reforms that mainstream economists believe would make the biggest difference, such as raising the future retirement age and changing from wage indexing to price indexing, need to receive political consideration. In contrast, the politically salient alternatives of repealing the Bush tax cuts or relying on a free lunch from the stock market are much less sound economically.

CHAPTER 48

AMERICA IS MENTALLY ILL

America's most expensive health care problem is mental illness. I'm not referring to depression, schizophrenia, or other commonly-diagnosed psychological disorders. I am talking about the neuroses that cause us to remain attached to a complex system of corporate and government involvement, rather than relying on individuals to make their own choices about health care and health insurance.

How Health Care Ought to Work

"How much more could be accomplished if all the money and time now being wasted were put in the hands of individual patients, who could then make their own health care choices? The government and corporations would be eliminated as third-party payers, and would no longer face uncontrolled health care expenses; health care options would multiply to meet the preferences and needs of individual patients; and the insurance industry, once freed of mandates, could offer a wider variety of coverage to meet the budgets and circumstances of individual clients."—Ron Bailey[215]

People should pay for their own health insurance. The typical policy would be "catastrophic coverage," meaning that you are covered for large medical expenses. However, catastrophic coverage means that deductibles are high, so that if you have only modest medical expenses in a given year you pay them yourself. Of course, people should be free to choose medical plans with low deductibles, but those plans will tend to be expensive and inefficient.

Poor people should receive vouchers that enable them to obtain catastrophic coverage. These vouchers will be financed by taxpayer money, of course. Because hospitals are not going to refuse to treat people, everyone should be required to obtain catastrophic coverage, just as every driver is required to obtain auto insurance.

Health care benefits paid by businesses should be taxable to individuals. This would eliminate the tax advantage to business-paid health care, which in turn would lead to companies dropping health care as a benefit. This would get ordinary companies out of the health care business. It would eliminate the situation in which a change of employer automatically means having to reconfigure your health coverage.

A health care system in which government involvement is limited to providing vouchers to the poor would be better for the poor as well as more efficient in many respects than what we have today. Unfortunately, mental illness blinds many people to the feasibility and wisdom of such an approach.

Fear of Losing Employer Coverage

After over half a century of employer-provided health care coverage, the American people have developed a phobia of paying for health insurance themselves. In 1994, when I left Freddie Mac to start my own business, I obtained catastrophic coverage for my family of five for less than $4000 a year (rates have gone up since). To me, this seemed like a trivial expense when compared to the salary that I was giving up, which had been close to $100,000 a year. Yet when my friends expressed concern about the risks I was taking, it was always over losing health benefits, never over giving up my salary.

Basic economic theory says that employers could make their employees better off by giving them cash income rather than the in-kind benefit of health care coverage. Employees could use the cash to purchase health care coverage directly from insurance companies, which would result in a more efficient system. What precludes this from happening today is the tax deduction that employers receive for providing health care benefits, which in turn are *not* treated as taxable income by employees. This tax subsidy distorts the market for health care, raising the cost of health care for everyone.

The Delusion of Collective Affordability

In a previous chapter, "The Statism Trap," I alluded to the problem of socialized medicine. When that essay first appeared on the World Wide Web, one reader provided aggressive feedback. He was adamant that health care is so expensive that the only way people can afford it is if the government pays the bill.

Anyone who believes that we can afford collectively what we cannot afford individually is delusional. Based on my experience with the reader's feedback, this delusion appears to be untreatable. However, I think it is important to point out this peculiar mental illness.

Suppose that a group of friends is getting ready to go out for dinner. At first, they consider a fancy restaurant, but then it is pointed out that the price of a meal there is higher than anyone in the group can afford. Somebody pipes up and says, "That's ok. We can just split the check." Does that make sense?

Paying for health care with taxpayer dollars means splitting the check for health care. Health care costs do not diminish. Quite the contrary. Just as splitting the check at a restaurant tends to lead people to order more expensive meals than what they would order on their own, insulating individuals from the cost of health care decisions tends to make them less cost-conscious in their health care choices.

Health care differs from a restaurant meal in that one family may end up with unusually large expenses, due to a severe illness. However, we can pool our risks of severe illness with catastrophic health insurance coverage. Thomas Sowell[216] points out that this is how auto insurance works, "but our automobile insurance does not cover gasoline or oil changes." Health care policies that pay for routine doctor visits are the equivalent of auto insurance that covers gasoline and oil changes.

When the government pays, health care's lack of affordability becomes a self-fulfilling prophecy. In health care, as in other things, government is the high-cost producer (see chapter on "Government: The High-Cost Producer").

Paternalism

Any attempt to inject market discipline in health care is denounced as an assault on the poor. Somehow, self-interest cannot be trusted when what is at stake is a "basic need." As my earlier adversary put it, "Is there something more valuable than keeping people alive and healthy that society should be paying for?"

This form of mental illness might be called paternalistic paranoia. It is the belief that the market is out to get people, so the government must step in and make choices for them.

Instead, we might want to consider how the choices that people make reveal their own beliefs about what is valuable. W. Michael Cox and Richard Alm, in *Myths of Rich & Poor*, pointed out that in 1994 over 90 percent of poor households owned a color television. The majority of the poor owned microwave ovens, VCR's, and cable television hookups. Almost three-fourths of such households owned one or more cars. From this sort of data, one must infer either that there *is* something more valuable than health care coverage or that poor people have obtained enough coverage and are moving on to meeting other needs.

We could provide for the health care needs of the poor at far less cost by using vouchers in a market setting rather than using pervasive government intervention. However, as Sowell writes,[217] "here, as elsewhere, the poor are being used as excuses to fasten a whole system of controls on all of us. The left uses the poor as political human shields."

Chapter 49

Health Insurance Do-Nots

"Forget about the haves and the have-nots. America now faces a divide between do's and do-nots . . . Conservatives, Sawhill argues, will need to spend more generously on child care subsidies and wage supplements and last-resort jobs to get the poor working (jobs bring mainstream values as well as money). Liberals will need to accept that money without behavioral change is useless or worse."—Jonathan Rauch[218]

Columnist Jonathan Rauch points out that poverty is dominated by behavioral factors. The best anti-poverty program would be to increase work and reduce out-of-wedlock births. This approach of looking at "do-nots" vs. "have-nots" ought to be applied to health insurance.

A new Census report found that the number of Americans without health insurance has increased. Interestingly, the number *with* health insurance also increased.[219] This fact did not receive as much notice.

In any case, the supporters of the nanny state reacted predictably to the news. The New York Times editorialized,[220] "The lack of health insurance, a problem once confined mostly to the poor and nearly poor, has reached into the lower middle classes, most notably to those earning $25,000 to $49,999 a year, and even to some above $50,000. It is a problem that needs to be addressed by Congress and the administration, which have thus far sat mostly on the sidelines."

More Mental Illness

In the chapter "America is Mentally Ill," I wrote that our health care policy reflects mental illness. The fundamental problem is that we believe that health insurance is something that only should be received as a gift—never obtained for oneself. Thus, we immediately assume that when a family does not have health insurance, they are to be pitied for not having received the gift, rather than being blamed for not having taken responsibility.

After the Census report was announced, the evening News Hour on PBS featured a young man (he appeared to be about 30) without health insurance who had been diagnosed with melanoma. The focus of the feature was the financial hardship that the man was going to have to undergo, including putting his family deeply into debt.

While I truly feel sorry for this man, I have to say that the worst of the financial burden of his illness was avoidable. When he was healthy, he could have obtained health insurance. Instead, he chose to spend his income on other things. He was a health insurance "do-not."

However, the thrust of the story was not, "Let this be a lesson to you. Buy health insurance, because you never know when you may need it." Instead, as in the *Times* editorial, the PBS story treated the man as a victim because he did not have employer-provided or government-provided health insurance.

Redistributing Health Insurance

In fact, everyone in the country pays for health insurance, whether or not they have it. When you pay for goods and services, part of the cost is the cost of employer-provided health insurance. In addition, everyone who is on a payroll pays taxes for Medicare, which provides health coverage for the elderly.

In the chapter "Bleeding-heart Libertarianism," I argued that the welfare state redistributes poverty and may make it worse. Many people find this counterintuitive.

However, health insurance is a prime example of welfare state policies that impoverish some at the expense of others. The taxes that a young middle-class family pays to provide health coverage to the elderly (many of whom are well off) is money that the family cannot use to buy its own health insurance. Corporate employees have their health care subsidized by people who work for small businesses and the self-employed, even though the latter may have lower incomes.

The *Times* is right to note that the middle classes are squeezed today. However, as my essay pointed out, that squeeze comes from the welfare state. If instead we had the bleeding-heart libertarian approach to taxation, the middle classes would have more after-tax income to spend on health care.

Mandatory Health Insurance

I believe that some form of catastrophic health care coverage ought to be mandatory. This is a departure from pure libertarianism.

Mandatory health insurance would eliminate the problem of "do nots." One paternalistic argument for mandatory health insurance is that people who do not choose insurance are taking an irrational gamble. Like the cancer victim profiled on PBS, they do not appreciate health risks until it is too late to insure against them.

My argument for mandatory health insurance is slightly different. I believe that it is inevitable that taxpayers will offer some assistance to people with low incomes. Given that this is the case, then taxpayers have the right to insist that this government assistance should be spent responsibly. Although it is paternalistic, mandatory health insurance at least treats health care as a purchase and not a gift. If instead we think of health care as something to be provided to us, and we think of those without health insurance as "have-nots" rather than "do-nots," then we are headed toward socialized medicine. Given the natural tendency for the health care sector to grow as new technologies develop, and given the way in which third-party payment for health care services stimulates demand, this means that our economy will become less and less free. That will turn all of us into have-nots.

Chapter 50

Phase Out Medicare

The most critical economic issue for the 21st century is socialized medicine. Largely because of Medicare, the default scenario for the United States in the middle of the century is that government spending on health care will be about 10 percent of GDP. It could be twice that under a "single-payer" system, as endorsed by many on the left.

With Republicans in control of Congress and the Presidency, this may be the last chance to change course in this country. If we continue on the path of socialized medicine, there is every reason to fear that the United States will fall into the debilitating, low-growth, over-taxed trap that has Europe and Japan in its grip.

If the Bush Administration is looking for a bold economic agenda, then I believe that the best choice would be to take steps to return health care to the private sector. The most effective way to do this would be to raise the Medicare eligibility age for everyone under the age of 50.

Bigger than Social Security

In a paper on "Fiscal and Generational Imbalances," economists Jagadeesh Gokhale and Kent Smetters calculate that the present value of the excess of future government liabilities relative to tax revenue is $44.2 trillion, of which $36.6 trillion is accounted for by Medicare. Thus, the problem of future deficits is mostly attributable to Medicare, which has much higher unfunded liabilities than even Social Security.

Robert Fogel[221] says that the health care sector of the economy is undergoing a secular increase, which he believes could take it from 14 percent of GDP today to 21 percent of GDP later in this century. My guess is that if he is correct, then Medicare spending alone will be more than 10 percent of GDP.

How to Phase Out Medicare

I believe that if we are going to stay out of the government-expansion trap that has been set for us, and the high-tax future that it implies, we will have to do more than just tinker with Medicare at the margins. We need to phase it out. (Actually, what I am proposing would reduce the size of Medicare, but not phase it out completely.)

The most practical way to phase out Medicare is to raise the age of eligibility, so that people spend more of their lives paying for their own health insurance and less of their lives taking government money. However, it seems to me that it would be unfair to change the terms of the social contract for people who are within 15 years of the traditional retirement age of 65. Therefore, I would start to phase out Medicare for people aged 50 and younger.

I would immediately raise the Medicare eligibility age to 75 for everyone aged 50 and younger. Then, I would index the eligibility age to average longevity, so that the eligibility age continues to rise as longevity increases. If longevity continues to increase at the rate of about 1/4 year per year, then the eligibility age would rise at that rate.

Once you reach 50, your eligibility age would be locked in. For example, someone who is 46 today would be given an initial eligibility age of 75. However, by the time they reach 50, the eligibility age might have increased to 76. At that point, that person's Medicare eligibility would be locked in to age 76.

For Social Security, a similar change to the retirement age would be an effective way to move in the direction of privatization. Moreover, David Levine[222] estimates that by a much less Draconian increase in the Social Security retirement age (moving it to 70 in the year 2030), we could eliminate the projected deficit in that program.

The Sugar Coating

The Medicare phase-out would produce long-term benefits for the economy, but it offers relatively little in terms of short-term economic or political advantage. One short-run gain might come from lower long-term interest rates, as the bond market calculates the reduction in future government liabilities. However, particularly given the high unemployment rate, we should be looking for a sugar coating for the phase-out plan. I have two proposals in that regard.

First, I would propose eliminating the Medicare tax, which would lop about 1.5 percentage points off of the odious payroll tax. In the short run, I would recommend not cutting spending elsewhere, and instead letting this serve as an economic stimulus. Once the unemployment rate falls to a more reasonable level, we could try to find spending cuts elsewhere in the government Budget to offset the shortfall in payroll tax revenues.

The second sugar-coating proposal would be a new government-matching IRA account for people born in 1953 or later (i.e., those affected by the increase in the Medicare eligibility age). The idea would be to encourage people under the age of 50 to save money for their old age by providing both tax advantages and government matching funds. These savings accounts would help people to support themselves until they reach the age when they are eligible to receive Medicare.

Conclusion

Willie Sutton said that he robbed banks "because that's where the money is." In the 21st century, the size of government will be determined by the mix between public and private spending on health care, because that is where the money will be. Under current policy, those of us who favor a smaller government are on a losing course. Our number one priority should be to phase out Medicare.

Chapter 51

The Great Race

In 2003, the moviegoing public was treated to a depiction of the rivalry between two Depression-era horses—War Admiral and Seabiscuit. One can view the future outlook for the United States economy as a similar contest, in this case between Moore's Law and Medicare.

Of all of the possible indicators that might be used to assess the success of the economy, I would select the ratio of government outlays to GDP. If this ratio gets to be too high, then the economy will collapse under the weight of the taxes needed to fund the government. The lower the ratio, the more confidence I have in the sustainability of the economy.

Some historical behavior of the ratio of government spending to GDP is shown in the following table.

Year	Percent of GDP spent on Social Security, Medicare, and Education*
1960	5.8
1970	8.6
1980	10.2
1990	10.9
2000	11.5

*Education spending includes only state and local government expenditures on education.

LEARNING ECONOMICS

This table understates spending on what I call the Welfare State, because it excludes Medicaid, Federal spending on education, and various subsidies to education and health care that are embedded in the tax code. However, it does indicate the general upward trend in government spending on health, education, and retirement benefits. All three components are a growing share of the economy.

War Admiral vs. Seabiscuit

For the next fifty years, I see two major factors at work. One factor makes me optimistic. The other factor makes me pessimistic.

The optimistic element in the outlook is technological progress, particularly in computing. The economy should grow faster than ever, because of Moore's Law (see Chapter on "Rationally Exuberant"). Increased computing power is going to fuel the economy in a number of ways.

- The technology of the late 1990's has so far only been adopted and utilized effectively in a few industries. That means that we still have in front of us much of the gains from diffusion of current technology. Classic economic studies of hybrid corn[223] and the dynamo[224] support this view of gradual adoption of technology.
- We are in the early stages of a revolution in wireless communications. At a conference in 2003, Microsoft's Maria Fernandez speculated on a future in which most of the devices connected to the Internet will be unmanned sensors and radios, acting autonomously. Along these lines, we have seen descriptions of potential uses for radio chips in passports,[225] currency,[226] keeping track of personal possessions,[227] and numerous commercial applications.[228]
- Advances in computer processing are helping to drive advances in biotechnology. As Randall Parker put it,[229]

there are "signs that biotechnology is going to advance at rates which are analogous to the way electronics technology has been advancing for decades. If that is the case we should expect to see the costs for taking apart and manipulating biological systems to drop by orders of magnitude while the speed of doing so rises by orders of magnitude as well."
- Nanotechnology,[230] which is another beneficiary of improved computing, seems to be advancing even faster than was expected a few years ago.

But if Moore's Law is the economy's War Admiral, then Medicare is government's Seabiscuit. A new study by Jagadeesh Gokhale and Kent Smetters[231] shows just how large Medicare looms in the future. They argue that the present value of the difference between future Medicare obligations and future Medicare tax receipts is a staggering $36.6 trillion. This swamps all other future Budget issues, including the current national debt. The comparable fiscal imbalance in Social Security is only about $7 trillion in their estimate.

Gokhale and Smetters estimate that it would take a permanent tax increase of more than 6 percent of GDP to fund the fiscal imbalance in Medicare. If we take the structure of Medicare as given, and if economic growth fails to accelerate, then I believe that the liberals who argue for the repeal of the Bush tax cut are correct. The Gokhale-Smetters calculations show that what we need instead is a large tax *increase*, and the longer we wait to enact this tax increase, the larger it will have to be.

A Scenario Analysis

One way to summarize the possible outcomes of the great race is to consider four possible scenarios, based on different assumptions about the key drivers of Moore's Law and

Medicare. This scenario analysis is presented in the following table.

Four Scenarios	Moore's Law Fails	Moore's Law Succeeds
Medicare Is Reformed	Low Gear	Capitalist Utopia
Medicare Is not Reformed	Economic Implosion	Affordable Welfare State

By Medicare reform, I mean something like my proposal to phase out Medicare (see chapter on "Phase Out Medicare"). Reform means that health care decisions are made in the private sector, and it means that twenty years from now the cost of treating the elderly is not paid for by taxes on the young.

By Moore's Law succeeding I mean more than just that the cost of computer processing continues to fall. I mean that the applications enabled by faster computing pan out and have a significant impact on increasing productivity. Although government policy can affect this somewhat, I believe that for the most part the success or failure of Moore's Law will depend on conditions in science, technology, and the private sector.

I believe that if we have both Medicare reform and success with Moore's Law, then the economy will win its race with government decisively, leading to what I call Capitalist Utopia. As individuals, we will enjoy high incomes, with the median household in thirty years living better than someone in the top 20 percent today. Those Baby Boomers who save prudently in response to the planned phase-out of Medicare will find health care affordable, thanks to a high rate of return on savings and new medical technologies that reduce treatment costs. However, Boomers who do not save for retirement will cry out for government support, and they will be filled with resentment for their "rich" (i.e., prudent-saving) counterparts.

At the other extreme, if Moore's Law fails and Medicare is not reformed, then the tax burden on the working population will increase beyond anything that has been seen in a viable economy, which means that we could see an Economic Implosion. Many of the most creative, hard-working people will be driven out of the mainstream economy. Some may go abroad, to take advantage of low-tax havens. Others will work underground, in a growing black-market sector. This in turn will force the government to raise tax rates further, driving more productive workers away, in a vicious downward spiral. Health care is rationed, and its quality deteriorates for everyone.

An intermediate scenario is one in which Medicare is reformed but Moore's Law fails. I call this "Low Gear," because the economy will still function, but economic growth will be slow. Even Baby Boomers who have saved prudently will find in their retirement years that after they pay for health insurance they have little discretionary income.

A better intermediate scenario is one in which Moore's Law succeeds but Medicare is not reformed. Paying for the Baby Boomers' health care requires a large increase in tax *revenues*, but the impact on tax *rates* is mitigated by the high level of GDP. Thus, I call this scenario "Affordable Welfare State."

Medicare Hedgehog?

In terms of Isaiah Berlin's famous metaphor,[232] President Bush has been called a "hedgehog," meaning that he has a narrow focus. In foreign policy, his focus has been on defeating the forces of terror, and this strikes me as correct.

In domestic policy, the President's focus has been on tax cuts, which makes me nervous. Although the intent is to hold down government as a share of GDP, the tax cuts may fail to do so. For one thing, the size of the Bush tax cuts is overblown.[233] More important, in the absence of Medicare reform, it is very doubtful that even those modest tax cuts can be sustained.

I wish that instead of remaining a tax-cut hedgehog, President Bush would become a Medicare-reform hedgehog. Otherwise, we had better hope that Moore's Law beats Medicare in the great horserace.

Chapter 52

The World's Nicest Holding Pen

"Because maybe college isn't the be-all and end-all that parents make it out to be. You know, I mean, maybe once you get past the rhetoric of all these great books that nobody reads, college is basically just a holding pen for 18-to 22-year-olds."—Dawson[234] *("Future Tense," episode #404, "Dawson's Creek.")*

College tuitions have increased at a rate of 2 or 3 percent more than general inflation over the past thirty years, according to Cornell University's Ron Ehrenberg.[235] This means that the real cost of going to college has nearly doubled in that span.

When a price increases by this magnitude, it is important not to lose track of the law of supply and demand. A clear implication of basic economics is that it is impossible to explain the increase in college costs by looking at only one factor. This type of sustained price increase can only occur if *both* demand is rising *and* costs are going up. Without cost increases, higher demand would induce more supply, with only modest price changes. Without increased demand, cost increases would translate into a market with fewer consumers, rather than more consumers paying higher prices.

In this essay, I want to make two points. First, "college" is a different good than it was thirty years ago, when I was an undergraduate. Second, college is an information industry that operates by industrial-age methods.

The Rise of Aesthetics

Virginia Postrel's book, *The Substance of Style*,[236] argues that the aesthetic component of consumption has increased dramatically in recent years. I have yet to read the book, so that I do not know whether it uses college as an example. However, having heard Postrel outline her book's thesis in a talk, I believe that it makes for a good fit.

Here are some of the ways in which the aesthetic aspect of college has changed in thirty years, without necessarily changing what used to be the substance of college:

- **Food.** I can remember when the Swarthmore cafeteria only offered one choice at dinner, such as liver and onions, or veal cutlet (known as "vile cutlet"). If you did not like that, you got a slice of bread and smeared on some industrial peanut butter from a large vat. Nowadays, students get the types of food choices that one sees in suburban mall food courts.
- **Facilities.** Fitness centers resemble expensive health clubs. The University of Maryland's performing arts center is as luxurious as the Kennedy Center. Swarthmore has a magnificent auditorium that seats several hundred—and is almost always empty at a college that prides itself on small classes.
- **Ethnic solidarity.** Postrel argues that consumers use aesthetics to express their identity. Her bumper-sticker phrase that describes the identity-driven motive for consumption is, "I like that. I'm like that." This is very evident on college campuses, where there are special buildings for the African-American student union, for Jewish students, and for other segments. Ethnic-group clubs are

the most thriving student organizations on campus. One of my academic friends wryly notes that "there is a dean for all three genders, for each ethnic group, and for every intersecting combination." Entire academic departments, such as Black Studies or Women's Studies, have emerged to serve no purpose other than "I like that. I'm like that."
- **Professional sports.** The University of Maryland cannot provide housing for all of the students who would like to live on campus. However, it was able to afford a new stadium and a new arena for its football and basketball teams.
- **Urban settings.** Students want access to clubs, restaurants, and a variety of entertainment. New York University and Boston University are brimming with applicants, while small midwestern colleges are finding themselves at a competitive disadvantage.

These aesthetic values were not forced onto college students unwillingly. On the contrary, colleges that are deficient in aesthetics pay a price in terms of lower application rates. If college is a holding pen, then it is populated by 18- to 22-year-olds who insist that it should be a pleasant, comfortable, and entertaining one.

I am not trying to say that the college experience ought to revert to some mythical past in which students experienced a monastic existence. Granted, I have strong philistine tendencies. But rather than make a value judgment, I wish to make the point that college represents a different bundle of services than it did thirty years ago, and part of where the increase in tuition goes is to pay for this rise in aesthetics.

Industrial-Strength Education

Education is at the center of the information age, and it is a driving force in economic growth. The information age is characterized by economies of scale, with diseconomies of scope.[237] Ironically, college education is stuck in some industrial-era habits.

To take advantage of economies of scale, information-age companies must make their products inter-operate. Cell phone calls have to reach people with different providers. Computer software companies must go as far as they can to make their products inter-operable without eliminating proprietary advantages altogether. In the 1990's, Microsoft thrived because its competitors failed to provide the level of inter-operability with third-party hardware and software that the Evil Empire delivered. The Internet took off because its protocols provide inter-operability.

Colleges are not inter-operable. My daughter's calculus course at the University of Rochester could not be used to meet the math requirement at the University of Maryland. You would think that she was trying to repair a General Motors car with a Ford part. In higher education, inter-operability actually has declined in the past thirty years. When I was in college, it was relatively easy to transfer and stay on track to graduate in four years. Now, doing so can be difficult or even impossible.

If colleges pursued inter-operability, then courses would be less location-dependent. If freshman economics is going to be taught in large lecture format, then instead of 20 universities each putting a professor in front of 250 students, a single lecture could be broadcast to all 5000 students. My daughter's economics class was given by that distinguished lecturer, A. Warm Body, who seems to wind up teaching the majority of courses nowadays. With modern communication technology, this is inexcusable.

To reduce diseconomies of scope, colleges have to limit their course offerings. A college cannot offer a large variety of disciplines, sub-disciplines, and cross-disciplines in a cost-effective manner. Specialization is inevitable. This increases the value of inter-operability. If students can construct special majors or take special courses by taking advantage of resources at other institutions, that will be more cost-effective than trying to have every college be all things to all students.

Another key to avoiding diseconomies of scope is the ability to let go of poorly-performing professors and uncompetitive departments. The information age rewards dynamic excellence, not stable mediocrity.

The sectors of our economy that are growing most rapidly are characterized by the highest rate of failure. Economic growth is a process of trial-and-error learning. If errors are not corrected and failures are not quickly shut down, then experiments become too costly to conduct. If most new businesses fail, then most new academic departments should fail, also. Without a process for quick failure, institutions have to be somewhat reluctant to create new departments.

Jack Welch of General Electric reportedly decreed that if a division of GE was not in the top three in its market, then that division would be sold. No such ruthlessness exists in academia. Mediocrity and failure are tolerated indefinitely.

A Future of Outsourcing?

Colleges today are in a position to continue to increase tuition charges. They have successfully met the demand for the aesthetic qualities desired by parents and students. They have achieved market dominance by becoming highly attractive holding pens.

On the other hand, the ability of college to provide educational substance at reasonable cost is diminishing. To me, this suggests that in the future colleges will turn increasingly to outsourcing. Rather than rely on an internally-selected faculty, a college might turn to a specialized supplier. That supplier might provide instructional videos and software in addition to live professors. Rather than enjoy the privilege of institutional tenure, professors might sell their lecture time through agencies that book popular speakers.

In the information age, many manufacturing companies have become supply-chain integrators. You might hire consultants to design a product, go to China to manufacture it, hire a logistics specialist to ship it, and rely on a value-added reseller to market it. I could see colleges going down the same path. A generation from now, the most successful colleges may be the ones that provide the best aesthetics, while outsourcing the actual function of education.

Chapter 53

Efficiency, Entrepreneurship, and Education

Sometimes, you will hear a governor talk about the need to entice more entrepreneurs to his state. In my opinion, if you really want to bring entrepreneurs into your state, you should enact a school voucher program that enables entrepreneurs to compete with public schools on a level playing field.

Since I sold my business, I have said that I have no plans to become a serial entrepreneur. However, I am attracted by the notion of starting a school. Unfortunately, Montgomery County, Maryland is so heavily Democratic that even charter schools are viciously opposed by the local authorities.

As an economist, I tend to look at education from the standpoint of efficiency and equity. This essay will examine the case for vouchers in terms of efficiency, which means the quality of education relative to cost. My next essay will look at the issue of equity, which means the role of education in affecting the distribution of income and wealth.

Big Profit Margins

I started examining this issue back in 2000, when my youngest daughter was in sixth grade in the local public schools. When the school held its annual parent night, we got

LEARNING ECONOMICS

to meet the teachers. The science teacher mentioned casually that over the course of a day she teaches 180 students.

I was surprised by the figure of 180 students per day. From an educational perspective, this seems like too many. How can a teacher assign and grade homework from 180 students?

However, what really struck me about the teaching load was its economic implications. It made me think in terms of the key operating ratios in Montgomery County Public Schools.

There are about six academic classes in a day in middle school. Therefore, the middle school science teacher handles 1/6th of the total teaching for each of her 180 students. So we can say that she accounts for 30 "student-years" worth of education.

In 2000, the county spent about $8,000 per year on each student. Multiplying 30 student-years by $8,000 gives $240,000, which represents the annual "sales per teacher" for the County.

Meanwhile, the cost per teacher, including salary and benefits, was probably not more than $80,000 a year. In other words, the County's primary cost is $80,000, and they mark it up all the way to $240,000. What a business! A consulting firm would love to have those kind of profit margins.

For comparison, consider Sandy Spring Friends School, where our oldest daughter went to high school. Tuition was $14,000 a year, which at first makes it appear more expensive. However, the number of students that a teacher sees in a day is much lower. I believe that 60 per day is a conservative estimate. Again, we take 1/6th of that to get "student-years," because there are about six academic periods per day. This gives us 10 student-years per teacher at Sandy Spring. Multiplying by tuition, "sales per teacher" amounts to something like $140,000 per year.

Teachers are paid less at Sandy Spring, so that the cost per teacher might be just $60,000, including salary and benefits. Nonetheless, it is not as good a business as the public school. The public school charges a $160,000 markup over its direct cost ($240,000-$80,000), while Sandy Spring has a profit margin per teacher of only $80,000 ($140,000-$60,000).

Of course, what I am calling "markup" or profit margin actually is overhead. My point is that public schools have a lot of overhead.

The County will tell you that the overhead is necessary to handle "special needs" and diversity. In fact, there clearly are programs in the budget that reflect these issues.

For example, the western half of the County traditionally has been more affluent and less diverse than the eastern half, where I live. These disparities give rise to special needs.

The special need that the County identified was that the affluent white kids from the western half require enrichment programs, such as advanced mathematics and science. They also need to visit schools in our half of the county in order to make their parents feel less guilty.

To meet these special needs, the County set up "magnet" programs in some of the schools in our half of the county. The rich white kids who require advanced mathematics instruction are brought over in buses every day to their special math programs. At lunch, they get to see our "diverse" population.

My guess is that this is not the most efficient way to meet the special needs of the affluent white kids and their parents. Instead, the school system might have offered the special math programs in the local schools in the western half of the County, and sent the kids on occasional field trips to our half in order to see children of other backgrounds.

A Voucher System

More generally, what if we had a voucher system in place in Montgomery County? What would happen to private schools, public schools, and teachers?

Let us assume that the public schools all would be taken over by private entrepreneurs. There might emerge a variety of school formats, but I want to speculate about the average school.

My guess is that the "profit margin" or "markup" would fall. It would fall for the former public schools, because of competitive pressure. It would fall for private schools, because they would tend to become larger, helping to create economies of scale. (Some classes at Sandy Spring have only a handful of students, which is educationally unsound as well as economically unsustainable.) Let us assume that the markup per teacher would settle at $60,000 per year.

The number of student-years per teacher probably would end up somewhere between the 10 that we see at Sandy Spring and the 30 that we see in public school. I would hope that it would end up closer to the Sandy Spring figure. Let us say that it turns out to be 15.

If the number of student-years per teacher ends up at 15, then we will need many more classroom teachers than currently are supplied by public schools. Some of these teachers would come from cutbacks in overhead, as administrators return to the classroom. However, many of the new teachers would have to come from the market. This would require higher salaries. Let us assume that the total cost per teacher would have to rise to $90,000 per year.

Adding the teacher salary of $90,000 to the markup of $60,000 gives $150,000 per year as the basic operating cost per teacher in our hypothetical average post-voucher school. If a teacher handles 15 students, then to get $150,000 we need to charge $10,000 a year. If students receive only an $8,000 voucher, then on average families will have to pay an additional $2,000 a year on top of their vouchers. In other words, we cannot double the number of teachers per student simply by increasing efficiency. More money must be spent as well.

Opponents argue that vouchers cannot possibly work. As an economist, I find their arguments untenable. Markets work, and prices adjust. The bloated overhead of public schools (and, to a lesser extent, of private schools) can be cut. Teacher salaries can be increased. And parents can supplement public expenditures.

You will hear people scorn vouchers by saying that "there are not enough private schools." The point of this essay is that with plausible adjustments the market could make every school a private school.

CHAPTER 54

EQUITY, ENTREPRENEURSHIP, AND EDUCATION

Many people appear to oppose school vouchers on equity grounds. However, it is difficult to pin down this argument.

One voucher proponent tells me that he is opposed to markets in education, because "Markets create winners and losers." However, he is opposed to all markets for this reason. His point of view appears to be that markets are the poison apple of inequality in a Garden of Eden of natural prosperity. Given his lack of intellectual rigor, it is not surprising that he sends his children to private schools even as he denounces the voucher movement.

Instead, I take it as given that markets provide efficiency and innovation. The question then becomes, where would you oppose a market?

For example, I oppose a market in professional baseball. I do not care about other sports, but in baseball I value equity and tradition more than efficiency and innovation. I would like to see the cities own the teams, with revenue sharing and no free agency for players. That would lead to team continuity and to fewer advantages for big-market teams.

In education, I also value equity. However, in contrast with baseball, I do not dismiss innovation and efficiency. In baseball, if there is no innovation, and the quality of play holds steady, that is acceptable. Not so with education, where I believe that we need progress. Therefore, the case for a public sector monopoly in education is not as strong.

In education, there are two equity issues. One issue pertains to parental income. How much do we want the quality of a child's education to depend on the income of his or her parents? The other issue pertains to learning disabilities. How much spending on children with special needs is appropriate to compensate for their disabilities?

Our current educational system is regressive with respect to income. People with higher incomes tend to live in areas with higher property tax revenues, so that their children tend to benefit from more resources spent on schools.

With respect to learning disabilities, our system provides some special programs. However, it also has special programs for children who are gifted. In that sense, our current system includes regressive as well as progressive components.

With a voucher system, one could have somewhat more confidence in the equity of education. For example, we could give larger vouchers to people who have less income with which to supplement a voucher. In addition, we could give larger vouchers to students with learning disabilities.

My guess is that many people would be willing to pay a huge premium in order for their children to attend schools that are regarded as the best. Wealthy families might be willing to pay tuition of $25,000 or more per year. It would be difficult to offer that much in vouchers to poor people to enable them to compete.

The case for enabling poor people to compete to send their children to good schools is that the schools are a major transmission mechanism for inequality. If you have the choice between leaving your child a million dollars or leaving her with a good education, chances are that the latter will have a more enduring effect on her well-being.

Therefore, it is conceivable that we would want to enact a "luxury estate tax" on private school tuition. If the tuition is above, say, $20,000, some of the tuition might be taxed. The revenue from this tax could be used to increase the money that is available for vouchers for low-income parents.

Determining the size of supplements for learning disabilities would be a challenge. As best as I can figure it, some government bureaucracy would have to identify the most desirable level of supplementary funding for a given disability. For example, the government might decide that a certain disability requires 40 hours a year of tutoring, at $25 an hour, or $1,000 in additional spending. Then parents of children with that disability would receive an additional $1,000 in voucher money.

Ultimately, the parents of children with learning disabilities would determine the types of programs that their kids receive. Relative to the educational enhancements used by the bureaucrats to set the amount of the supplement, parents could choose special programs that are more intensive, less intensive, or different altogether.

The voucher supplements associated with each disability would have to be sufficient to motivate schools to offer services for the learning disabled. If hardly any private schools offer programs for a learning disability, then this is a sign that the funds for that disability are not sufficient.

It would be a challenge to determine the amount of voucher supplement for each learning disability. These supplements would have to be based on difficult judgments about ethics and money. However, in our current education system, the same sorts of judgments are made. They are implicit in the programs that are provided to the learning disabled.

I do not know how to define perfect equity in education, and even if we could define it I doubt that we could achieve it. Our current education system is regressive with respect to income and not clearly progressive with respect to learning disabilities. With a voucher system that varies the amount of the voucher based on parents' income and on learning disabilities, we could arrive at a system that is more equitable.

CHAPTER 55

MANDATORY LIBERTARIANISM

"I'm a geneticist," the woman said, as she began an impassioned speech against vouchers and school choice. "I don't want to see schools where students are not taught evolution. And I want to make sure that they get sex education and learn to use a condom."

The setting was a debate over vouchers between Tanya Clay of People for the American Way[238] (opposed) and Marie Gryphon[239] of the Cato Institute (in favor). It was held at a meeting of "Coffee and Politics" in Washington, DC. (It seems like all groups that meet in the District cater to a singles-bar demographic. I felt conspicuously middle-aged and married.)

"I'm an economist," I wanted to reply. "I don't want to see schools where students are not taught libertarianism." Unfortunately, mandatory libertarianism is too much of an oxymoron. But if I could propose a required course in libertarianism for all Americans, here are some ideas that I would want students to take away.

1. Government cannot be relied upon as benevolent.

A useful way to think about the scope of government is to ask what would happen if a particular government power were exercised by someone with whom you disagree. The geneticist should consider that giving government control over the curriculum for science or for sex education is not a guarantee that she will be happy with the curriculum. The balance of political forces could lead to teaching creationism and abstinence. Furthermore, even if her views prevail, those who are on the other side and who are equally passionate should have their rights respected.

Actually, I agree with Neil Postman,[240] who argues that schools should teach both creationism and evolution. The point is that students should learn to make up their own minds. But I believe that parents should be allowed to send their children to any schools they want. That includes schools that teach principles contrary to libertarianism and to American values. I just have to hope that young people receive enough exposure to good values to overcome the occasional bad school.

2. Government Is fallible.

Ultimately, it is people who make decisions in markets and in government. People are fallible in both settings. The difference is that in a market setting mistakes are corrected more quickly than in a government setting. Thus, even if markets were wrong 9 times out of 10 and government were right 9 times out of 10, over time markets would achieve better outcomes. On a small scale, the persistence of government mistakes can be seen in the mohair subsidy.[241] On a large scale, it can be seen in the between $30 and $50 billion dollars[242] wasted on renewable energy without providing any power that is economically viable.

3. Individuals are well motivated.

Most of the "coffee and politics" attendees were anti-vouchers. They expressed a strong distrust of individual choice. Ms. Clay said that the "single mom with two jobs

LEARNING ECONOMICS

does not have time" to choose the best school for her children. Others expressed similar concerns. However, when Prashant Kothari[243] asked how many of the twenty-odd attendees planned to have children in the DC public schools one day, no one raised their hand to express personal confidence in public schools for their future children.

I have confidence that people will make thoughtful decisions concerning their children. Consider a neighborhood couple, who are very left-wing and very committed to the public school system. She is a long-time public school teacher. He recently stopped going to his synagogue and started going to Quaker meetings because he was upset that his rabbi did not oppose the war in Iraq. For their own children, they chose a Jewish private school—obviously not for the religious education. On the other hand, even though I favor vouchers (see chapter on "Efficiency, Entrepreneurship, and Education"), we sent our children to the public school because we did not want the ethnic and economic homogeneity that comes with a private school under today's regime of very limited choices among private schools.

The point is that when people make decisions about their own children, they seem to make them with great care and a fair amount of wisdom. They certainly seem less dogmatic and hypocritical than when they make decisions about other people's children.

4. Markets deliver goods and services.

As Julian Sanchez[244] pointed out at the meeting, none of the voucher opponents could envision a viable free market in schools. Instead, they thought of vouchers as a pure transfer of funds from existing public schools to existing private schools, with no response of supply and demand in either.

Economists understand that a decentralized, impersonal market is capable of delivering goods and services. People who do not understand markets cannot really imagine how they work. They can only picture central planning to produce goods and Authority Ranking to make sure that they are distributed.

Ms. Clay and other opponents asserted that there could not possibly be enough private schools to support a voucher system. However, if education were completely privatized, then every school would be a private school by definition. All of the schools that exist today would still exist. Of course, parents would attempt to leave some existing schools and send their children to other schools. This increase in demand for alternatives to existing schools would induce today's private schools to expand as well as stimulate entrepreneurs to create new private schools. Ultimately, a better school system (as judged by parents as consumers) would be created by the same mechanism that delivers Australian clementines to an economics professor in Berkeley California (see the introduction to Part 1 of this book).

The Voucher Debate

Overall, considering that vouchers are viewed as a "radical" idea in education, the case against them is remarkably flimsy. Yes, it is possible that abusive or incompetent parents could make bad choices for their children, but taking the choice away from every parent because of the potential bad choices of a few seems unwarranted. Yes, it is possible that some children will go to schools where they do not learn the theory of evolution, but today many children go to schools where they do not even learn to read and write. Yes, it is likely that a privatized education system will not give everyone an equal education, but neither does today's system (see chapter on "Equity, Entrepreneurship, and Education").

The one argument against vouchers that was raised that I found challenging was an argument that school competition is limited by geography and transportation. People may find that when the costs of transportation are included, they have only one or two viable options for schools. If these sorts of local monopolies were to emerge, we might fail to see results that are as satisfying as from a strongly competitive market. But I suspect that in reality we would see much more powerful effects from competition.

The opponents of vouchers claim to want to protect us from the risk that vouchers will be an educational and/or ethical failure. However, I cannot shake the feeling that what they really fear is that libertarianism in education would be a practical and moral success.

Chapter 56

True or False: Does Standardized Testing Promote School Reform?

Many conservative education reformers, including President Bush, advocate the use of standardized testing as a tool for evaluating school performance. My knee-jerk liberal friends oppose it. The teachers' unions oppose it.

Ordinarily, this line-up of supporters and opponents would lead me to favor standardized testing. However, having thought about the issue, I believe that standardized testing should be opposed by conservatives—at least by those of us with a libertarian bent.

I have three perspectives on this issue. I can speak to it as an econometrician, as a teacher, and as a parent.

Signal and Noise

As a econometrician, I am prepared to argue that the signal to noise ratio in standardized testing is simply not high enough to support the burdens that its proponents place on it. The random variation in school-wide test scores can be quite high. There are some schools where the annual student turnover rate exceeds 30 percent, which has major effects both on the education process itself and the measurement of results. Even for a stable population, it would take years to obtain a reliable test average.

Even worse, in statistical terminology, school test results are an observational study as opposed to an experiment. In an experiment, the researcher is able to choose two equivalent groups, and have only one factor (the "treatment") differ between the two groups. In an observational study, the effect of the treatment (the school) is blended in with myriad other factors. These factors undermine the reliability of any conclusion that one might attempt to draw.

There are schools where education is taking place, but the population has so many deficits that the scores will indicate a failing school. Conversely, there are school populations which could score well even if classes were conducted by gerbils.

Teacher Accountability

Standardized testing is not a requirement for teacher accountability. There are many alternatives available.

For example, one way to hold teachers accountable is by having outside evaluations. Suppose that you teach a statistics class that is at an advanced high school level, but you did not want to teach to the AP test. Your school could contract with me for an outside evaluation. I could ask to see a copy of your final exam along with your grading criteria. I could review a random sample of the students' papers to make sure that your grading followed your plan. I could look at the overall results on the exam. Using this information, I could make a determination as to whether the material you offered is sufficiently rigorous and whether you were successful in teaching the concepts that you chose to emphasize.

School Accountability

Only a politician could argue that standardized testing is necessary in order to hold schools accountable. Accountable to whom, other than politicians? Test scores are not an accountability tool for parents, who should be the customers of the school system.

To be sure, some parents do use test scores. They will move into school districts with higher test scores. However, the parents who make such a move do not care whether those test scores reflect anything that the school is doing. These parents are not doing educational research. They are simply guessing that their child is better off in the high-scoring school—if nothing else the child will be exposed to high-achieving peers.

For the standardized testing approach to accountability, success *by definition* means making schools responsive to top-down control. In the case of the Bush Administration "reforms," standardized testing increases the leverage of the Federal government over local schools. Any conservative ought to think twice about supporting such a trend.

I believe that schools ought to be accountable to parents. I think that much of what is wrong with public schools today can be traced to the ways in which parents have become disempowered by politicians and special interests:

1. **Large school districts smother parents with bureaucracy.**

School principals feel more accountable to their administrators than to parents. Many policies are set externally and are beyond the control of the school's teachers or principal.

2. **Teachers' unions can control school boards.**

It only bothers me a little that in Montgomery County, Maryland where I live, the teachers' union endorses a slate of school board candidates. It concerns me a lot that nobody ever wins other than the candidates they endorse. There is a diversity of interests in school governance, and that diversity is not represented on the school board. There is no check on the Kudzu-like bureaucracy of curriculum specialists and cluster coordinators, which serves no purpose other than union featherbedding.

3. State and Federal programs come with strings attached.

Not content with local school performance, the state and Federal government layers have stepped in to "help." This gives schools another constituency of educrats to whom they must answer, further diluting parents' influence.

The forces of centralized control and top-down management of schools are strong already. I can see how standardized testing might help them, but do they need any more help?

The Right Focus

My personal inclination is to support school choice, with so-called "progressive vouchers" (meaning that voucher support would vary inversely with family wealth). However, even within the framework of public schools, my guess is that the route to improvement is more parental empowerment, not centralized testing.

In the 1950's and 1960's, "local control" of public schools got a bad name, because it was associated with racial segregation. But local control itself is a virtue, not a vice. Today, we need to find a way to bring back local control without returning to segregation.

In our school district, the knee-jerk liberal parents complain vociferously about standardized testing. I think that a significant part of their opposition to standardized testing reflects frustration over the ways that parents have been marginalized by the modern public school machine. I share that frustration.

Imagine what might happen if power over schools were re-distributed back to parents. This would require breaking large school districts down to a size that enables meaningful participation by parents. It would require that any state or Federal funding come with no strings attached. It would require local leaders willing to stand up to bureaucracy and union featherbedding.

I think that the focus of school reform ought to be on stripping away the centralized power structures and re-empowering parents. Standardized testing feels to me more like part of the problem than part of the solution.

Chapter 57

Government: The High-Cost Producer

As an economist, I am dismayed by the cavalier way in which politicians add to the roster of goods and services provided by the government. I cringe when I hear an official begin a sentence with the phrase "We need ___" where the blank might be filled in with "prescription drug coverage," "day care," "alternative sources of energy," or—most alarmingly—"to spend more money on education."

The political appeal of public provision of goods and services is that the recipients have the illusion of a free lunch. If you are paying hundreds of dollars a year for prescription drugs, and suddenly the government pays the cost, it seems as though you are getting something for nothing.

In fact, public provision of goods and services is anything but a free lunch. There is a textbook economic argument that shifting the method of funding goods and services from private-sector prices to public-sector taxes is very costly. There are at least three ways in which shifting from private provision to public provision lowers economic efficiency.

Inefficient Production

Compared with the private sector, government is not as motivated to select the most efficient production methods.

Nor is the government as flexible and motivated to continuously improve its production processes.

In fact, inefficiency in government is so ingrained that people often take it for granted. For example, blogger Kevin Drum[245] responded to a complaint by a taxpayer about the apparent failure of his satisfaction with government services to rise along with his tax bill by saying that compared with forty years ago, "much of the [increase in taxes] comes from the fact that we pay government employees more, just the same as we pay private sector employees more these days too thanks to rising GDP and increasing prosperity. School teachers, for example, are no longer expected to do their jobs for $15,000 per year."

Overlooked in Drum's analysis is the fact that the reason that private sector wages have risen is because productivity has gone up. The rise in private-sector productivity drives up private-sector wages, forcing government salaries to increase in order to keep pace.

In fact, if public-sector productivity were rising at the same rate as private-sector productivity, then a taxpayer could enjoy either a higher level of services, a lower level of taxes, or both. However, as the example of teachers illustrates, public-sector productivity lags far behind private-sector productivity. Because wages cannot be held down in line with low productivity gains, the cost of government services rises over time. Among economists, this phenomenon is known as Baumol's cost disease.[246]

Over-consumption

Demand is self-limiting when the consumer bears the cost of goods and services. The number of books that I purchase each month depends on my calculation of the benefit of owning the books relative to their cost. If the cost exceeds the benefit, then I stop buying.

On the other hand, if the government paid for my books, I would buy many more of them. Only storage considerations would limit my purchases.

Over-consumption tends to occur whenever government provides goods and services. For example, health care expenditures are on a sharply rising trend. There are many reasons for this, but one of them is the fact that many people feel that they are insulated from the cost of their lifestyle and health care decisions. When the government pays for health care, all of us pay more, and none of us has enough incentive to make choices that could lower the cost.

When demand is not self-limiting, it is up to the government to determine the level of its provision of goods and services. As blogger Kevin Brancato puts it[247], "how-on earth, not utopia—is it possible for the government to know if it is producing efficiently? Should it produce the good at all, charge more, or charge less?"

In the private sector, firms that are unable to provide goods at prices that cover their fixed and variable costs are forced to shut down. This prevents over-consumption. There is no comparable mechanism at work in the public sector.

Tax Distortions

Even if the government were to choose the most efficient production methods and limit output to prevent over-consumption, there would still be a reason to prefer private-sector pricing to taxpayer finance. That is because a dollar of tax revenue costs more than one dollar to collect.

An obvious cost of collecting taxes is compliance cost. Both the government and individuals have to put resources into the tax collection process.

A less-obvious cost of collecting taxes is the distortionary effect that they have on the economy. If you tax something, you get less of it. The income and payroll taxes punish work and thrift, which we otherwise would like to encourage. Even the real estate property tax is distortionary, because it reduces the incentive for owners to improve their properties. Taking into account distortions, the economic cost of $1.00 of tax revenue might be something like $1.25 or $1.50.

Education, Costs, and Benefits

All of these factors—inefficient production, over-consumption, and tax distortions—make government the highest-cost producer in the economy. Therefore, instead of looking for new opportunities to provide goods and services using tax revenues, politicians should be looking to hold government production to minimal levels.

For example, politicians talk about spending more on education as if this were a good thing. In fact, the more that the government substitutes public for private spending on education, the more resources it shifts to the high-cost producer.

There are public benefits to education, but those benefits are limited. By public benefits, I mean the benefits that do not accrue to the individual being educated. I have an incentive to obtain as much education as will benefit me. However, to the extent that my education also benefits you, then you might be willing to pay something to have me educated. Only this additional external benefit justifies taxpayer funding for education.

When the issue is formulated in these terms, it suggests a limited, narrow role for the government in supporting education. The government probably should provide support to poor people for obtaining education, because they otherwise may obtain sub-optimal amounts due to cash constraints. Beyond that, the case for government involvement in education becomes more difficult to make.

If we combine the limited extent to which education is a public good with the factors that make government the highest-cost producer, it becomes almost certain that the cost-benefit calculation for additional government spending on education is negative. In fact, on both equity and efficiency grounds, we would be much better off if we got the government out of the schooling business, except for need-based assistance to the poor and learning disabled.

Conclusion

Politically, it seems as though any attempt to shrink government is unthinkable. Democrats appear to be happy to tax and spend. Republicans appear to be happy to tax-cut and spend. But economists are obliged to remind everyone of the adverse consequences of shifting economic activity to the highest-cost producer.

A Final Note

If you have finished the other chapters in this book, then you probably have done some hard thinking. I hope that all along you were questioning my reasoning and composing responses and exceptions to my arguments. I hope that I have stimulated you to study economics further, not simply accept my ideas as the final truth. I would rather that you disagree intelligently than follow blindly.

Economics is both philosophical and computational. This book is heavy on the philosophy and light on the math. Should you wish to pursue your studies further, then I recommend learning the mathematical concepts of economics. College textbooks are one avenue for acquiring those concepts. Another source would be the study guides for high school AP economics.

I would warn you that standard textbooks and this book offer different perspectives. The textbook approach to economics studies the market as an *allocation* mechanism. The idea is to show how a given amount of resources can be used efficiently.

What I have come to appreciate even more is that the market is a *learning* mechanism. It encourages experimentation, keeps what works, and discards the rest. Conveying that concept of economics was my main purpose in writing this book.

For most of human history, market learning proceeded so slowly as to be scarcely noticeable. Today, the process is almost incomprehensibly fast. Children used to have to acquire knowledge from their elders. Now, it is often the parents and the grandparents who must ask for help with using the Internet or taking advantage of the features on a cell phone.

For centuries, family memories consisted of oral history. In the past few hundred years, people could write down their stories. Since the late 1800's, we have had photo albums. In the middle of the twentieth century, we took home movies. In the 1980's, we put family memories onto videocassette tapes. Already, those have to be discarded in favor of DVD's. And it is reasonable to wonder if those will not be superseded within a decade.

Because the pace of change is accelerating, I believe it is important to have the perspective of the market as a learning mechanism. In the 21st century, the processes by which we continue to accumulate and apply knowledge will play a major role in shaping our lives.

ENDNOTES

PART 1—What's Different About Economics—Introduction

1. Brad Delong, "A Brief Hayekian Moment," July 16, 2003, *Semi-Daily Journal*, http://www.j-bradford-delong.net/movable_type/2003_archives/001779.html.
2. Alan Page Fiske, "Human Sociality," *Relational Models Theory Overview*, http://www.sscnet.ucla.edu/anthro/faculty/fiske/relmodov.htm.
3. Stephen Pinker, *The Blank Slate*, (Viking Press, September, 2002), p. 234.

Sweetwater vs. Saltwater

4. Bjorn Lomborg, *The Skeptical Environmentalist: Measuring the Real State of the World* (Cambridge University Press; Reprint edition, September, 2001).
5. Delong, "Eldred v. Ashcroft: Could Congress Make Copyright Perpetual and Absolute if It Wanted To?" *The Semi-Daily Journal*, August 13, 2002, http://www.j-bradford-delong.net/movable_type/archives/000488.html.
6. "The Bank of Sweden Prize in Economic Sciences," *Nobel e-Museum*, http://www.nobel.se/economics/laureates/2002/public.html.
7. David Friedman, *The Hidden Order: The Economics of Everyday Life*, (Harper Business, August, 1997), p. 3.
8. DeLong, "Nobel Prizes in Economics," *The Semi-Daily Journal*, October 18, 2002, http://www.j-bradford-delong.net/movable_type/archives/001010.html.

9. Gary Becker, Interview with "The Region," *Federal Reserve Bank of Minneapolis*, June, 2002, http://www.minneapolisfed.org/pubs/region/02-06/becker.cfm?js=0.
10. Hal Varian, "For Too Many, Social Security Is Main Retirement Plan," *New York Times*, December 20, 2001, http://www.nytimes.com/2001/12/20/business/20SCEN.html?ex=1073538000&en=c183b85132927572&ei=5070.
11. Varian, "Investor Behavior Clouds the Wisdom of Offering Wider Choice in 40l(k)'s," *New York Times*, February 14, 2002, http://query.nytimes.com/gst/abstract.html?res=FB0E15F93C5B0C778DDDAB0894DA404482.
12. Edward Prescott, "Prosperity and Depression," Working Paper 618, January, 2002, Richard T. Ely Lecture, *Federal Reserve Bank of Minneapolis*, Research Department, http://research.mpls.frb.fed.us/research/wp/wp618.pdf.
13. Robert Solow, Interview, September, 2002, *Federal Reserve Bank of Minneapolis*, http://minneapolisfed.org/pubs/region/02-09/solow.cfm.
14. Jane S. Shaw, "Public Choice Theory," *The Library of Economics and Liberty*, The Concise Encyclopedia of Economics, http://www.econlib.org/library/Enc/PublicChoiceTheory.html.
15. Paul Krugman, "For Richer," *New York Times*, October 20, 2002, http://query.nytimes.com/gst/abstract.html?res=FA0F1EF83A5E0C738EDDA90994DA404482.
16. Kling, "Microsoft and the Anointed," Nov. 8, 1999, *Arguing in My Spare Time*, No. 2.21, http://www.arnoldkling.com/~arnoldsk/aimst2/aimst221.html.

The Omniscient Voyeur

17. Iain Murray, "Hating Why They Hate Us," February 1, 2003, *Tech Central Station*, http://www.techcentralstation.com/020103B.html.
18. "Emigration: Immigration and Emigration by Decade 1901-1990," *Immigration Information*, http://uscis.gov/graphics/shared/aboutus/statistics/Est2000.pdf

19 "Illegal Immigrants," *Immigration Information*, http://uscis.gov/graphics/shared/aboutus/statistics/2000ExecSumm.pdf

20 Paul Anthony Samuelson, "Revealed Preference," *The Library of Economics and Liberty*, The Concise Encyclopedia of Economics, From the CEE biography, http://www.econlib.org/cgi-bin/search.pl?query=revealed+preference&results=0&book=Encyclopedia&andor=and&sensitive=no.

21 "About School Choice," *Milton and Rose D. Friedman Foundation*, http://www.friedmanfoundation.org/schoolchoice/the_truth/index.html.

22 Don Peck and Ross Douthat, "Can Money Buy Happiness?" *Atlantic Monthly*, January/February 2003, Vol. 291, Iss. 1, pg. 42, 2. See also David G. Myers, "The Disconnect Between Wealth and Well-Being: It's Not the Economy, Stupid," http://pqasb.pqarchiver.com/theatlantic/index.html?ts=1044142443.

23 Prescott, Working Paper 618, p. 25, http://research.mpls.frb.fed.us/research/wp/wp618.pdf

24 Richard Layard, "Happiness: Has Social Science a Clue?," "What Is Happiness? Are We Getting Happier?" Lecture 1, delivered at Lionel Robbins Memorial Lectures, London School of Economics, March 3–5, 2003, http://cep.lse.ac.uk/events/lectures/layard/RL030303.pdf, "Income and Happiness: "Rethinking Economic Policy," Lecture 2, February 27, 2003, http://cep.lse.ac.uk/events/lectures/layard/RL040303.pdf, and "What Would Make a Happier Society," Lecture 3, March 5, 2003, http://cep.lse.ac.uk/events/lectures/layard/RL050303.pdf.

Type C and Type M Arguments

25 The unofficial Krugman archive, "The Tax-Cut Con," originally published in the *New York Times, September 14, 2003*, http://www.pkarchive.org/economy/TaxCutCon.html.

There Is No Labor Shortage

26 Herbert Stein, *Washington Bedtime Stories* (Free Press, 1986), p. xi.

Quack Economic Prescription

27 Marc Siegel, "This Doesn't Have to be the Price We Pay," *Washington Post*, June 22, 2003, http://www.washingtonpost.com/ac2/wp-dyn?pagename=article&node=&contentId=A17936-2003Jun20&notFound=true.
28 Jane Galt, "Asymmetrical Information," July 19, 2002, http://www.janegalt.net/blog/archives/001111.html#001111.
29 "Importation Is Not the Answer." Prescription Drugs, *Galen Reports*, July 16, 2003, http://www.galen.org/pdrugs.asp?docID=507.

Economics vs. Populism

30 Walter Russell Mead, *Special Providence: American Foreign Policy and How it Changed the World* (Knopf, 2001) p. 311.

Economic Attribution Errors

31 Malcolm Gladwell, *The Tipping Point*, (Back Bay Books, January, 2002), p. 6.
32 Paul Krugman, "Deficit Attention Disorder," originally published in the *New York Times*, March 26, 2000, *The Unofficial Paul Krugman Archive*, http://www.pkarchive.org/column/32600.html.
33 Alan Kohler, "More Warnings of Downward Market Trends," June 10, 2002, *ABC Online Home*, Inside Business, http://www.abc.net.au/insidebusiness/content/2002/s694354.htm.
34 Brad DeLong, "By Contrast the Economist Presents a Good Analysis of the Dollar-Euro," *The Semi-Daily Journal*, July 16, 2002, http://www.j-bradford-delong.net/movable_type/archives/000360.html.
35 Douglas W. Elmendorf, Jeffrey B. Liebman, and David W. Wilcox, "Fiscal Policy and Social Security Policy During the 1990s," paper presented at Harvard University, June 27-30, 2001, http://www.ksg.harvard.edu/cbg/Conferences/economic_policy/elwrevisedcbg.pdf, August, 2001.

36 Greg Mankiw, "American Economic Policy in the 1990s," paper presented at Harvard University, June 27-30, 2001, http://www.ksg.harvard.edu/cbg/Conferences/economic_policy/MANKIW.pdf, May, 2001.

PART II—Growth, Technological Progress, and Decentralized Innovation—Introduction

37 Delong, "The Real Shopping Cart Revolution," March, 2003, *Wired Magazine*, http://www.wired.com/wired/archive/11.03/view.html?pg=5.
38 Virginia Postrel, "The Scene," December 11 and December 13, 2002, *Dynamist.com*, http://www.dynamist.com/scene/cheap.
39 Delong, "(One Piece of) the Real Headline News," December 13, 2002, *The Semi-Daily Journal*, http://www.j-bradford-delong.net/movable_type/archives/001260.html.

Growth Across Time

40 Delong, "Growth: An Introduction," *Macroeconomics*, Introduction, http://www.j-bradford-delong.net/macro_online/gt_primer.pdf.
41 Delong, ibid., p. 2.
42 Ward Nicolson, "Longevity and Health in Ancient Paleolithic vs. Neolithic Peoples," 1997 and 1999. *Beyond Vegetarianism*, http://www.beyondveg.com/nicholson-w/angel-1984/angel-1984-1a.shtml.
43 Niall Ferguson, *The Cash Nexus*, (Basic Books, March, 2001), p.34.
44 Delong, "A Long Boom?" Talk given at Haas Business School Leading Edge Conference, September 18, 1999, http://econ161.berkeley.edu/Comments/long_boom.html.
45 Ray Kurzweil, *The Age of Spiritual Machines*, (Viking Press, January, 1999) p. 3.

Progress and Displacement

46 Stan Bernstein, "Burned by CD Burners," September 24, 2002, *Washington Post*, http://www.washingtonpost.com/ac2/wp-

dyn?pagename=article&node=&contentId=A57856-2002Sep23&notFound=true.

[47] Janis Ian, "The Internet Debacle—An Alternative View," first appeared *Performing Songwriter* magazine, May 2002, *Janis Ian Articles*, http://www.janisian.com/article-internet_debacle.html.

[48] David Gruber and Jonathan Cutler, "Health Policy in the Clinton Era, Once Bitten, Twice Shy," paper presented at Harvard University, June 27-30, 2001, http://www.ksg.harvard.edu/cbg/Conferences/economic_policy/CUTLER-GRUBER.pdf.

[49] Robert Fogel, et al, "A Nobel Roundtable," Third Quarter, 2002, *The Milken Institute Review*, http://www.milkeninstitute.org/publications/review/2002_9/76-86.pdf.

Rationally Exhuberant

[50] Gordon Moore, "Moore's Law," *Internet.com Webopedia*, http://www.webopedia.com/TERM/M/Moores_Law.html.

[51] Delong, "Productivity Growth in the 2000s," Draft 1.2, March, 2002, http://www.j-bradford-delong.net/Econ_Articles/macro_annual/delong_macro_annual_05.pdf.

[52] Intel, *Microprocessor Hall of Fame*, http://www.intel.com/intel/intelis/museum/exhibits/hist_micro/hof/.

[53] William D. Nordhaus, "The Progress of Computing," *Yale University and the NBER*, August 30, 2001, http://www.econ.yale.edu/~nordhaus/homepage/prog_083001a.pdf.

[54] Delong, "The Economic History of the 20th Century: Slouching Towards Utopia," January 24, 1997, http://www.j-bradford-delong.net/TCEH/Slouch_title.html.

The Elastic Economy

[55] Charles Wilson, "The Columbia World of Quotations," as quoted in *New York Times*, February 24, 1953, http://www.bartleby.com/66/76/64876.html.

56 Mark Gongloff, "U.S. Jobs Jumping Ship," *CNN Money*, March 13, 2003, http://money.cnn.com/2003/03/13/news/economy/jobs_offshore/index.htm.
57 Ahmed, March 19, 2003, http://www.winterspeak.com/2003_03_01_archive.html#90560141.

What Causes Prosperity?

58 Donald Rumsfeld, Secretary of Defense, Veterans Day speech, November 11, 2002, *U.S. Department of Defense*, http://www.defenselink.mil/speeches/2002/s20021111-secdef.html.
59 Robert Mundell and Milton Friedman, "One World, One Money," May, 2001, *Policy Options*, http://www.irpp.org/po/archive/may01/friedman.pdf.
60 J. Bradford Delong and Barry Eichengreen, "Between Meltdown and Moral Hazard: Clinton Administration International Monetary and Financial Policy," May 27, 2000, http://www.j-bradforddelong.net/Econ_Articles/CIEP_eich_del.html.
61 Ronald Bird, "Finding Gold in the Melting Pot," review of *Heaven's Door: Immigration Policy and the American Economy* by George J. Borjas (Princeton University Press, 1999), *In Review*, Vol. 23, No. 3, p. 67, http://www.cato.org/pubs/regulation/regv23n3/bird.pdf.
62 Peter S. Goodman, "China's Bank Bind," November 15, 2002, *Washington Post*, http://www.washingtonpost.com/ac2/wp-dyn?pagename=article&node=&contentId=A56594-2002Nov14&notFound=true.
63 Russ Mitchell, "All the T in China," October 3, 2002, *Smartmoney.com*, http://www.smartmoney.com/Techwise/index.cfm?story=20021003.
64 Ralph Peters, "Spotting the Losers: Seven Signs of Non-Competitive States," Spring, 1998, "*Parameters, U.S. Army War College Quarterly*,http://carlisle-www.army.mil/usawc/parameters/98spring/peters.htm.
65 Delong, "The Last Development Crusade," August 5, 2001, http://econ161.berkeley.edu/TotW/Easterly_neoliberal.html.

The Statism Trap

[66] Krugman, "The Fear Economy," originally published in the *New York Times*, September 30, 2001, http://www.pkarchive.org/economy/FearEconomy.html.

[67] Krugman, "Fear of a Quagmire," *New York Times*, May 24, 2003, http://www.nytimes.com/2003/05/24/opinion/24KRUG.html?ex=1073710800&en=d31721b1d040afe0&ei=5070.

[68] Ken Henry, "Economic Prospects and Policy Challenges," speech to the Australian Business Economists, May 20, 2003, *Australian Government, The Treasury*,http://www.treasury.gov.au/documents/639/HTML/docshell.asp?URL=speech_%20main.asp.

[69] Prescott, Working Paper 618, http://research.mpls.frb.fed.us/research/wp/wp618.pdf.

[70] FDIC, "The S & L Crisis: A Chrono-Bibliography," December 20, 2002, *FDIC*, http://www.fdic.gov/bank/historical/s&l/.

[71] Kling, "Celebrate Diversity," May 19, 2003, *Tech Central Station*, http://www.techcentralstation.com/051903C.html.

[72] Edward O. Wilson, *The Future of Life*, (Knopf, January, 2002).

Substitution, Technological Change, and the Environment

[73] *www.anti-lomborg.com*, http://www.mylinkspage.com/lomborg.html.

[74] Kling, "Lomborg's Lessons," April 2, 2002, *Tech Central Station*, http://www.techcentralstation.com/040202D.html

[75] Ray Kurzweil, "The Singularity: A Talk with Ray Kurzweil," March 25, 2001, *Edge*, http://www.edge.org/3rd_culture/kurzweil_singularity/kurzweil_singularity_index.html.

[76] Alan Blinder, "The Internet and the New Economy," paper prepared for the Internet Policy Institute, January, 2000.

Nonlinear Thinking

[77] *Pop! Tech*, http://www.poptech.org/.

78 Geoffrey Ballard, *General Hydrogen*, http://www.general hydrogen.com/html/GeoffreyBallard.html.
79 Katie Hafner, "The Revolution Is Coming, Eventually," *New York Times*, October 19, 2003, http://query.nytimes.com/gst/abstract.html?res=F30E13FB395A0C7A8DDDA90994DB404482.
80 Moore, ibid.
81 Delong, "Productivity Growth in the 2000s," ibid., http://www.j-bradford-delong.net/Econ_Articles/macro_annual/delong_macro_annual_05.pdf.
82 Aubrey de Grey, "A Cure for Aging," August 6, 2003, *The Speculist*, http://www.speculist.com/archives/000056.html.
83 Peter D. Ward and Donald Bryson, *The Life and Death of Planet Earth: How the New Science of Astrobiology Charts the Ultimate Fate of Our World* (Times Books, 2003), http://www.poptech.org/speakers.cfm?page=speaker_detail&id=97 .
84 Christine Peterson, *Foresight Institute*, http://www.foresight.org/FI/Peterson.html.

Hayek, Stiglitz, and Michael Powell

85 F. A. Hayek, translated by Marcellus S. Snow, "Competition as a Discovery Procedure," *The Quarterly Journal of Austrian Economics*, Vol. 5, No.3, Fall, 2002, http://www.mises.org/journals/qjae/pdf/qjae5_3_3.pdf.
86 Joseph E. Stiglitz, "Information," *The Library of Economics and Liberty*, The Concise Encyclopedia of Economics, http://www.econlib.org/library/Enc/Information.html.
87 DeLong, "Stiglitz, Globalization and its Discontents," June 9, 2002, *The Semi-Daily Journal*, http://www.j-bradford-delong.net/movable_type/2003_archives/000398.html.
88 David S. Isenberg and David Weinberger, "Don't prop up phone firms; let them fail," *USA Today*, November 13, 2002, http://www.usatoday.com/news/opinion/2002-11-12-oped-isenberg_x.htm.
89 Roy Mark, "FCC Proposes More Spectrum for Mobile Broadband," March 14, 2003, *Internet News.com*, Wireless, http://www.internetnews.com/wireless/article.php/2109731.

PART 3—Moore's Law, Progress, and Displacement—Introduction

[90] Jon "Hannibal" Stokes, "Understanding Moore's Law," February, 2003, *Ars Technica,* http://arstechnica.com/paedia/m/moore/moore-1.html.

Listen to the Technology

[91] Tim O'Reilly, "Inventing the Future," April 19, 2002, *O'Reilly Network,* http://www.oreillynet.com/pub/a/network/2002/04/09/future.html.
[92] James Taranto, "Best of the Web Today," *Opinion Journal,* http://www.opinionjournal.com/best/.
[93] "Inside the Blogsphere Panel," *Microcontent News,* http://www.microcontentnews.com/entries/20020629-914.htm.
[94] Peter Francese, "Continuous Market Research Meets the Test of Time," 2002, *Presstime,*http://www.naa.org/Presstime/PTArtPage.cfm?AID=2021.
[95] *American Demographics,* review, *Epinions.com,* http://www.epinions.com/mags-review-167A-BA6E58A-39C38489-prod1.
[96] Vin Crosbie, "What Newspapers and Their Websites Must Do to Survive," USC Annenberg, *Online Journalism Review,* http://www.ojr.org/ojr/business/1078349998.php.
[97] Dan Kohn, "Steal this Essay3: How to Finance Content Creation," December, 28, 2002, *DanKohn.com,* http://www.dankohn.com/archives/000278.html.

The Internet Packet Express

[98] Bob Frankston, *Comments from Frankston, Reed, and Friends,* http://www.satn.org/. See also: http://www.frankston.com/public/Writings.asp, David P. Reed, *Reed's Locus,* http://www.reed.com/dprframeweb/dprframe.asp, and Bricklin's at Dan Bricklin, *Writings,* http://www.bricklin.com/writings.htm.

The Wireless Last Mile

99 http://www.longbets.org/.
100 Moore, ibid.
101 Andy Chapman, "Prediction," *Longbets*, 2002, http://www.longbets.org/13.
102 Jeffrey K. MacKie-Mason and Hal Varian, "Some Economics of the Internet," paper for the Tenth Michigan Public Utility Conference, November, 1992, revised February 17, 1994, http://www-personal.umich.edu/~jmm/papers/Economics_of_Internet.pdf.
103 Kevin Werbach, "Radio Revolution," *New America Foundation*, Page: 38 http://werbach.com/docs/RadioRevolution.pdf.
104 Timothy J. Shepherd, Ph.D., comments before the Spectrum Policy Taskforce related to the Commission's Spectrum Policy issues, ET Docket No. 02-135, *Federal Communications Commission*, http://gullfoss2.fcc.gov/prod/ecfs/retrieve.cgi?native_or_pdf=pdf&id_document=6513201206.

Asymptotically Free Goods

105 Simson Garfinkel, "The Internet Amenity," *Technology Review*, March 2002.
106 Walter Y. Oi, "A Disneyland Dilemma: Two-Part Tariffs for a Mickey Mouse Monopoly," The Quarterly Journal of Economics, 1971, Vol 85, Issue 1, pp. 77-96, *EconPapers*, Page: 38 http://econpapers.hhs.se/article/tprqjecon/v_3a85_3ay_3a1971_3ai_3a1_3ap_3a77-96.htm.

Legamorons in a Trackable Society

107 Dana Blankenhorn, "Wanna Catch the Sniper?," October 15, 2002,*Corante Tech News*, http://www.corante.com/mooreslore/8861.
108 David Brin, website, http://www.davidbrin.com/.
109 Brin, *The Transparent Society*, (Perseus Publishing, June, 1999).

110 Pat Gelsinger, "Expanding Moore's Law: A History of Proving the Skeptics Wrong—Moore's Law Extends and Expands for the Future," *Intel*, http://www.intel.com/labs/eml/patinterview.htm.

111 Jon Udell, "The Atomic, Subatomic, and Galactic Structure of Things Today," October 14, 2002, iDiscuss, Jon Udell's Weblog, *InfoWorld*, http://weblog.infoworld.com/udell/2002/10/14.html.

Metaphors for Intellectual Property

112 Ahmed, February 28, 2003, http://www.winterspeak.com/90363421.

113 James V. Delong, "Defending Intellectual Property," Competitive Enterprise Institute, http://www.cei.org/pdf/2368.pdf.

114 Michele Bodrin and David K. Levine, *Economic and Game Theory Intellectual Property Page*, http://levine.sscnet.ucla.edu/general/intellectual/intellectual.htm.

115 Douglas Clement, "Creation Myths: Does Innovation Require Intellectual Property Rights?" March, 2003, *ReasonOnline*, http://www.reason.com/0303/fe.dc.creation.shtml.

116 Kling, "Content Is Crap," January 13, 2003, *Tech Central Station*, http://www.techcentralstation.com/011303A.html.

117 Clay Shirky, "The Case Against Micropayments," December 19, 2000, *O'Reilley P2P*, Page: 38 http://www.openp2p.com/pub/a/p2p/2000/12/19/micropayments.html.

The Club vs. the Silo

118 Lawrence Lee, *Tomalak's Realm*, http://www.tomalak.org/.

119 Postrel, *Dynamist.com*, http://www.dynamist.com/weblog/index.html.

Equilibrium in the Market for Rock 'n' Roll

120 Ted Nugent, "Cat Scratch Thiever," March 13, 2001, *Opinion Journal*, http://www.opinionjournal.com/extra/?id=85000700.

121 Kling, "Effective Tournaments," October 26, 1999, *Arguing in My Spare Time*, No. 2.20, http://arnoldkling.com/~arnoldsk/aimst2/aimst220.html.
122 Jakob Nielsen, website, http://www.useit.com/
123 Shirky, "Power Laws, Weblogs, and Inequality, February 8, 2003, *Clay Shirky's Writings About the Internet*, Page: 38 http://www.shirky.com/writings/powerlaw_weblog.html.

Moore vs. Plato

124 Merle Kling, "The Intellectual: Will He Wither Away," originally appeared in *The New Republic*, April 8, 1957, transcribed by Arnold Kling, April 28, 2003, http://arnoldkling.com/~arnoldsk/aimst5/klingm.html.
125 Moore, ibid.
126 EconLog: Library of Economics and Liberty, website, http://econlog.econlib.org/.
127 Frederick Turner, biography, http://www.techcentralstation.com/bioturnerfrederick.html.
128 Galt, April 30, 2003, http://www.janegalt.net/blog/archives/004125.html.
129 Will Wilkinson, *The Fly Bottle*, April 23, 2003, http://willwilkinson.net/flybottle/200180042.
130 Ronald Bailey, *Reason Online*, http://www.reason.com/rbmain1.shtml.

Roll Over, Ricardo

131 David Ricardo, Esq., "On the Principles of Political Economy and Taxation," *The Library of Economics and Liberty*, The Concise Encyclopedia of Economics, http://www.econlib.org/library/Ricardo/ricP.html.
132 Michael Lind, "Are We Still a Middle-Class Nation?, January/February 2004, *The Atlantic*, http://www.theatlantic.com/issues/2004/01/lind.htm.

[133] Senator Charles Schumer and Paul Craig Roberts, "Exporting Jobs Is Not Free Trade," January 7, 2004, *International Herald Tribune*, http://www.iht.com/articles/123898.html.
[134] Fiske, ibid.
[135] Krugman, "Ricardo's Difficult Idea," http://www.pkarchive.org/trade/ricardo.html.
[136] Lind, ibid.
[137] Real State of the Union Conference, *New America Foundation*, http://www.newamerica.net/index.cfm?pg=event&EveID=331.
[138] Daniel Davies, "The War on (some kinds of) Theory," December 15, 2003, *Crooked Timber*, http://www.crookedtimber.org/archives/001010.html.
[139] "Free Trade in the New Global Economy," transcript from Brookings Briefing tape recording, (The transcription reads "margin of product" instead of "marginal product."), *The Brookings Institution*, http://www.brookings.edu/dybdocroot/comm/events/20040107.pdf.

Don't Smoot the Weasels

[140] Robert J. Samuelson, "Great Depression," *The Library of Economics and Liberty*, The Concise Encyclopedia of Economics, http://www.econlib.org/library/Enc/GreatDepression.html.
[141] Scott Ott, "Rumsfeld Sorry for Axis of Weasels Remark," January 22, 2003, *Scrappleface*, http://www.scrappleface.com/MT/archives/000608.html.

Please Outsource to My Daughter

[142] Alan Blinder, "Free Trade," *The Library of Economics and Liberty*, The Concise Encyclopedia of Economics, http://www.econlib.org/library/Enc/FreeTrade.html.
[143] Phylis Schafly, "When White-Collar Jobs Follow the Blues," June 2, 2003, *Townhall.com*, http://www.townhall.com/columnists/phyllisschlafly/ps20030602.shtml.

144 Glenn Harlan Reynolds, "Outsourcing and Elections," June, 25, 2003, *Tech Central Station*, http://www.techcentralstation.com/062503A.html.
145 Prashant Kothari, *Finding My Voice*, http://www.prashantkothari.com.
146 String Information Services, http://www.stringinfo.com/.
147 Derek Lowe, "Passed on Without Comment," June 29, 2003, *Corante Tech News*, http://www.corante.com/pipeline/42154.

Manufacturing a Crisis

148 Rodney Brooks, "Beyond Computation: A Talk with Rodney Brooks," *Edge, The Third Culture*, http://www.edge.org/3rd_culture/brooks_beyond/beyond_p6.html.
149 President George W. Bush, "President's Remarks on Labor Day," speech to Ohio Operating Engineers, Richfield Training Center, Richfield, Ohio, September 1, 2003, *The White House*, http://www.whitehouse.gov/news/releases/2003/09/20030901.html.
150 Bureau of Labor Statistics, *U.S. Department of Labor*, http://www.bls.gov/webapps/legacy/cesbtab1.htm.
151 Bruce Bartlett, "Manufacturing Is Not in Trouble," April 14, 2003, *Townhall.com*, http://www.townhall.com/columnists/brucebartlett/bb20030814.shtml.
152 David N. Thompson and Gregory K. Ottosen, *The Real New Economy*, (Crossroads Research Institute, 2003).
153 Marshall Brain, "Robotic Nation," http://marshallbrain.com/roboticnation.htm.
154 James D. Miller, "Robot Economics," August 19, 2003, *Tech Central Station*, http://www.techcentralstation.com/081903C.html.

The Language Barrier

155 Krugman, "Want Growth, Speak English: That Certain Je Ne Sais Quoi of Les Anglophones," 1999, http://www.pkarchive.org/global/english.html.

[156] Delong, "The View From 2023," *The Semi-Daily Journal*, January 27, 2003, http://www.j-bradford-delong.net/movable_type/archives/001488.html.
[157] Kling, "The Internet and Productivity," January 31, 2003, *EconLog*, http://econlog.econlib.org/archives/000015.
[158] Kothari, January 18, 2003, http://prashantkothari.blogspot.com/88253641.
[159] Joel Mokyr, *The Gifts of Athena* (Princeton University Press, November, 2002).
[160] Nick Schulz, "What You Don't Know *Can* Hurt You," January 6, 2003, *Tech Central Station*, http://www.techcentralstation.com/010603D.html.
[161] Sheizaf Rafaeli, http://gsb.haifa.ac.il/~sheizaf/.
[162] Nicholas Negroponte, "Being Global," *MIT*, http://www.mit.edu:8001/people/davis/NegroponteLec.html.

The Balance of Saving

[163] Kenneth Rogoff, "The Debtor's Empire," October 20, 2003, *Washington Post*, http://www.washingtonpost.com/ac2/wp-dyn?pagename=article&node=&contentId=A50923-2003Oct19&notFound=true.

Labor Force Capacity Utilization

[164] Business Cycle Dating Committee, "The NBER's Recession Dating Procedure," October 21, 2003, *NBER*, http://www.nber.org/cycles/recessions.html.
[165] Federal Reserve Statistical Release, "Industrial Production and Capacity Utilization," December 16, 2003, *Federal Reserve*, http://www.federalreserve.gov/releases/G17/Current/.
[166] U.S. Department of Labor, "Employment, Hours, and Earnings," June 6, 2003, *U.S. Bureau of Labor Statistics*, http://www.bls.gov/webapps/legacy/cesbtab5.htm.
[167] U.S. Department of Labor, ibid.

168. Delong, "Third Quarter Productivity Growth," October 23, 2002, *Semi-Daily Journal*, http://www.j-bradford-delong.net/movable_type/archives/001091.html.

The President's Macroeconomic Report Card

169. George Akerlof, "State of the Economy," conference call transcript, August 12, 2003, *Economic Policy Institute*, http://www.epinet.org/webfeatures/viewpoints/economy_transcript_20030812.pdf.
170. Krugman, "Fiscal Policy and Employment: Simple Analytics," April 28, 2003 http://www.wws.princeton.edu/~pkrugman/fiscal.html.
171. Akerlof, ibid.
172. Paul Kasriel and Asha Bangalore, "Bill Clinton Was the Luckiest President in the Post-WW II Period," April 11, 2003, *The Northern Trust Company*,http://www.financial-planning.com/northerntrustinvestments/docs/clinton041103.pdf.
173. Federal Reserve Constant Maturity Index, *Federal Reserve*, http://www.federalreserve.gov/releases/h15/data/m/tcm10y.txt.
174. "U.S. Unemployment Rate, SA, Percent," Economic Time Series, *Economagic.com*, http://www.economagic.com/em-cgi/data.exe/feddal/ru.
175. Akerlof, ibid.
176. Delong, "Third Quarter Productivity Growth," ibid.

The Great Displacement

177. Alexander J. Field, "The Most Technologically Progressive Decade," *American Economic Review*, September 2003.
178. "The Great Depression," *Wikipedia*, http://en2.wikipedia.org/wiki/Great_Depression.
179. Erica L. Groshen and Simon Potter, "Has Structural Changed Contributed to a Jobless Recovery?, August, 2003, *Federal Reserve Bank of New York*, http://www.newyorkfed.org/research/current_issues/ci9-8.html.
180. Harold L. Cole and Lee E. Ohaian, "The Great Depression in the

United States from a Neoclassical Perspective," Federal Reserve Bank of Minneapolis Quarterly Review, Winter, 1999, Vol. 23, No. 1, pp. 2-24, *Federal Reserve Bank of Minneapolis*, http://minneapolisfed.org/research/qr/qr2311.pdf.

[181] Krugman, "Mind the Gap," August 16, 2002, *New York Times*, http://www.pkarchive.org/column/081602.html.

Can Greenspan Steer?

[182] Delong, "How Large Is the Output Gap?" August 16, 2002, *Semi-Daily Journal*, http://www.j-bradford-delong.net/movable_type/archives/000520.html.

[183] Delong, "Productivity Growth in the 2000s: What Will It Be? March 30, 2002, *Semi-Daily Journal*, http://www.j-bradford-delong.net/movable_type/archives/week_2002_03_24.html.

[184] Delong, *Macroeconomics*, ibid, p. 271.

[185] Richard Berner and David Greenlaw, "How Low Can Yields Go?" August 16, 2002, *Morgan Stanley Global Economic Forum*, http://www.morganstanley.com/GEFdata/digests/20020816-fri.html.

[186] Rich Miller, "Bond Vigilantes Are Getting Restless," April 1, 2002, *Business Week*, http://www.businessweek.com/bwdaily/dnflash/apr2002/nf2002041_6855.htm.

The Bitterness of Supply-Siders

[187] Edmund L. Andrews, February 27, 2003, "A Salesman for Bush's Tax Plan Who Has Belittled Similar Ideas," *New York Times*, http://www.nytimes.com/2003/02/28/business/28ECON.html?ex=1074229200&en=626ea280165d7c15&ei=5070.

[188] James D. Gwartney, "Supply Side Economics," *The Library of Economics and Liberty*, The Concise Encyclopedia of Economics, http://www.econlib.org/library/Enc/SupplySideEconomics.html.

[189] Raymond J. Keating, "A Walk on the Supply Side," originally published in *The Freeman*, May 1995, Vol. 45, No. 5, a publication of the Foundation for Economic Education, *Liberty Haven*, http:/

/www.libertyhaven.com/theoreticalorphilosophicalissues/supplysideeconomics/walksupply.html.

190. Delong, "The Real Supply Siders," March 3, 2003, *Semi-Daily Journal*, http://www.j-bradford-delong.net/movable_type/2003_archives/000837.html.

191. Friedman, "What Every American Wants," January 19, 2003, *Opinion Journal*, http://www.opinionjournal.com/editorial/feature.html?id=110002933.

192. Kling, "The Internet and Productivity," January 31, 2003, *EconLog: Library of Economics and Liberty*, http://econlog.econlib.org/archives /000015.html.

193. "Exploding Deficits, Declining Growth: The Federal Budget and the Aging of America," March, 2003, Policy Statement by the Research and Policy Committee of the Committee for Economic Development, *CED*, http://www.ced.org/docs/report/report_deficit.pdf.

Would Keynes Change His Mind?

194. John Maynard Keynes, *The Columbia World of Quotations*, (Columbia University Press, 1996), *Bartleby.com*, http://www.bartleby.com/66/23/32523.html.

195. Kling, "Basic Supply and Demand," reader comment, April 28, 2003, *Econlog*, http://econlog.econlib.org/archives/000405.

196. Governor Ben S. Bernanke, "Deflation: Making Sure It Doesn't Happen Here," November 21, 2002, remarks before the National Economists Club, Washington D.C., *The Federal Reserve Board*, http://www.federalreserve.gov/boarddocs/speeches/2002/20021121/default.htm.

197. Keynes, "Economics A-Z," *Economist.com*, http://www.economist.com/research/Economics/alphabetic. cfm?LETTER=K.

What's Your Margin of Safety?

198. Benjamin Graham, *The Intelligent Investor* (Harper Business, July, 2003), *Watermark Capital Management, Inc.* http://www.watermark.ca/philosophy.html.

199. Bill Gross, "Dow 5000," Investment Outlook, September, 2002,

Pimco Bonds, http://www.pimco.com/LeftNav/Late+ Breaking+ Commentary/IO/2002/IO_09_2002.htm.

The Dollar Bubble and the Bond Bubble

[200] Stephen Roach, "Cracking Denial," January 18, 2002, *Morgan Stanley,* http://www.morganstanley.com/GEFdata/digests/20020118-fri.html.
[201] billmon, "The Economic Limits of the Empire," June 12, 2003, *Whiskey Bar,* http://billmon.org/archives/000233.html.
[202] J. Huston McCulloch, "The U.S. Real Term Structure of Interest Rates," October 31, 2003, *Department of Economics, Ohio State University,* http://economics.sbs.ohio-state.edu/jhm/ts/ts.html.
[203] Robert Solow, archived, http://straitstimes.asia1.com.sg/m expired content/0,4393,,00.html.

Bleeding Heart Libertarianism

[204] Stefan Sharansky, "My Blog and Welcome to It," June 1, 2002, *Shark Blog,* http://www.usefulwork.com/shark/archives/000001. html.
[205] Karl Kraus, quoted in "Politics, Politician, and Government," *Quotable Quotes,*http://www.info.bw/~jacana/QuotesP.htm.
[206] Jodie T. Allen, "Negative Income Tax," *The Library of Economics and Liberty,* The Concise Encyclopedia of Economics, http://www.econlib.org/library/Enc/NegativeIncomeTax.html.

A Social Security Policy Primer

[207] Galt, "Required Reading for Discussions of Pensions and Demographics,"*Assymetrical Information,* June 21, 2003, http://www. janegalt.net/blog/archives/004221.html.
[208] Maureen Culhane, "Global Aging—Capital Market Implications," February 8, 2001, *Goldman Sachs*http://www.ced.uab.es/jperez/PDFs/GoldmanSachs.pdf.
[209] John F. Cogan and Olivia S. Mitchell, "The Role of Social Security

in Economic ReforM: Perspectives from the President's Commission," NBER Work Paper No. W9166, September 2002, *NBER*, http://papers.nber.org/papers/W9166.
[210] Galt, "Found: $12 Trillion," *Asymmetrical Information*, June 18, 2003, http://www.janegalt.net/blog/archives/004214.html.
[211] Michael J. Boskin, "Deferred Taxes in the Public Finances," January 2003, NBER Working Paper, http://emlab.berkeley.edu/users/burch/e231_sp03/Boskin.pdf.
[212] Solow, archived, http://straitstimes.asia1.com.sg/mexpiredcontent/0,4393,00.html.
[213] Kling, "Social Security Privatization," June 12, 2003, *Econlog*, http://econlog.econlib.org/archives/000160.html.
[214] Peter Ferrara, "A Progressive Proposal for Social Security Private Accounts," IPI Policy Report, No. 176, *Institute for Policy Innovation*, http://www.ipi.org/ipi/IPIPublications.nsf/PublicationLookupFullText/60F897580B4B619186256 D40007266DF.

America Is Mentally Ill

[215] Ronald Bailey, "Free Market Health Care," May 28, 2003, *Reasonline*, http://www.reason.com/rb/rb052803.shtml.
[216] Thomas Sowell, "Universal Health Care, Part II," May 7, 2003, *Townhall.com*, http://www.townhall.com/columnists/thomassowell/ts20030507.shtml.
[217] Thomas Sowell, "Universal Health Care, Part III," May 8, 2003, *Townhall.com*, http://www.townhall.com/columnists/thomassowell/ts20030508.shtml.

Health Insurance Do-Nots

[218] Jonathan Rauch, "Forget about Haves and Have-Nots, Do-s and Do-nots," September 29, 2003, *The Atlantic*, http://www.theatlantic.com/politics/nj/rauch2003-23-09.htm.
[219] Kevin Brancato, "U.S. Population with Health Insurance: Number Up, Percentage Down," September 30, 2003, *Truck and Barter*, http://www.truckandbarter.com/106492213853139855.

[220] "The Health Insurance Crisis," October 2, 2003, *New York Times*, http://www.nytimes.com/2003/10/02/opinion/02THU2.html?ex=1074315600&en=dd69075f50b7844a&ei=5070.

[221] Fogel, "A Nobel Roundtable," Third Quarter, 2002, *The Milken Institute Review*, http://www.milkeninstitute.org/publications/review/2002_9/76-86.pdf.

[222] David A. Levine, "The Other Social Security Solution," Third Quarter, 2002, *The Milken Institute Review*, http://www.milkeninstitute.org/publications/review/2002_9/17-27.pdf.

The Great Race

[223] Nina Brown, "Zvi Griliches: The Diffusion of Hybrid Corn Technology, 1957," *Center for Spatially Integrated Social Science*, http://www.csiss.org/classics/content/37.

[224] Paul A. David, "The Dynamo and the Computer: An Historical Perspective on the Modern Productivity Paradox," *The American Economic Review*, Volume 80, Issue 2, May, 1990, pp. 355-361., http://www.compilerpress.atfreeweb.com/Anno%20David%20The%20Dynamo%20and%20the%20Computer%20An%20Historical%20Perspective%20on%20the%20Modern%20AER%201990.htm.

[225] Vandana Sinha, "Passports to get Facial Biometrics," July 22, 2003, *Washington Technology*, http://www.washingtontechnology.com/news/1_1/daily_news/21271-1.html.

[226] Winston Chai, "Radio ID Chips May Track Banknotes," May 22, 2003, *CNET News.com*, http://news.com.com/2100-1017-1009155.html.

[227] Michael Singer, "Woz to Wield a Personal Wireless System," July 21, 2003, *Wi-Fi Planet*, http://www.wi-fiplanet.com/news/article.php/2238121.

[228] Scott Granneman, "RFID Chips Are Here," June 27, 2003, *The Register*, http://www.theregister.co.uk/content/55/31461.html.

[229] Randall Parker, "Will Biological Technologies Advance as Rapidly

as Electronic Technologies?" August 31, 2002, *FuturePundit.com*, http://www.theregister.co.uk/content/55/31461.html.
230 *Small Times*, http://www.smalltimes.com/.
231 Jagadeesh Gokhale and Kent Smetters, "Fiscal and Generational Imbalances," *The AEI Press*, 2003, http://www.aei.org/docLib/200307161_smetters.pdf.
232 Sir Isaiah Berlin, "The Hedgehog and the Fox," (Simon and Schuster, 1953), excerpt on *Idris Hsi's website*, http://www.cc.gatech.edu/people/home/idris/Essays/Hedge_n_Fox.htm.
233 Kling, "Krugman and the Blowfish," *Arguing in my Spare Time*, No. 4.08, March 10, 2001, http://arnoldkling.com/~arnoldsk/aimst4/aimst408.html.

The World's Nicest Holding Pen

234 "Future Tense," *Dawson's Creek Script Archives 404*, http://www.geocities.com/dwscrk/404.htm.
235 Ron Ehrenberg, "Tuition Rising: Why College Costs So Much," Exploring the Future of Higher Education, 2000 Papers, Chapter 5, *Forum Strategy Series*, Vol. 3, (Jossey-Bass, 2002), http://www.educause.edu/ir/library/pdf/ffp0005.pdf
236 Postrel, *The Substance of Style, How the Rise of Aesthetic Value Is Remaking Commerce, Culture, and Consciousness* (Harper Collins, September 2003).
237 Kling, "Thoughts on Scale, Scope, and Bureaucracy," *Arguing in My Spare Time,"* No. 15, http://arnoldkling.com/~arnoldsk/scale.htm.

Mandatory Libertarianism

238 *People for the American Way*, http://www.pfaw.org/pfaw/general/.
239 Marie Gryphon, *The Cato Institute*, http://www.cato.org/people/gryphon.html.
240 Neil Postman, "Building a Bridge to the 18th Century: How the Past Can Improve Our Future," (Knopf, September, 1999).

241 "Fleecing Taxpayers Mohair Subsidies," *Green Scissors*, 2002, http://www.greenscissors.org/agriculture/mohair.htm.

242 Robert L. Bradley, Jr., "Renewable Energy—Why Renewable Energy Is Not Cheap and Not Green," *National Center for Policy Analysis*, http://www.ncpa.org/~ncpa/studies/renew/renew2.html.

243 Kothari, ibid.

244 Julian Sanchez, *Julian's Notes and Lounge*, http://www.juliansanchez.com/links.html.

Government: The High-Cost Producer

245 Drum, ibid., 12:30 p.m., http://calpundit.blogspot.com/92667886.

246 Kenneth A. Shaw and Dan A. Black, "Why College Costs So Much?" College Times, April 8, 2001, *New York Times*, http://www.nytimes.com/2001/04/08/college/08ED-VIEW.html?ex=1074315600&en=56487ab92cf385a2&ei=5070.

247 Kevin Brancato, April 15, 2003, *Truck and Barter*, http://truckandbarter.blogspot.com/92658235.

INDEX

Ahmed, Zimran 94, 159
Akerlof, George 241, 245
Alm, Richard 296
Anderson, Martin 256

Bailey, Ronald 173, 293
Baily, Martin Neil 185, 189
Ballard, Geoffrey 115, 118
Bangalore, Asha 242
Barro, Robert 99
Bartlett, Bruce 200
Baumol, William 338
Becker, Gary 26, 257
Berlin, Isaiah 310
Bernanke, Ben 264
Berner, Richard 253
Bernstein, Stan 82
Blankenhorn, Dana 154
Blinder, Alan 13, 113, 116, 195, 285, 292
Boldrin, Michele 160, 161
Bono, Sonny 25
Boskin, Michael 289, 290
Brain, Marshall 202
Brancato, Kevin 339
Brin, David 154, 176
Brooks, Rodney 199, 202
Buchanan, James 29

Burns, Arthur 65
Bush, George 42-44, 58-61, 66, 67, 120, 123, 193, 199, 221, 222, 232-236, 241-245, 256, 270, 290, 310-311, 332-334

Card, David 42
Chapman, Andy 144
Churchill, Winston 164, 246
Clay, Tanya 327
Clement, Douglas 160
Clinton, Bill 57, 65, 121, 122, 185, 235, 242
Cogan, John F. 288, 290
Cole, Harold L. 250
Copps, Michael 120, 123
Cox, W. Michael 296
Crosbie, Vin 136
Culhane, Maureen 286, 287
Cutler, David 85

David, Paul 89
Davies, Daniel 187
Dawson's Creek 312
De Grey, Aubrey 117
De Soto, Hernando 99
DeLong, J. Bradford 19, 26, 27, 64, 71, 72, 74-77, 87-90, 99, 102, 116, 121, 204, 205, 239, 252-253, 257
DeLong, James V. 27, 159
Douglass, Frederick 78
Douthat. Ross 34
Drum, Kevin 338

Easterly, William 99
Ehrenberg, Ron 312
Ehrlich, Paul 111
Elmendorf, Douglas W. 65

Evans, Don 199

Ferguson, Niall 77
Fernandez, Maria 307
Ferrara, Peter 290
Field, Alexander J. 246, 249
Fiske, Alan 21, 184
Fogel, Robert 85, 303
Francese, Peter 135
Frankston, Bob 140
Freud, Sigmund 173, 175
Friedman, David D. 26
Friedman, Milton 11, 26, 28, 30, 220, 246, 257, 280

Galt, Jane 53-54, 172
Garfinkel, Simson 148, 149
Gelsinger, Pat 155
Gibson, William 12
Gilder, George 100, 115
Gladwell, Malcolm 63
Glassman, James 227
Gokhale, Jagadeesh 302, 308
Gore, Al 241
Graham, Benjamin 265, 266
Greenlaw, David 254
Greenspan, Alan 57, 66, 251
Groshen, Erica L. 248
Gross, Bill 265-269
Gruber, Jonathan 85
Gryphon, Marie 327-330
Gwartney, James D. 257

Hafner, Katie 115
Hassett, Kevin 227

Hayek, Friedrich 19, 120-123
Heilbroner, Robert 13
Henry, Ken 104
Herz, J.C. 165
Hillenbrand, Laura 160
Hubbard, Glenn 256
Hundt, Reed 122, 123

Ian, Janis 83
Isenberg, David 123

Kahneman, Daniel 25
Kaplan, Robert 99
Kasriel, Paul 242
Keating, Raymond 257
Keynes, John Maynard 28, 60, 104, 122, 220-222, 230, 232-236, 241, 244, 246, 250, 260-264
Kindleberger, Charles 220, 221, 249
Klein, Naomi 82
Kling, Merle 172
Kohn, Dan 138
Kothari, Prashant 196, 329
Kraus, Karl 279
Krol, Ed 140
Krueger, Alan 42
Krugman, Paul 30, 41-46, 64, 103-106, 184-189, 204, 252-253
Kurzweil, Ray 78, 81, 111, 116, 176

Layard, Richard 36
Lee, Lawrence 166
Lee, Susan 256-258
Lessig, Lawrence 25
Levine, David 304

Levine, David K. 160, 161
Liebman, Jeffrey B. 65
Lind, Michael 183-191
Lindsey, Brink 105
Lomborg, Bjorn 25, 94, 108-111
Lucas, Robert E., Jr. 28

MacKie-Mason, Jeffrey K. 145
Mankiw, Greg 66, 256, 257, 259
Martin, Kevin 120
Marx, Karl 23, 121
McArdle, Megan 172
McCulloch, J. Huston 272, 273
Mead, Walter Russell 57-62
Miller, James 202
Mitchel, Olivia 288, 290
Mitchell, Joni 82
Modigliani, Franco 28
Mokyr, Joel 205
Moore, Gordon 14, 84, 87-90, 116, 127-129, 132, 144-147, 172-176, 245, 253, 292, 306-311
Moore, Stephen 256
Murray, Iain 32

Negroponte, Nicholas 206
Nicholson, Ward 76
Nielsen, Jakob 170, 224, 225
Nixon, Richard 65
Nordhaus, William 88
Norlin, Eric 157
Nugent, Ted 168

Ohanian, Lee E. 250
Oi, Walter 150

O'Reilly, Tim 133
Ott, Scott 192
Ottosen, Gregory K. 201

Parente, Stephen 99
Parker, Randall 307
Parker, Randall E. 246-249
Parsons, David 127
Peck, Don 34
Peters, Ralph 99, 100
Peterson, Christine 118
Pinker, Steven 22, 184
Postman, Neil 328
Postrel, Virginia 71, 166, 313
Potter, Simon 248
Powell, Colin 44
Powell, Michael 120-124
Prescott, Edward 28, 34, 99, 105, 106

Rafaeli, Sheizaf 206
Rauch, Jonathan 298
Reagan, Ronald 48, 256
Reed, David 140, 148
Reynolds, Glenn 197
Ricardo, David 183-191, 257, 258
Roach, Steve 64, 270, 272
Roberts, Paul Craig 183-191
Rogoff, Ken 212, 213
Roosevelt, Franklin 247, 250
Rubin, Robert 57
Rumsfeld, Donald 96

Saffran, Bernard 36
Samuelson, Paul 11

Samuelson, Robert J. 227
Sanchez, Julian 329
Schultz, Nick 206
Schumer, Charles 183-191
Sharkansky, Stefan 279
Shepard, Timothy J. 146
Shiller, Robert 90, 233-234
Shirky, Clay 164, 171
Siegel, Mark 52-56
Simon, Julian 111
Smetters, Kent 302, 308
Smith, Vernon 25
Snow, C.P. 172
Solow, Robert 28, 87, 115, 274, 289
Sowell, Thomas 30, 296, 297
Spence, Michael 205
Stein, Ben 256
Stein, Herbert 29, 47, 51, 64
Stephenson, Neal 175
Stiglitz, Joseph 120-123
Stokes, Jon 127

Taranto, James 135, 139
Thompson, David N. 201
Tobin, James 28, 233, 246

Udell, Jon 157

Varian, Hal R. 145

Ward, Peter 118

Weinberger, David 157
Werbach, Kevin 145

Wilcox, David W. 65
Wilkinson, Will 172, 173
Wilson, Charlie 91
Wilson, Edward O. 25, 108
Woodward, Bob 66

Yardeni, Edward 254

Printed in the United States
32754LVS00008B/40-162